Muted Voices

THE SPECTRUM SERIES

〜〜〜〜〜〜〜〜〜〜〜〜〜〜〜〜〜〜〜〜〜〜〜

Race and Ethnicity
in National and Global Politics

Series Editors

Paula D. McClain　　　**Joseph Stewart Jr.**
Duke University　　　*University of New Mexico*

The sociopolitical dynamics of race and ethnicity are apparent everywhere. In the United States, racial politics underlie everything from representation to affirmative action to welfare policymaking. Early in the twenty-first century, Anglos in America will become only a plurality, as Latino and Asian American populations continue to grow. Issues of racial/ethnic conflict and cooperation are prominent across the globe. Diversity, identity, and cultural plurality are watchwords of empowerment as well as of injustice.

This new series offers textbook supplements, readers, and core texts addressing various aspects of race and ethnicity in politics, broadly defined. Meant to be useful in a wide range of courses in all kinds of academic programs, these books will be multidisciplinary as well as multiracial/ethnic in their appeal.

TITLES IN THE SERIES

Muted Voices: Latinos and the 2000 Election edited by Rodolfo O. de la Garza and Louis DeSipio

Latino Politics in America: Community, Culture, and Interests by John A. García

The Navajo Political Experience, Revised Edition by David E. Wilkins

Asian American Politics: Law, Participation, and Policy edited by Don T. Nakanishi and James S. Lai

American Indian Politics and the American Political System by David E. Wilkins

FORTHCOMING TITLES

Media & Minorities by Stephanie Greco Larson

Muted Voices

Latinos and the 2000 Elections

〰〰〰〰〰〰〰〰〰〰〰〰〰〰〰〰〰〰

EDITED BY
Rodolfo O. de la Garza
and
Louis DeSipio

ROWMAN & LITTLEFIELD PUBLISHERS, INC.
Lanham • Boulder • New York • Toronto • Oxford

ROWMAN & LITTLEFIELD PUBLISHERS, INC.

Published in the United States of America
by Rowman & Littlefield Publishers, Inc.
A wholly owned subsidiary of
The Rowman & Littlefield Publishing Group, Inc.
4501 Forbes Boulevard, Suite 200, Lanham, Maryland 20706
www.rowmanlittlefield.com

P.O. Box 317, Oxford OX2 9RU, UK

British Library Cataloguing in Publication Information Available

Library of Congress Cataloging-in-Publication Data

Muted voices : Latinos and the 2000 elections / edited by Rodolfo O.
de la Garza and Louis DeSipio.
     p. cm.—(The spectrum series, race and ethnicity in national
  and global politics)
  Includes bibliographical references and index.
  ISBN 0-7425-3590-8 (cloth : alk. paper)—ISBN 0-7425-3591-6 (pbk. :
alk. paper)
    1. Hispanic Americans—Politics and government—20th century.
2. United States—Politics and government—1993–2001.   3. Elections—
United States—History—20th century.   I. De la Garza, Rodolfo O.
II. DeSipio, Louis.   III. Series.

E184.S75M88 2004
324.973'0929'08968—dc22

                                        2004006817

Printed in the United States of America

∞ ™ The paper used in this publication meets the minimum requirements of
American National Standard for Information Sciences—Permanence of Paper
for Printed Library Materials, ANSI/NISO Z39.48-1992.

Contents

Figures and Tables

~~~~~~

Introduction: Awaited Voices

Latinos and U.S. Elections

ROBERT Y. SHAPIRO

~~~~~~

THIS IS AN EXCITING TIME TO BE A STUDENT OF ETHNIC AND RACIAL politics in the United States. As already described in the recent textbook accounts, changing demographics and long-term trends in immigration—legal and otherwise—are harbingers of mass level changes in electoral politics and participation in the United States (Abramowitz 2004: 60–63). Or are they? If they are, the kind of change may continue to be a gradual one, more evolutionary in contrast to the politically realigning shocks of the past—less striking and more gradually evolving than the electoral mobilization of African Americans that occurred in the 1960s, as the Democratic Party became unequivocally the party of civil rights and as the issue of racial equality became a signature issue dividing the parties (Carmines and Stimson 1989). A good case can be made that the Democratic Party should command for the long term, and overwhelmingly, the support of Latinos who have now nudged out African Americans as the largest distinguishable racial and ethnic group (as delineated by the U.S. census) and thereby augment the party's national strength that was weakened by the loss of support from white southerners. Indeed, there has been visible discussion of "the emerging Democratic majority" toward which such population trends are expected to contribute (Judis and Teixeira 2002).

But Democrats should hold off on any exuberance. Political scientists, to be sure, should treat this as an open empirical question. What has happened thus far, as the title of this timely volume suggests, has been much more constrained and muted. Louis DeSipio and Rodolfo O. de la Garza describe this well in chapter 1. At some point in the future, differential rates of population growth and laws of large numbers should—or at least may—fully amplify Latinos' voices. While not the kind of extreme case that might be projected for differences in population growth of Jews versus Arabs in Israel and Palestine, the use in the future of the terms "majority" to describe white Americans, and "minority" to describe Latinos—to say nothing of Latinos and African Americans taken together (even putting aside Asian Americans and others)—may seem noticeably out of place. But short of this, how can we best understand what DeSipio and de la Garza and other authors in this volume see as constraining the impact of Latinos in American national elections as we move further into the twenty-first century?

An answer can be found by considering the history of research in the relatively new field of study of Latino politics. Beyond this particular history, if the broader discipline of political science is worthy of its name, it should also be able to provide useful guidance. That is, to understand the politics we need to draw on the other relevant political science where we can.

De la Garza and DeSipio have helped lead the field of Latino politics that has now—at the start of a new century—broadened and diversified in ways to which this introduction cannot do justice (for a fuller review, see de la Garza 2004; on minority and immigrant political participation, see Park and Vargas-Ramos 2002). It has come a long way from F. Chris Garcia and de la Garza's early book *The Chicano Political Experience: Three Perspectives* (1977), which attempted to integrate Latino politics into mainstream political science debates in the 1960s and 1970s on the relevance of pluralist theory. Some important themes and tensions cited in this book have remained. The book offered a further challenge to the pluralist paradigm that was being questioned as part of the tumultuous debates of the 1960s involving African Americans, women, and others—and especially on university campuses. Garcia and de la Garza brought Mexican American politics—and by extension Latino politics—into the debate about the lack of power of certain groups in America. The book also added its own social science emphasis and presentation of a good deal of data and other evidence. Furthermore, its emphasis on the *Mexican* American and immigrant experience raised questions and tensions about eventually referring to the field as "Latino politics." Although Garcia and de la Garza set a tone that has remained in contemporary research—one of possible optimism with regard to the prospects for Latino political power—they described the data and evidence that revealed political weaknesses and posed a significant challenge for the future. Specifically, it was imperative to make important distinctions between state and local versus national politics. While large numbers and concentrations of Mexican American and other Latino citizens and voters could gain power in states and localities, their prospects in national politics were less clear because of the way in which political leaders and others choose to mobilize—or not mobilize—Latinos and the way they may attempt to play off different racial and ethnic groups against each other. These weaknesses remained visible and thematic in later work, continuing in the present volume.

Subsequently, research on Latino politics developed slowly along different tracks that corresponded to different focuses of political science research on public opinion and political behavior. One important track, less directly examined in this book on elections, was the study of political attitudes and values of different Latino groups, as they compared to each other as well as to whites and African Americans. Building on survey studies that were previously limited to a few localities, de la Garza and a team of colleagues were able to obtain support for a broader national study. This led to a major breakthrough in studying Latino political attitudes and behavior nationally with the 1989–1990 Latino National Political Survey (LNPS), which allowed researchers to compare political attitudes, values, and political behavior of Mexican Americans, Cuban Americans, Puerto Ricans, and Anglos nationally. Perhaps most important, this enabled researchers to determine to what extent particular attitudes of Latinos could be call "pan-ethnic"— common to all Latinos—or whether differences between and among the different Latino groups defied this kind of classification.

The LNPS data, which is reported in *Latino Voices* (de la Garza et al. 1992), were the first to show persuasively that there were clear differences among Latinos, with Cuban Americans standing apart from Mexican Americans and Puerto Ricans in ways we now widely acknowledge. Other more subtle and not so subtle differences across Latino groups and Anglos were analyzed and described, as well as important similarities with Anglos' attitudes. One particularly important journal article "Will the Real Americans Please Stand Up: Anglo and Mexican-American Support of Core American Values" (de la Garza, Falcón, and Garcia 1996) demonstrated strikingly that, after multivariate analysis, Mexican Americans were equally or even more supportive of the fundamental American values of individualism and patriotism than Anglos. This suggested much about American values, ethnic identity, and especially the nature of self-selection among immigrants, the nature of acculturation, and the nature of the immigrant experience more broadly. In another article, de la Garza (1995) emphasized the basic differences between Puerto Ricans and Anglos in their support for American values of individualism, patriotism, and tolerance of the rights of groups they dislike, with Puerto Ricans as much less supportive. These differences are, however, attributable to whether individuals are native-born American and use English as their main language, and to their levels of education and income. These Anglo-Latino comparisons as well as the intraethnic ones have challenged stereotypes used to characterize immigrant or migrant Latino groups. Moreover, they leave open such questions more broadly about immigrants and their values and political attitudes, and perhaps most important, in the case of Latinos (and, indeed, other pan-ethnic categorizations) the similarities with Anglos that have been found raise questions about whether it is possible to emphasize a distinctive "Latino politics."

Latino Voices and the findings from its data drove home the importance of doing valid and reliable survey research on Latino public opinion and behavior. This goes beyond the argument that Latinos should "speak in their own voice, just as polls give voice to other Americans" (Pachon and de la Garza 1998: 2). Latinos' opinions and votes need to be measured and reported accurately, without misrepresentations of them as apparently occurred in the case of voting on ballot propositions that affected the Latino community in California in the 1990s (1998).

While basic research on Latino political attitudes and values is important in understanding the tensions they may create with respect to assimilation and with regard to potential conflicts with whites and African Americans on political issues and the policy agenda, what matters most for real-world politics are observable indications of Latino political power, including high rates and levels of political participation. De la Garza, DeSipio, and their collaborators have focused on this in a series of books, of which this volume is the latest. These works have continued to find recurring patterns of political behavior and recurring themes. These include, most notably, the still limited political clout that Latinos have, despite immigration, other demographics and trends, and political changes that seemingly point in the opposite direction. With regard to voting and other forms of political participation, de la Garza and colleagues repeatedly emphasize the need for much further mobilization efforts by Latino groups and elites. In this context, some data and statistical analyses are misleading: they seem to show increasing voter participation among Latinos, suggesting that mobilization efforts have been effective and may be less necessary in the future. These results appear to be artifacts of measurement error: the inflated findings are based on self-reports about voting, not actual—*validated*—voting behavior (Abramson, Aldrich, and Rohde 2003: 77–82, 311–312nn15–19; Shaw, de la Garza, and Lee 2000). The political science lesson learned is that researchers need to be cautious, and whenever possible they should rely on actual election returns and related data, exit poll results (interviews with individuals who have just voted), and reports of voting by survey respondents that have been *validated.*

In the series of books on the elections since 1988, de la Garza and DeSipio with different teams of authors have followed these threads in full and rich ways, with the emphasis through the 1996 volume on the irony that, thus far, Latinos have become more important in various aspects of economic, social, cultural, and political life, but they have remained without much political influence in presidential politics. That is, the central question that remains is will population increases among Latinos ultimately lead to persistent and substantial influence in national elections. De la Garza and DeSipio's volumes have addressed this across elections, bringing to light certain patterns in the behavior of the political parties and political leaders.

Beginning in *From Rhetoric to Reality: Latino Politics in the 1988 Elections* (1992), the 1988 election volume, de la Garza and DeSipio track the impact of Latinos from the primaries (where Michael Dukakis benefited from Latino support in key states) through the general election and subsequent gains for Latinos based on indicators such as cabinet appointments. The 1990 election volume, *Barrio Ballots: Latino Politics in the 1990 Election* (de la Garza, Menchaca, and DeSipio 1994), which was part of the Latino Political Ethnography Project and also benefited from the LNPS project, was the first to emphasize the failure of Latino efforts to mobilize voters, the critical political importance of citizenship for Mexican immigrants, and how the redistricting efforts connected to the Voting Rights Act may have had the unintended effect of decreasing the competitiveness of elections and thereby lessening the incentives for parties and politicians in particular localities and more generally to engage in large-scale voter mobilization efforts. De la Garza and DeSipio (1993) elaborate on this further in a *Texas Law Review* article, in which they even suggest, to emphasize the severity of the mobilization problem, that voting by noncitizens be allowed in subnational elections—a possibility that has been suggested by others ten years later.

The 1992 election volume *Ethnic Ironies: Latino Politics in the 1992 Elections* (de la Garza and DeSipio 1996) continues to examine these phenomena and themes. De la Garza's chapter in the volume makes one pattern and theme in the series of books on the elections quite clear: the *variable* nature of the behavior of the parties and their candidates toward the role Latinos play in the elections. The irony that emerged in 1992 was that Latino voters were more influential and played a greater role in the national as well as state elections, even though Latino leaders and organizations played less of a formal role in the campaign. The Democrats did not target any effort toward the Latino vote; rather, Latinos were treated like any other Democratic constituency. This suggests that Latino voters were, in fact, part of the mainstream Democratic electorate. Thus, Latinos were mobilized through a more general process of outreach. Ironically, too, in this case Latinos mattered less in determining the outcomes of the states with the largest Latino populations than in states with significant but smaller numbers. In contrast, again owing to the variable nature of party and candidate behavior, de la Garza and DeSipio's 1996 volume reflected its title, *Awash in the Mainstream: Latino Politics in the 1996 Elections* (de la Garza and DeSipio 1999): the Latino vote received no special attention by the parties and candidates in the big election picture. In short, key indicators could readily be cited that illuminated the problems with voter mobilization: voter turnout declined in fully fifteen of seventeen competitive House districts, where Latino voters presumably could have made a difference.

This new volume on the 2000 election could well refer again to "ironies" in its title. De la Garza and DeSipio begin their overview chapter by emphasizing how fully unusual and distinctive the election was: both parties tried to win the Latino vote. Latinos had become a key part of the electorate—from the standpoint of campaigning. In the end, once the vote was untangled and fully—though not necessarily accurately—counted, the impact of the Latino vote overall was not enormously different from previous elections. Why was this?

Short of any large nationwide swelling in the numbers of Latino voters, the political rules, institutions, and structure matter in a very big way, especially in how voters in states are not fully counted through the electoral college. Had Vice President Al Gore won the presidency based on the popular vote alone, or as the result of Cuban Americans in Florida realigning with the Democratic Party, there might be a compelling new, though still tentative, story to tell about Latinos and American elections.

As elections stand, the rules and structure continue to interact with the demographic and electoral geography that tends to compartmentalize the effect of Latino electoral power largely within a limited set of states and localities as the chapters in this volume show. Missing from this discussion are a number of large and nationally visible industrial and heartland states. While a lot of important politics is local—with due respect to former House Speaker Tip O'Neill—and occurs in the states examined in the chapters of this volume, the national scene and the national political agenda are of great concern with regard to broad matters of equality and other issues and policies of concern to Latinos. The respect and influence that Latinos have had has come significantly from population—numbers and growth—not necessarily from more organized demands being made independently on the political parties.

Under what conditions might greater attention be paid to such concerns and demands of Latinos? As de la Garza and DeSipio's account and several of the chapters directly show or suggest, the basic conditions are in place. Political changes are poised to come with the effect of population growth being augmented by increasing rates of political mobilization and the use of Latinos' resources in politics. This requires, however, that rates of Latino participation, as measured in terms of multiple activities and multiple dimensions, increase beyond the increments of Latino population growth.

A key political element that has emerged and is in place is summed up by the observation that both Democratic and Republican candidates felt compelled to campaign in Spanish. The Republican Party wants to compete for Latinos' votes beyond those of Cuban Americans, as George W. Bush did in campaigning for governor in Texas. Furthermore, even taking into account the distinctiveness of New York City and state politics, the fact that Republican governor George Pataki and Mayor Michael Bloomberg were reelected and elected, respectively, with substantially increased percentages of the Latino (heavily Puerto Rican) vote relative to the support Republicans had received historically, suggests the options and opportunities that are open to the Republican Party. This would allow, as de la Garza and DeSipio note, Latinos to "begin playing a more substantive role in the Republican Party than in the past." This would, in turn, compel the Democrats to follow suit even more aggressively than they have. The questions left, of course, are: What mobilization strategy to use and how to implement it, and to what extent will this lead to actual empowerment?

There are a number of forces working against this empowerment that are well known to political scientists, though these are not always easy to weigh precisely in explaining the political behavior—or lack thereof—of Latinos or individuals in other groups. The most well-known ones are the socioeconomic resources, education and income, and in addition, other personal, "civic" related, or "social capital" resources in which Latinos as well as others lag behind (Burns, Schlozman, and Verba 2001; Putnam 2000; cf. Fuchs, Shapiro, and Minnite 2001). Attention to such resources can only take the analysis so far, since as education and income have increased nationally, participation has not also increased. If the reason for this is in fact that "sorting" and competitive processes occur that keep the barriers up to many individuals, not just Latinos who have not long been part of the mainstream (Nie, Junn, and Stehlik-Barry 1996), then it is necessary to look at other factors bearing directly and separately on Latinos' involvement in politics (though applicable to other immigrant-related populations as well).

One obvious factor is American citizenship status, for reasons that include it as a legal requirement for voting and also the way it affects how individuals interact with other citizens in economic, social, and political life (Segura et al. 1999; Fuchs, Shapiro, and Minnite 2001). Another is English-language proficiency, not only as a necessary resource for following politics and voting, but also as an indicator of ease of interactions and involvement for individuals in social and civic life, going beyond their immediate Latino community.

Both citizenship and language proficiency, and their consequences for political involvement, are options available, in particular, to Latinos of all ages (with the exception of citizenship for some illegal immigrants). Age itself, that is *age cohort*, is another factor. As de la Garza and DeSipio fully note, Latinos are much younger compared to non-Hispanic whites and blacks, and this raises the broader questions about how newly arrived or first-generation immigrants are socialized politically in the United States (see Jackson 2003, on the age effect). In a review essay, de la Garza (2004) aptly observes that the importance of opportunities and mechanisms for socialization have not been fully recognized in understanding the barriers to Latino political incorporation and empowerment. There are, however, other broader phenomena that very likely magnify the consequences of this claim as it is restricted to Latinos and perhaps other immigrant-related groups.

The broader trends that must be taken into account concern, most of all, socialization processes as they have affected *all* new cohorts of young adults nationwide, among which Latinos are a part. There are wider trends at work, not just those affecting Latinos. From the standpoint of political science, there is nothing striking about this claim; in this context, Latinos are considered as part of the mainstream in addition to being possibly affected in distinctive ways. The general trend is that new cohorts of adults have been participating less in politics—have lower rates of voter turnout—than previous generations and especially compared to the New Deal and World War II generation. While Robert D. Putnam (1995, 2000) sees this as part of declining social capital in the United States, regardless of its cause(s), the trend is clear and compelling: the youngest American adults are the least likely to vote and this participation has not thus far increased as they age to reach the levels of older cohorts, despite the higher levels of education of new generations. It remains an open question as to whether they or the next young cohorts will catch up. Thus, arguments concerning the lack of socialization or the impediments to political socialization of Latinos has to be assessed in this context. The barriers to Latinos and the difficulties of expanding their mobilization into politics and thereby increasing attention to them may be more closely related to current national trends in which the kinds of processes of political socialization that occurred in the past through the family and communities and political parties and other organizations that pulled people into politics. Newly naturalized immigrants as well as the children of foreign-born parents may be caught within the decline in socialization and mobilization processes nationally. What is clear is that future research on this as it pertains to Latinos should approach this from the broader political science perspective and compare the attitudes and behavior of Latinos with those of the rest of the population at large. It may, however, be the case that the particular acculturation of Latinos may have separate adverse effects (Michelson 2003b).

The question thus becomes how to break out of this general pattern of decline. How might this national trend and also the trends among Latinos (and other immigrant groups) be reversed? Reversing these trends is a major challenge for twenty-first-century American politics, and recent research suggests that this will be tough going. Since the 1960s, the public's trust and confidence in the country's political leaders and its politics has declined, and the public has shown its disdain for political conflict and polarization (Nye, Zelikow, and King 1997; Jacobs and Shapiro 2000). Some analysts have identified the predisposition that Americans now have to avoid political conflict since it makes them very uncomfortable (Hibbing and Theiss-Morse 2002)—though we cannot tell whether this has long been the case—when this began and how long it has

been so. To overcome this would seem to require a complete transformation of American politics, offsetting forty years of recent political history. Or, more modestly, as the same analysts suggest, we
might start by changing what schools teach about civic life and
real-world politics. These are enormous challenges and difficult expectations to fulfill, and even if this began to alter the mass public's
attitudes and behavior, the effects on Latinos and others may still
be uncertain.

One trend affecting new generations that political scientists have
devoted special attention too is the apparent decline in efforts by political parties, organized groups such as labor unions (related to the
gradual decline in percentage of workers who are union members),
and others to *mobilize* potential voters (Rosenstone and Hansen
1993). While it is true that the political parties and campaigns, as
noted earlier and as the chapters that follow reflect, visibly attempt
to engage voters and compete for votes, spending all-time record
amounts of money on this, it is the *method* of campaigning and mobilization that has changed. Money is spent on television ads, direct
mail, public appearances, and phone banks. What is missing, however, are the kinds of in-person contacting and canvassing that have
long been known to be effective in mobilizing voters. Some field experiments have confirmed this in the case of local elections (Green,
Gerber, and Nickerson 2003), and other research has begun to show
the effectiveness of this in the case of mobilizing Latino voters even
in more rural areas (Michelson 2003a).

The effectiveness of this personal contact has to do with the
added salience and importance that gets attached to voting by
virtue of the contact alone. This kind of mobilization may occur
devoid of any politically important content of an election itself
that might motivate citizens further. Further research could re-
veal—and some evidence already exists—that mobilization efforts
that are likely to be most effective are those that can emphasize
substantive politics and issues that can arouse voters. Some research has already found that the *threat* imposed by ethnically or
racially charged ballot propositions in California captured the attention of and mobilized Latinos, especially recent immigrants
who are among the least likely to vote (Pantoja and Segura 2003;
Pachon and de la Garza 1998). The mobilizing effect of threat has
its basis in the psychology of emotions that can draw individuals'

attentions to important problems and concerns, and these can affect individuals' behaviors directly and autonomously (Marcus, Neuman, and MacKuen 2000). One recent study showed how telephone contacting and mobilization can be effective in the kind of politicized context that has existed in California since the mid-1990s (Ramirez 2002). Other researchers have argued more broadly about the importance of the social and political context for mobilization and participation (see Leighley 2001; Vargas-Ramos 2003).

These reflections on Latino politics and other themes and concerns of political scientists provide one backdrop for the chapters that follow, and they raise questions for future observations and research beyond this volume. The influence of Latinos in U.S. elections requires attention to population growth and to political party strategies and tactics in election years that this volume covers well. Population growth does not automatically lead to electoral power, since such empowerment requires an increase in the number of Latino *voters*. Changes in the number of actual voters hinges on changes in the numbers of those who are citizens and how effectively processes of political socialization and mobilization lead citizens ultimately to vote. The fact that the following chapters focus on how the election played out at the state level confirms both the importance and constraint of geography that bears on the overall political clout of Latinos. The influence of Latinos on party politics in particular states does not necessarily translate to empowerment nationally. The latter requires Latinos being a force to reckon with in additional states. Will migration and further population growth move in this direction? Even if so, these demographic changes are not enough. Political science research on voter mobilization and on how individuals and groups respond to threat suggests scenarios that could change the dynamics and fabric of American politics. We await to see how this plays out in the next presidential election.

NOTE

I thank Rodolfo O. de la Garza and Louis DeSipio for their comments and for inviting me to contribute this introduction.

1

Between Symbolism and Influence

Latinos and the 2000 Elections

LOUIS DESIPIO and RODOLFO O. DE LA GARZA

THE 2000 PRESIDENTIAL RACE WAS LIKE NO OTHER IN AMERICAN history. It was the longest, the most expensive, and, ultimately, the most contested of the nation's fifty-four presidential elections. In the end, the winner's margin was, depending on one's perspective, 537[1] Florida voters or the vote of just one Supreme Court justice.

The race was also distinctive from another perspective. It was the first election in which the candidates of both major national parties campaigned in a foreign language, specifically Spanish. Additionally, this was the first time that the Republican Party systematically reached out to the Hispanic[2] community, and it was the first time that winning the Hispanic vote was an explicit objective of both major parties. Consequently, this campaign stands out as a new benchmark indicating that Latinos have become a significant component of the electorate.

As noteworthy as the tenor of the 2000 campaigns was from a Hispanic perspective, it must be emphasized that Latinos did not have an enhanced impact on the results of the election. Despite some hints at the beginning of the campaign season that because of their numbers Latinos would have a significant impact on the election's outcome, their eventual role looked much like that of previous presidential races. The causes for this relative unimportance can be found both inside and outside Latino communities. Latino demographic characteristics continue to create barriers to full empowerment. While these demographic traits could be overcome, candidates and political institutions failed to mobilize Latino voters and noncompetitive races dampened the incentives to mobilize. The electoral college and the laws of most states allocating electoral college votes on a winner-take-all basis discount total popular votes received in favor of the number of states won. Finally, Latino leaders and organizations failed to mobilize Latino adults to overcome these factors.

In regards to changes from previous election cycles resulting from Latino-led efforts, there were few. Latinos did not have a major voice in campaign strategy in either the Al Gore or George W. Bush campaigns or in either major party, and neither national nor local Latino leadership played a major role in mobilizing Latino voters outside of some nontraditional and small Latino communities in highly competitive states (such as Wisconsin). Thus, while there is no doubt that partisan outreach to Latino communities was at an all time high in 2000, and that both campaigns were respectful rather than hostile to Latino culture and related policies such as bilingualism and immigrant rights, this was the result of Latino population growth rather than of the parties responding to organized demands from the Latino community.

These two observations about the Latino role in the 2000 elections—new levels of campaign and party concern about Latino sensitivities and Latino influence no greater than in past races—may seem contradictory. They are related to the extent that the Latino role in the campaign and its outcome reflect Latino initiatives versus their just being there. That their importance is a result of the changed tone of the campaign represents the latter. That is, the changed tone of the Republican campaign may be seen as a Republican initiative to prevent Mexican Americans from mobilizing against them as they had against Pete Wilson in California in 1994 and, then, against Republicans more broadly in 1996. It also reflected the belief that a substantial number of Mexican Americans could be wooed away from the Democrats. In either case, the impetus for this change came from the Republicans and was not in response to any Hispanic-driven initiative. In sum, it may be argued that the role that Latinos played in 2000 did not change significantly from what it had been previously. Furthermore, given the key roles that Hispanics played in the 1996 Democratic campaign, it may be argued that their importance within that party declined.

In this chapter, we seek to do two things. First, we seek to advance the theoretical discussion of Latinos and national elections. We evaluate how Latinos interact with the opportunities presented in national election cycles to reshape Latino influence on national and local politics. Second, we use the 2000 elections as a case study to advance our understanding of how candidates and political institutions reach out to Latinos and how Latinos organize to influence national political debates and the choice of the president. The 2000 presidential election is the fourth national campaign we analyze in this manner (de la Garza and DeSipio 1992, 1996, 1999; for an evaluation of Latino influence in an off-year election, see de la Garza, Menchaca, and DeSipio 1994).

LATINO PARTICIPATION IN NATIONAL ELECTIONS

The seeds of Latino involvement in national politics were planted in the 1930s (Pycior 1997). The first comprehensive effort to mobilize Latinos as a cohesive electorate occurred in 1960 in support of John F. Kennedy's presidential campaign (I. García 2000). Yet, it is only in the modern era—since the extension of the Voting Rights Act to Latinos in 1975—that it is possible to speak of a national "Latino" as opposed to Mexican American or Cuban American politics that has a predictable impact on candidates' strategies and electoral outcomes. Equally important, it is only in this contemporary era that reliable data are available to measure Latino participation and candidate choice in national as well as state and local contests. Thus, the eight national contests since 1976 offer a template on which theories of national Latino politics are built.

Our studies of these elections have identified three patterns of Latino participation and nonparticipation. One is almost entirely externally driven. In response to increasingly sophisticated efforts by candidates and campaigns to reach out to Latinos, the Latino vote takes on strategic importance in some electoral outcomes. The 1992 race, which was close nationally and in states with large Latino populations, is an example of this pattern, particularly on the Democratic side where the Bill Clinton campaign experimented with two models of Latino outreach (discussed later on). Second, again in selected cases, Latinos have organized to influence outcomes, though this phenomenon is much more common at the local rather than the national level. The 1988 Texas Democratic primary offers an example. Hispanic leaders organized Latino voters to support Michael Dukakis in the state's primary. Finally, in some cases little effort is made to win Latino votes, and Latinos do little internal organizing to shape the electoral outcome. The 1996 Bob Dole presidential campaign offers a clear example of a weak outreach effort; Latino leaders did little to influence either the Democratic or Republican campaigns in 1996.

As is evident in the 2000 race, outreach does not guarantee that Latinos will be influential in shaping outcomes. Although the Latino vote has increased from election to election in the period we have studied, Latino nonvoters—that is, eligible Latinos who do not go to the polls—have increased at an equally rapid pace (see table 1.1). Between 1976 and 2000, the number of Latino voters recorded in the Current Population Survey (CPS) increased by approximately 183 percent from 2,098,000 to 5,934,000.[3] In the same period, the number of adult U.S. citizen nonvoters increased by almost 176 percent. In 2000, the adult U.S. citizen nonvoters exceeded the number of voters by 1.3 million. Adult noncitizens increased even more rapidly, from 1.9 million to 8.4 million in this twenty-four-year period. Thus, while electoral institutions have increased their sophistication at reaching out to Latinos and the number of Latinos voting has increased, there is still no pattern of overall Latino electoral mobilization that reaches more than a small share of Latino adults.

Candidate and Campaign Outreach to Latinos in Presidential Elections

Over the four presidential elections that we have studied most closely, the most dramatic change that we have observed is the development of targeted strategies to recruit Latino voters. In the period between 1988 and 2000, candidates and their parties have ex-

Table 1.1   Latino Adult Voters, Adult Citizen Nonvoters, and Adult Non–U.S. Citizens, 1976–2000

	Latino Voters	Latino Adult Citizen Nonvoters	Latino Adult Non–U.S. Citizens
1976	2,098,000	2,620,000	1,876,000
1980	2,453,000	3,112,000	2,645,000
% Change 1976–1980	+16.9%	+18.8%	+41.0%
1984	3,092,000	3,622,000	3,027,000
% Change 1980–1984	+26.0%	+16.4%	+14.4%
1988	3,710,000	4,368,000	4,815,000
% Change 1984–1988	+20.0%	+20.6%	+59.1%
1992	4,238,000	4,540,000	5,910,000
% Change 1988–1992	+14.2%	+3.9%	+22.7%
1996	4,928,000	6,281,000	7,217,000
% Change 1992–1996	+16.3%	+38.3%	+22.1%
2000	5,934,000	7,224,000	8,440,000
% Change 1996–2000	+20.4%	+15.0%	+16.9%
% Change 1976–2000	**+182.8%**	**+175.7%**	**+349.9%**

Notes: Current Population Survey (CPS) voting data likely overreport turnout and the U.S. citizen population. Despite this overreporting, it is the only source that allows comparison of Latino turnout and nonparticipation across elections.

The CPS is based on a survey of approximately 80,000 individuals conducted in the weeks after the election. Small sample sizes for specific subsets of the Latino adult population, such as non–U.S. citizens, ensure that the reported voting, nonvoting, and non–U.S. citizenship rates are estimates. We would encourage looking at trends, as opposed to specific year to year changes.

Sources: U.S. Bureau of the Census (1978; 1982; 1986; 1990; 1994; 1998; 2002c); Current Population Survey (Series P-20).

perimented with at least three outreach strategies. Candidates have run Latino-specific campaigns to reach Latino voters from within the presidential campaign that have paralleled and often been linked to other group-specific campaigns. In 1996, for example, Dole's Latino campaign was located in an office with other interests (such as blacks and farmers) and competed with these groups for access to campaign funds. Second, some campaigns have incorporated Hispanic mobilization efforts into multiple aspects of the campaign, which diminishes the importance of the Latino-specific overtures. The 1992 and 1996 Clinton campaigns exemplify this model of outreach. A third model that we have observed is to rely on party-coordinated campaigns to reach out to Latino voters instead of developing specific Hispanic initiatives. The 1996 Clinton campaign and 2000 Gore and Bush campaigns relied extensively on party coordinated campaigns.

Traditionally, campaigns to reach Latino voters were not well integrated into the broader campaigns. As a result, the Latino message was not well integrated into the broader themes of the campaign. Prior to 1988 when Latino outreach was rare, Latino campaigns often had an ad hoc character that did not facilitate broader incorporation into the general campaign (I. García 2000). In the most narrow cases, these outreach efforts were not comprehensively designed "Latino campaigns," but were instead isolated visits to Latino populations often at the end of the campaign when candidates were scrambling for every possible vote (Rosales 2000). We have characterized this traditional pattern, which is not unheard of in contemporary Latino politics, as "taco politics" (de la Garza, Menchaca, and DeSipio 1994).

In the contemporary era (beginning roughly in 1988), several campaigns have tried to distinguish the Latino message from that of the broader campaign. In at least one case, this worked well—Dukakis's 1988 campaign in the Texas primary, when a successful narrow and focused effort to win Latino votes allowed him an unexpected win in a southern primary (de la Garza 1992). Usually, however, campaigns that distinguish the Latino message see conflict between the Latino and mainstream messages. In George H. W. Bush's 1992 presidential race, a series of Latino-themed events focusing on Bush's connection to Latinos, such as his support for bilingual education and affirmative action (relative to his opponent, Clinton), may have appealed to Latinos, but alienated many whites who also attended the rallies (de la Garza and DeSipio 1996: 28). Whatever their overall Latino strategy, however, throughout the modern era, candidates—and particularly Republican candidates—have targeted a unique message to Cuban Americans.

The 1990s have seen a significant change in how campaigns package their Latino message. The success of Clinton's effort to mainstream Latino outreach in his 1992 campaign perhaps sealed the fate of the older model of ethnic-specific campaign messages. Despite his "campaign for all Americans," leaders of Latino organizations successfully demanded that a parallel Hispanic-specific outreach organization be created. Clinton's success in presenting a similar message to all audiences marginalized the more traditional campaign outreach structure developed in response to Hispanic leaders' demands. The existence of a Hispanic campaign notwithstanding, in 1992 Latinos became part of the broader Clinton message. By 1996, the Latino message was central to the Clinton campaign message and more targeted efforts—such as Spanish-language media outreach—were left to the Democratic Party. His opponent in 1996, Dole, ran a more traditional, ethnically distinct campaign to reach Latinos, but this effort was not funded and failed completely to win Latino votes for the Dole campaign. In 2000, both major candidates made their Latino outreach message, which emphasized candidate bilingualism and tolerance of immigrants, part of their broader campaign messages. This allowed both candidates, and Bush in particular, to use their core campaign message to make direct appeals to the Latino community without alienating white voters.

Message, of course, is just one aspect of Latino outreach. The second dimension of the Latino campaign that has changed over the period of our observation is where the Latino campaign is positioned within the broader campaign. As with efforts to shape the campaigns' Latino messages, early campaigns relied on ad hoc structures to situate Latino campaigns. By 1988, it was customary to name the Latino campaign (usually with the *Viva!* nomenclature) and to locate it within the campaign as part of a group-based outreach. In the contemporary era, this is the default campaign style. In 1988, both George H. W. Bush and Dukakis relied on it, as did Bush in 1992 and Dole in 1996. To the extent that candidates in the primary campaigns sought Latino votes (a rarity for reasons analyzed later on), they, too, set their Latino outreach mechanisms apart.

Beginning in 1992, however, a new model of Hispanic involvement in presidential campaigns emerged, particularly in Democratic campaigns. While targeted "Latino campaign" initiatives remain, they no longer serve as the only focus for campaign outreach to Latino votes. Second, Latino participation in the campaign is no longer restricted to Latino outreach initiatives.

Clinton's two campaigns appear to have institutionalized this new model. Initially, the leaders of his general election campaign tried to do away with a specific office for Latino outreach. The

Clinton campaign failed in this under pressure from the leaders of Latino organizations. It succeeded dramatically in the other dimension, however, which was placing Latinos throughout the campaign structure. So, when the Clinton campaigns needed insight into reaching Latino voters, multiple perspectives were available. More importantly, perhaps, many state campaign directors were Latino, both in states with large and small Latino populations. By the 2000 race, when Latino votes were actively sought (at least initially) by both campaigns, the Clinton model was the norm.

The 1990s also saw a second change in the management of outreach to Latino communities (one that paralleled a restructuring of presidential campaigns generally). Candidates, and particularly Democratic candidates, came to rely increasingly on their parties' coordinated campaigns. These were efforts funded by the parties to get out the vote for the entire party ticket. Through the 1990s, these efforts became more sophisticated at identifying Latinos likely to vote and informing them of reasons why they should vote for the party's ticket. Given their focus, though, these efforts neglect Latinos not likely to vote (except, perhaps, for newly registered voters). Even voter registration efforts funded through the coordinated campaigns are crafted to reach primarily likely future voters. Both candidates relied on the coordinated campaigns extensively in 2000 as had Clinton in 1996. The coordinated campaigns usually served as the organizing body for tours of Latino influentials that did the last-minute get-out-the-vote campaigns in Latino communities nationwide. They also produced the vast majority of bilingual election materials used as part of the presidential campaigns.

In general, with the exception of outreach to the Cuban American community in Florida, Republicans have invested less to win Latino votes in presidential elections. In the past, Republicans either (1) ignored Latinos, (2) disenfranchised Mexican Americans, (3) pursued Latino votes while showing no respect for Latino cultural practices, or (4) included among the contenders for the party's nomination individuals such as Pat Buchanan and Pete Wilson, who promoted their candidacies with explicit anti-immigrant slogans, and incorporated these anti-immigrant slogans into the party's platform. The 2000 race was unique in that all such practices were repudiated to varying degrees by the Bush campaign. It used bilingualism throughout the campaign, including in venues where few spoke

Spanish. Equally importantly, it was tolerant of immigration at current levels and respectful of Mexican cultural practices.

These changes in Republican outreach, coupled with well-institutionalized outreach by Democrats that had begun in the 1992 and 1996 presidential races, made 2000 the most Hispanic-friendly campaign in the nation's history and could well serve as the model for future presidential elections.

In sum, the four presidential cycles that we have studied have seen both an expansion and contraction of Latino outreach. On the positive side, Latinos are less pigeon holed than they have been in most campaigns since 1988. Latinos now hold positions, and positions of power in some cases, throughout both Democratic and Republican campaigns. As a result, while offices designated as responsible for the Latino campaign remain, they are not the only voice mobilizing outreach to Latinos. On the other hand, the bulk of Latino outreach is now handled by the parties. The parties are narrow in their focus, seeking only to reach Latinos who are likely to vote. Although this segment of the Latino electorate continues to increase, the number of eligible nonvoters continues to grow as rapidly. As a result, campaign and party investment in outreach did not necessarily mean that presidential campaigns at the end of the twentieth century had become more likely to increase Latino turnout.

If future campaigns follow the outreach model evidenced in 2000, it is possible that Latinos will begin playing a much more substantive role in the Republican Party than they have in the past. That is, if Republicans invest in mobilizing Latinos, it seems inevitable that a new generation of Latino Republican political operatives will develop and articulate Latino perspectives on a range of issues that will be incorporated into the Republican agenda. If that occurs, we would expect the Democrats to follow suit. Should such a pattern develop, the 2000 campaign may come to be seen as a watershed of Latino political involvement. Until then, the conduct of this election and its outcome are but another example that increasing Latino electoral influence requires more than population growth.

LATINO VOTERS AND NONVOTERS

When do Latinos vote and when do they not participate? Ultimately, the answer to this question requires an assessment both of the reasons that all citizens, regardless of ethnicity, participate or not (De-Sipio 1996a) as well as the reasons unique to the Latino experience that may further dampen Latino electoral participation (Guerra and Fraga 1996; Shaw, de la Garza, and Lee 2000).

Among all racial and ethnic populations, voters are more likely to be found among the more affluent, the better educated, and the middle aged and old (Wolfinger and Rosenstone 1980). These patterns also apply to Latinos (see table 1.2). As Latinos are disproportionately likely to be younger, poorer, and less educated than the population as a whole, the impact of these demographic characteristics is greater for Latinos than for other groups (DeSipio 1996a). Clearly, each of these participation-dampening characteristics can be overcome at the individual or community level through individual interests or community mobilization (see Verba, Schlozman, and Brady 1995). That said, across multiple elections, demographic traits correlate with voting and Latinos are at a disadvantage.

Relative to non-Hispanic whites and blacks, Latinos are considerably younger. Approximately 19 percent of Latino adults are between the ages of eighteen and twenty-four, compared to 12 percent of non-Hispanic whites and 16 percent of non-Hispanic blacks. At the other extreme, just 37 percent of Latino U.S. citizen adults are forty-five or older. Among whites, 51 percent are forty-five or older. The differences in education and income are similarly dramatic. Nearly 15 percent of Latinos have nine or fewer years of education, compared to 4 percent of whites and 6 percent of blacks. Eleven percent of Latino adult U.S. citizens have college degrees or postgraduate work. The comparable figure for non-Hispanic whites is 26 percent. Among Latinos, 17 percent have family incomes of less than $15,000 per year. The comparable figures for whites is 6 percent. African Americans have a higher share of households with these very low incomes (20 percent). In sum, simply knowing the demographic profile of the Latino population predicts lower than average levels of electoral participation.

In addition to these characteristics that shape the likelihood of voting for all electorates, other traits are unique to Latinos (or to ethnic populations with a large share of immigrants). These characteristics further dampen their electoral participation. Most important among these is very high rates of non–U.S. citizenship. With a handful of exceptions in local elections, non–U.S. citizens cannot vote in

Table 1.2   Turnout Rates and Share of Adult Citizen Population for Age, Education, and Income Cohorts of Latinos, Non-Latino Whites, and Non-Latino Blacks, 2000

	Latino Adult		Non-Hispanic White Adult		Non-Hispanic Black Adult	
	Turnout %	Citizen %	Turnout %	Citizen %	Turnout %	Citizen %
Age						
18–24	25.6	(19.1)	38.1	(11.7)	36.2	(16.1)
25–44	43.2	(43.4)	57.8	(37.7)	56.5	(43.8)
45–64	55.8	(25.9)	69.7	(32.1)	65.5	(27.9)
65–74	61.1	(7.0)	73.7	(9.8)	69.2	(7.7)
75+	58.9	(4.5)	70.8	(8.8)	60.3	(4.5)
Education						
LT 9 years	38.5	(14.6)	38.5	(3.7)	47.0	(5.8)
9–12 yrs., no diploma	30.4	(17.1)	38.2	(8.3)	43.1	(14.8)
H.S. grad.	41.8	(32.8)	54.0	(33.3)	51.7	(35.0)
Some college	52.3	(24.1)	65.0	(28.6)	63.0	(29.4)
BA or equiv.	67.5	(7.6)	76.9	(17.5)	74.4	(10.5)
Advanced degree	73.8	(3.7)	83.4	(8.5)	78.6	(4.5)
Family Income (per year)						
LT $5,000	27.7	(2.9)	36.8	(0.8)	35.6	(3.9)
$5,000–$9,999	38.7	(5.1)	39.7	(1.6)	43.2	(7.6)
$10–$14,999	34.6	(9.1)	44.8	(3.3)	51.1	(8.7)
$15–$24,999	38.8	(15.3)	53.8	(7.5)	54.0	(13.3)
$25–$34,999	44.3	(14.8)	60.0	(10.6)	60.4	(12.7)
$35–$49,999	48.9	(15.3)	63.7	(15.0)	63.2	(13.8)
$50–$74,999	51.9	(15.6)	70.9	(20.1)	67.3	(15.2)
$75,000+	67.1	(13.6)	76.4	(26.5)	75.9	(11.3)
Refused	40.3	(8.3)	52.5	(14.6)	48.2	(13.4)

Note: The figure in parentheses is the share of the adult citizen population made up of that age, education, or income cohort.

Source: Authors' compilations based on U.S. Bureau of the Census (2002c: tables 2, 6, 9).

U.S. elections. Fully 39 percent of Latino adults nationally were thus excluded from electoral participation in 2000. Noncitizenship rates for non-Latino whites and blacks are 3.6 percent and 7.3 percent, respectively. Only Asian Americans exceeded the Latino levels of non–U.S. citizenship among adults. Approximately 41 percent of Asian Pacific Islander adults were not U.S. citizens in 2000 (U.S. Bureau of the Census 2002c).

The impact of noncitizenship on Latino eligibility to participate in elections varies across states (see table 1.3). In California, more than six in ten Latino adults were not U.S. citizens. There are more than twice as many noncitizen adults as voters. In New Mexico, on the other hand, just one in eight Hispanic adults is a noncitizen. Six of the states with large Latino populations have noncitizen adult populations that exceed the size of the Latino population who voted in 2000: Arizona, California, Florida, Illinois, New Jersey, and New York.

The impact of noncitizenship on Latino turnout nationally becomes clear when the reasons for nonvoting are examined (see table 1.4). In 2000, approximately 15.6 million Latino adults did not vote. Among these Latino nonvoters, non–U.S. citizens made up more than half (53.9 percent). Among non-Latino whites and blacks, 5.6 percent and 10.9 percent, respectively, of nonvoters were not U.S. citizens. Noncitizenship is the largest cause of nonvoting in Latino populations while the absence of registration among citizens characterizes white and black nonvoters who do not vote.

Noncitizenship spurs a second participation-dampening influence on Latino communities. In areas of the highest Latino concentration, there are significant shares of noncitizens as well as citizens who are less likely to vote because of demographic characteristics, such as youth, lower levels of formal education, and low incomes. These areas, thus, have a relatively low concentration of likely voters relative to the total population. Candidates are consequently less

Table 1.3   Latino Turnout and Noncitizenship by State, 2000

	Latino Adults	Latinos Voted 2000	Noncitizen Adults 2000
Arizona	910,000	247,000 (27.1%)	294,000 (32.3%)
California	6,514,000	1,597,000 (24.5%)	4,025,000 (61.8%)
Colorado	478,000	158,000 (33.1%)	129,000 (27.0%)
Florida	2,162,000	678,000 (31.4%)	897,000 (41.5%)
Illinois	771,000	218,000 (28.3%)	371,000 (48.1%)
New Jersey	583,000	179,000 (30.7%)	237,000 (40.7%)
New Mexico	484,000	191,000 (39.5%)	58,000 (12.0%)
New York	1,706,000	502,000 (29.4%)	629,000 (36.9%)
Texas	4,414,000	1,300,000 (29.5%)	1,241,000 (28.1%)

Note: Percentages reflect percentage of Latino adults who voted or who were non–U.S. citizens.

Source: Authors' compilations based on U.S. Bureau of the Census (2002c: table 4a).

Table 1.4   Reasons for Not Voting, by Race and Ethnicity, 2000

	Latino	Non-Hispanic White	Non-Hispanic Black
Total Nonvoters	15,664,000	58,566,000	10,838,000
	%	%	%
Not a U.S. citizen	53.9	5.6	10.9
U.S. citizen, not registered	35.8	70.3	66.9
Registered, did not vote	10.3	24.1	22.2
Reasons Registered Voters Report That They Did Not Vote			
Too busy	39.3	34.6	32.1
Not interested	10.8	13.3	10.2
Illness	8.2	11.2	12.8
Didn't like candidates/issues	4.1	6.0	3.5
Out of town	5.8	9.2	4.9
Forgot	7.0	4.9	7.5
Transportation problems	2.3	1.5	3.7
Inconvenient polling place/hours	1.1	1.2	0.7
Registration problems	4.8	3.4	4.1
Bad weather	0.2	0.2	0.1
Other reasons	9.2	8.2	8.1
Refused to answer	7.2	6.3	12.3

Source: Authors' compilations based on U.S. Bureau of the Census (2000c: tables 2, 12).

likely to invest the resources to conduct get-out-the-vote efforts in areas of high Latino concentration (de la Garza and DeSipio 1993; for a different conclusion based on recent Los Angeles County voting data, see Barreto, Segura, and Woods 2002). It is, of course, these areas that most need this outreach because they have more newly eligible voters (whether due to naturalization or citizens entering the ages of voter eligibility). Research shows that the one factor that will increase the likelihood of Latino voting that can be controlled by Latino communities themselves is personally contacting voters to encourage their turnout (Shaw, de la Garza, and Lee 2000). However, the low concentration of voters in high-density Latino neighborhoods makes this contact less likely.

What explanations do Latinos themselves offer for their failure to vote? In 2000, the Census Bureau asked registered voters who did not go to the polls why they did not vote (see table 1.4). Broadly, the reasons offered by Latinos were not distinct from those of whites and blacks. Latinos were slightly more likely to report that they were too busy to vote and somewhat less likely than non-Hispanic whites to report that they were either not interested in the outcome or that they didn't like the candidates.

The net effect of these demographic traits and ethnic character-istics is for Latinos to vote at levels lower than those for whites and African Americans. In 2000, for example, 27.5 percent of Lati-nos reported to the Census Bureau that they voted, compared to 60.4 percent of non-Hispanic whites and 54.1 percent of non-Hispanic blacks (U.S. Bureau of the Census 2002c: table 2). If the effect of non–U.S. citizenship is factored out, 45.1 percent of Latino citizens reported that they voted in 2000 (compared to 61.8 percent of non-Hispanic whites and 55.7 percent of non-Hispanic African Americans).

Certainly, this gap can be overcome in any election cycle if Latino citizens develop a heightened interest in the outcome of the race or if they are mobilized at new levels. The 2000 race spurred many observers to think that it might have been that year for two reasons. First, the number of Latinos eligible to vote increased more than it had in any previous four-year period. Second, the closeness of the race led many to believe that there would be extensive mobi-lization of Latinos.

The Latino population grows at a more rapid rate than the popu-lation as a whole. It is younger and family sizes are larger. Much of this growth is spurred by immigration, however, and thus does not directly increase the size of the potential electorate. Immigrants must naturalize before they vote. Mexican immigrants who are the great majority of the Latino immigrant populations take longer to naturalize than any other large immigrant group. This means that while the Latino population grows exponentially, the increase in el-igible voters is incremental.

This pattern changed somewhat as the 2000 elections ap-proached. More than in any previous four-year period, the number of naturalized Latinos increased substantially between 1996 and 2000. For a variety of reasons, however, naturalization began to surge in the mid-1990s (DeSipio 1996c). As a result, more than 2.7 million immi-grants naturalized between 1997 and 2000, a record for any four-year period in American history. Of these approximately, 1.1 million were Latinos and most of these were adults.[4]

Extensive mobilization within the Latino community around an issue or a candidate could spur more Latinos—and particularly more naturalized immigrants and other Latinos with lower incomes or less education—to go to the polls. Arguably, this happened in 1994 in California when Proposition 187 was on the ballot and community leaders invested heavily in public information campaigns and voter mobilization (Newton 2000).

The gap between Latino and Anglo turnout could also be overcome if a candidate, campaign, or party invested extensively in Latino mobilization to win in a close statewide race. The 1960 *Viva Kennedy!* campaign in Texas is perhaps the best example of this model for targeted Latino mobilization. Extensive mobilization, particularly of nontraditional voters, is, however, the exception in presidential politics. Going into the 2000 campaign, some thought that it might prove to be just this exception because of the closeness of the race and the uncharacteristic attention paid to Latinos by Republican candidates. In the end, mobilization was at traditional levels (sparse) and the gap between Latino and non-Latino turnout remained.

Latino Influence in Presidential Elections

Ultimately, outreach to Latinos and Latino efforts to convert potential voters into voters only matter to the degree that Latino voters influence electoral outcomes and have the chance to see the candidates of their choice elected, even over the opposition of non-Latino voters. Influence, however, can take several forms. In our research, we identify four possible forms of Latino voter "influence." At its strongest, influence occurs when some *new* characteristic of the Latino vote, either more Latinos voting or Latinos voting with a new partisan balance, can explain the victor's margin. Latino leaders often speak of Latino influence in this way, particularly in terms of Latinos switching their support from one party to the other (the "swing" vote), but we find no examples of this form of influence in presidential elections between 1988 and 2000. In the current configuration of the Latino vote, this form of influence is rare. Because the Latino electorate is small in most states, the form of influence only appears when the non-Latino vote is relatively evenly divided.

The second and third forms of influence are more common. The second form of influence is felt if the Latino vote as a whole shifts the result from what it would have been if only non-Latinos had voted. In this scenario, the outcome of the election would change if the winners' vote total minus his or her Latino votes is smaller than the loser's vote total minus his or her Latino votes. Clearly, this is an unrealistic scenario, assuming as it does that no Latino voting is a realistic expectation, but it does capture a form of influence inherent in the Latino vote.

The third model takes the thought experiment of the second a bit further. It looks at a form of influence held by the partisan minorities within the Latino electorate (Republican Latinos, except in Florida) and assesses what would happen if they did not vote for the winning candidate at the rate that they did. In a close race, a Republican victor (or Democrat in Florida) may owe his or her margin of victory to the 20 or 30 percent of Latino votes. Clearly, if no Latino had voted (scenario 2), this candidate still would have won because his or her opponent won many more Latino votes. Instead, this scenario for influence looks only at what would happen if the candidate receiving a minority of the Latino votes did not receive these votes (while the candidate who received the majority of Latino votes continued to do so). Despite this unrealistic assumption, we believe that this remains a valid form of influence because it suggests the importance of Latino votes to all major candidates. Candidates likely only to receive a minority of Latino votes cannot take those votes for granted in close elections.

These second and third scenarios for Latino influence are not real-world scenarios as Latinos do vote in large numbers and will vote in larger numbers in each forthcoming election. A significant share (approximately one-third) will support the Republican (or Democrat in Florida). As with the first scenario, for either of these to appear, the non-Latino vote has to be evenly divided.

We note also that when the victory margin in a state is very small, as it was in Florida (537 votes) and New Mexico (366 votes) in 2000, any cohesive electorate can claim that it gave the victor his margin. We discuss these two cases in greater depth later on and find that Latinos have some claim on the Bush Florida victory and the Gore New Mexico victory, but see this as a special case on influence (our fourth form) that only occurs when outcomes are razor thin and many exogenous factors can explain the outcome (such as Palm Beach County, Florida's notorious "butterfly ballots").

Overall, theoretically, we find Latinos can be said to have influence on electoral outcomes in slightly less than one in three states in presidential elections between 1988 and 2000 (eleven of the thirty-six state votes for president). Because of the absence of reliable polling data and estimates of Latino voting in states with smaller Latino populations, we limit our analysis to the nine states with the largest Latino populations. In no case did the first scenario appear—the victor's margin resulting from some *new* characteristic of the Latino vote. The election that came closest to this standard was in Arizona in 1996 when growth in Latino votes and a higher share of these votes going to the Democrats almost reached the Clinton margin of victory (31,215 votes). Seven of the cases of possible influence we have identified were examples of scenario 2—the result changing if no Latino had voted. Two are examples of scenario 3—the Latino vote for the candidate receiving the minority of the Latino vote disappearing or declining significantly. In two of the eleven cases, we see the final form of influence—very close state races in which all cohesive electorates can claim influence.

New Mexico has most often seen Latino influence on presidential election outcomes (see table 1.5). In three of the four elections that we studied, New Mexico Latinos influenced the outcome. Twice, the Latino margin for the Democrats was larger than the Democratic victory margin. The final election, in 2000, was quite close and Latinos undoubtedly contributed to the Democrat's narrow victory margin (a high share of New Mexico's Latino vote went to the Democrats, but overall Latino turnout may have declined in New Mexico).

In two states, California and Illinois, Latinos cannot be said to have had influence in any of the past four presidential elections. These two states, and the four others that have only had one competitive race over the four elections studied, are likely to have seen less efforts to mobilize Latinos than Florida, New Mexico, or Arizona (which had two of four competitive races).

The likelihood of influence at the state level clearly varies by election. The 1992 race was close nationally and this closeness

Table 1.5   Latino Influence in Presidential Elections, 1988–2000

	1988	1992	1996	2000
AZ	No Latino influence	Republican Latino voters ensure Bush win (Scenario 3)	Republican victory if no Latino voted (Scenario 2)	No Latino influence
CA	No Latino influence	No Latino influence	No Latino influence	No Latino influence
CO	No Latino influence	Republican victory if no Latino voted (Scenario 2)	No Latino influence	No Latino influence
FL	No Latino influence	Democrat victory if no Latino voted (Scenario 2)	No Latino influence	Republican 537 vote win includes Latino majority (Scenario 4)
IL	No Latino influence	No Latino influence	No Latino influence	No Latino influence
NJ	No Latino influence	Republican victory if no Latino voted (Scenario 2)	No Latino influence	No Latino influence
NM	No Latino influence	Republican victory if no Latino voted (Scenario 2)	Republican victory if no Latino voted (Scenario 2)	Democrat 366 vote win includes Latino majority (Scenario 4)
NY	Republican victory if no Latino voted (Scenario 2)	No Latino influence	No Latino influence	No Latino influence
TX	No Latino influence	Republican Latino voters ensure Bush win (Scenario 3)	No Latino influence	No Latino influence

Note: "No Latino influence" occurs when the winner's margin of victory is larger than the Latino vote; scenario 2—the winner changes if no Latino votes; scenario 3—the winner changes if no Latinos vote for the winner (but continue to vote for the second-place candidate); scenario 4—a close race in which a Latino majority voted for the winner (scenario 4 is a subset of scenario 2).

Sources: de la Garza and DeSipio (1992, 1996, 1999).

focused on states with Latino populations. In 1992, Latino voters were influential in six of the nine states with large Latino populations. No other election year saw more than two states in which Latinos influenced the outcome.

LATINOS AND THE 2000 ELECTIONS

At the beginning of the 2000 presidential race, it initially appeared that Latinos would enjoy a new prominence. As the campaign continued, the candidates and parties intermittently tied their fortunes to their success in winning Latino votes, but this interest in their votes rarely translated into an active campaign to win votes or mobilization efforts to convince nonvoters to join the electorate. Just as candidates and institutions exogenous to the community did little to give Latinos a substantive role in the campaign or its outcome, Latinos themselves did little to increase their impact. With the exception of dramatic efforts to register Latino voters, Latino elites and organizations did little to establish a unique Latino voice in either candidate's campaign. Thus, the promise of playing a prominent role both in the campaign and in the election's outcome dissipated into a significant if symbolic presence.

THE PRIMARIES

By the time the primary campaigns reached states with large numbers of Latinos, each party's race was largely done. As a result, Latinos had little formal influence in selecting their party's nominees. Their role in the primary season, however, should not be dismissed as irrelevant. Latinos took on a new symbolic role, particularly in the George W. Bush campaign, that will likely serve as the foundation for a new role for Latinos in presidential electoral politics.

In terms of their formal role, the first state to hold a primary that also had large numbers of Latinos was Florida. But, by this point, the front-runners were firmly established and the active primary campaign had ended. Florida Latinos simply confirmed the status of Vice President Gore for the Democrats and Governor Bush for the Republicans. Republican Latinos gave Bush 86 percent of their votes and Democratic Latinos gave Gore 91 percent of their votes. This pattern of the primaries being over before Latinos had a chance to vote was similar to all elections since 1988 (de la Garza 1992). Although there had been some hope among Latino activists that the pattern would change because of California's decision to move its primary to mid-March, the 2000 race reinforced yet again the fact that only the first five or six primaries or caucuses have any impact on determining the party nominees. As few Latinos reside in the states that traditionally hold these early primaries or caucuses, they have few opportunities to influence the selection of the parties' nominees.

Looking only at this formal role, however, neglects the new symbolic importance of reaching out to Latinos. Throughout the campaign, Bush staked his claim on the presidency in part on the notion that he could bring Latinos into the Republican fold. His belief that he could win 40 percent of the Latino vote and build a long-term connection between the Latino community and the Republican Party took several forms that began early in the primary season. While both candidates used Spanish to signify their concern for Latino issues, it was Bush's willingness to campaign in Spanish, however ungrammatical and accented his speaking may be, that signaled the symbolic significance of the Latino electorate. During one of the early Republican presidential debates, he answered a question in Spanish, much to everyone's surprise. While he would not win awards for his fluency, this Spanish-speaking ability indicated a linguistic tolerance that had long been absent among leading Republicans ("The Spanish Test" 1999). Bush used his Spanish at appearances before national and regional Latino organizations. Again, more than other recent Republican leaders, Bush accepted invitations to speak before the associations (as did Vice President Gore, but his appearances were more the norm for Democrats). Bush also used Spanish to deflect his opponents. When asked to debate Latino issues, he agreed, but only if the debate were conducted in Spanish. This was a safe offer on Bush's part as neither candidate could have conducted the debate in Spanish.

The Bush campaign also used Spanish, and by extension Latinos, quite strategically. Early in the race, for example, it ran Spanish-language radio and print advertisements in Iowa (Bustillo 1999). The small number of Latino Republicans, particularly Spanish-dominant Latino Republicans, who would likely vote in the state's Republican presidential caucus might make this expenditure seem foolhardy. Thus, its likely target was not Latinos. Instead, by reaching out to Iowa's relative handful of Latinos, the Bush campaign was able to generate extensive media coverage that showed it to be different, and arguably more moderate, than recent Republican campaigns. As a result, by reaching out to Latinos it was able to attract moderate white voters (who were the election's ultimate swing vote). The *New Republic*'s Michelle Cottle (2000) characterizes this tactic as the "ricochet pander."

Bush's Republican opponents did not cede the sole ability to win Latino votes for the party to Bush. John McCain trumpeted the fact that he had won 55 percent of the Hispanic vote in his last Arizona Senate campaign and spoke to the annual meetings of the National Council of La Raza and the League of United Latin American Citizens.[5]

Despite McCain's efforts, the media and punditocracy had ceded the leadership of Republican Latino outreach to Bush. They, uncritically, accepted his assertions that he could win an unprecedented share of Latino votes (based in large part on one faulty exit poll from the 1998 Texas gubernatorial race). While this ultimately proved untrue, its casual acceptance made Latinos appear to be more central to Bush's campaign than they eventually proved to be.

The Republican Party used the primary season to reinforce these candidate-driven efforts to win Latino votes (Meckler 2000b). In April, they began an ad campaign in selected markets targeted at Latinos. The message of the ad was: "This year I plan to keep an open mind and vote for the best person, and that includes Republicans." When this commercial was initially released, the Republicans promised that it would be the first wave of a $7 to $10 million media campaign designed to send a message that Latinos should look again at the Republicans.

Gore did not campaign as actively for Latino votes in the primaries; he ran no Spanish language ads and he spoke Spanish only before Latino audiences (and never more than two sentences at a time). We do not mean to suggest that he took Latino votes for granted. Instead, he organized to win their votes in the general election, but he recognized that they are a solidly Democratic electorate that would likely support his candidacy in November. Their votes, however, were less

important in his primary campaign against former New Jersey senator Bill Bradley.

Following the model of the Clinton campaigns, however, Gore
invested early in organization. This took three forms. First, he
sought the endorsement of every Latino Democrat elected official
and community leader of even modest prominence that he could
find. These endorsements, ranging from Latino members of Congress to elected members of sanitation boards in California, were
cataloged and released to the press. Second, he established a Latino
campaign within the broader campaign: *Ganamos con Gore!* This
top-down grassroots organization modeled on the Clinton campaign's *Adelante con Clinton!* offered the campaign a way to reach
out to Latinos when it needed to and a focus for Latinos seeking involvement in the campaign. Although *Ganamos* was never able to
position itself as centrally in the Gore campaign as *Adelante* did in
the 1996 Clinton campaign, it did represent a much greater organizational effort than anything in the Bush campaign. Because of the
nature of the primary season, *Ganamos con Gore!* did not play that
large of a role in the primaries, but was established and ready to hit
the ground running as the general election began. Finally, senior
Latino staff in the Clinton administration (many of whom were
alumni of the 1992 and 1996 campaigns) began meeting in early
1999 to form a Latino strategy that would be a resource for Gore
when he needed it (and a pressure group, if he failed to take the
Latino vote seriously).

Senator Bradley took his message of health care reform to Latino
audiences, particularly in California, but his "minority" outreach
was primarily directed to African Americans with whom he had a
longer term relationship (Brownstein 2000). Gore and Bradley held a
debate about urban and minority issues in Harlem prior to the New
York primary, but Latinos were a literal afterthought to both candidates in this debate. Often, they would add the phrase "and Latinos"
to a discussion of an issue facing African Americans. This debate,
and the primary elections more generally, received little attention
from Latino Democratic voters.

The major candidates were not the only players in the newly
emerging game of symbolic Latino outreach. Donald Trump began
his short-lived campaign for the Reform Party nomination with a
visit to the Bay of Pigs museum in Miami (Bragg 1999). He assured

his Cuban American audience that he supported the U.S. embargo on Cuba.

The primary season saw one issue with a particular Latino resonance. On Thanksgiving Day 1999, a young Cuban *balsero* was rescued at sea by the U.S. Coast Guard. While this event was not all that unusual, the media attention and geopolitics that followed made Elián González an international figure. Some months after his return to Cuba with his father, he may also have determined the outcome of the U.S. presidency.

From the start, Elián confounded traditional partisan positions on immigration. Republicans, including Governor Bush, tended to support his right to stay in the United States. Democrats, though notably not Vice President Gore, tended to cede to the boy's father (and only surviving parent) the right to determine his country of residence. The Justice Department quite actively supported the father's rights. Had the boy not been Cuban, this story would have been of little relevance to presidential politics, but because he was, his tragic story became fodder for a national discussion about immigration, refugee policy, and the role of Cuban Americans in immigration policy making. Gore distanced himself from the administration and spoke publicly of Elián's right to stay in the United States. Not surprising, this position satisfied few. Many Democrats saw Gore as pandering to the Cuban American community and it confirmed for many a perception that Gore would say anything to win support. Cuban Americans, however, were sufficiently disenchanted with the Clinton administration that Gore had little chance of winning their support. Although the Elián case had little impact on the primaries, it would come back to haunt the Gore campaign in the general election.

In sum, the primaries offered few opportunities for Latinos to influence the selection of candidates. The calendar of the primary elections and caucuses did not work to their advantage and, as had been the case in recent elections, the candidates had largely been selected before states with a large number of Latinos voted.

Nevertheless, the primary season offered several tantalizing hints as to the role that Latinos could play in the general election. First and most important, Latinos were central to the political calculus of the Bush campaign. This was a first for the Republican candidate. Second, the primary season introduced an issue—Elián

González—that would have repercussions in what became the most important state in the general election. Finally, despite the new interest in Latinos, particularly in the Republican side, there was little effort to mobilize their votes.

THE CONVENTIONS

Often, the period after the presidential primaries but before the general election begins in earnest allows candidates the opportunity to shore up their bases and to reach out to electorates who might shift their traditional partisan affiliations. In past campaigns, this period has seen the greatest level of candidate outreach to Latinos and 2000 was no different. Equally importantly, this period between the primaries and the general elections allows Latino elites their most public role: they are courted at conventions of Latino organizations and, to a lesser degree, at the national party conventions.

The late spring and early summer sees the national conventions of most of the national Latino organizations. Over the period that we have been studying Latinos and national politics, Democratic candidates have become increasing common visitors (in-person or electronically) at these events. In 2000, Gore was not their only presidential visitor. Instead, Bush was as common a speaker at these conventions as Gore. They each spoke before the League of United Latin American Citizens and the National Council of La Raza. Their speeches did not vary dramatically from organization to organization and emphasized the candidate's symbolic respect for the Latino community more than for ethnically targeted policy agendas. The appearances probably swayed few votes among the conference's attendees, but allowed each candidate—and particularly Bush—to demonstrate the inclusiveness of his campaign.

The Democratic and Republican conventions also offered an opportunity for the candidates and Latino elites to interact. Latinos were very much on display at each convention. While this was not all that unusual for the Democrats, the Republicans scored a major victory by displaying the party's inclusiveness. Unlike the past two Republican conventions, 2000 saw an event in which ethnic and racial diversity were praised and Latinos were present both on the dais and on the convention floor throughout the convention.

Overall, Latinos were slightly better represented at the Democratic convention. Approximately 10 percent of the 4,402 delegates and alternates to the Democratic convention were Latino. On the Republican side, 8.3 percent of the 4,338 delegates and alternates were Latino. These numbers were somewhat higher than in 1996, particularly on the Republican side. In 1996, 6 percent of Democratic delegates were Latino (9 percent of Democratic delegates *and* alternates were Latino). Just 2.3 percent of 1996 Republican convention delegates were Latino in 1996 (DeSipio, de la Garza, and Setzler 1999: 21–22).

Each party was careful to provide prominent speaking positions to Latinos. At the Republican convention, Texas representative Henry Bonilla, the only non-Cuban Latino congressman, was appointed as the convention cochair. He spoke from the dais as did George P. Bush (Bush's nephew, whose mother is Mexican American), musician Jon Secada, and a number of small business owners. The Republican convention also saw a first: California assemblyperson Abel Maldonado gave a speech from the dais in Spanish. The Republicans promoted this speech heavily in both the English and Spanish press as evidence of their new inclusiveness.

The Democratic convention saw a greater range of Latino speakers, including most sitting Democratic members of Congress, the AFL-CIO's Linda Chavez-Thompson, state-level Latino elected officials, and Latino musical performers. The chief executive officer of the Democratic convention was Lydia Camarillo, the former executive director of the Southwest Voter Registration Education Project. The Democrats had a more rigorously organized Hispanic Caucus of delegates that had daily meetings and drew prominent speakers to its caucus meetings.

The Bush campaign used its convention to conduct some Latino outreach. Bush's arrival in Philadelphia began with a "Latino rally." Nominally, the event was billed as a get-out-the-vote rally, though most of the attendees were convention delegates or Bush campaign staff. The rally included performances by Secada, Celia Cruz, and others. While this event reached few Pennsylvania Latinos and the audience was overwhelmingly Anglo, the press gave the rally a great deal of coverage, undoubtedly reinforcing the general public's perception that Bush was reaching out to Latinos.

The convention period offered some excitement for Hispanic Democrats for a final reason. The finalists for the vice presidential nomination included former New Mexico representative and Clinton cabinet member Bill Richardson. Although this was not the first time that a Latino had been a finalist for the vice presidency (Walter Mondale had considered Henry Cisneros), Richardson had greater governmental experience than Cisneros had in 1984 and the Latino vote had become more central to Democratic victory in the intervening years. In the end, Richardson's chances were undermined by that same governmental experience. Missing hard disks at the Los Alamos laboratory, reflecting a more general sense of mismanagement, did not bode well for Secretary of Energy Richardson (Plotz 2000).

Gore's selection of Joe Lieberman, however, also offered some potential strengths for Latino outreach. Lieberman had strong connections to Florida's Cuban American community. He also made support for immigration (and his wife's own immigration experience) part of the core campaign message that he provided in most speeches. Lieberman initially got off to a rocky start with black and Latino delegates; his support for affirmative action appeared tepid and he did not attend a meeting called by black and Latino leaders to discuss his candidacy (and his stand on affirmative action).

At the mass level, however, Lieberman won some support for the Gore ticket among Latinos. A Tomás Rivera Policy Institute survey found that the Lieberman nomination had no impact on approximately two-thirds of Latino voters (2000a). For the remainder, however, the nomination increased support for Gore among more than three in four respondents. Even among Cuban American voters, the net effect of the Lieberman nomination was positive.

This period between the primaries and the general election may not have won either candidate many new votes, but neither lost support either. Each candidate made the appropriate appearances before the national Latino conventions and guaranteed the Latino presence at the national party conventions. This very public courting of Latinos ensured that the press would continue to present the Latino vote as up for grabs and important to the outcome in November.

THE GENERAL ELECTION

As the general election campaign took off after Labor Day, Latinos lost the opportunity to be major players in its outcome. State-by-state polls showed where the contest would be fought. With two exceptions, these "battleground" states that would be the primary focus of the candidates' efforts for the next two months were not states with significant Latino populations. The exceptions, Florida and New Mexico, not withstanding, Latinos lived in states that were strongly in the camp of one candidate or the other and were not worth fighting for by the candidate who was behind. Instead, both candidates focused on the swing states in the upper Midwest, the Pacific Northwest, Pennsylvania, Missouri, and Iowa (as well as Florida and New Mexico). So, while some Latino issues came to the fore, the campaigns did not focus on the states with the largest numbers of Latino voters and thus they did not invest heavily in mobilizing their votes.

Within the competitive states, some regions or electorates were treated as particularly competitive. So, for example, in Florida Gore campaigned heavily among retirees, Jews, and Orlando-area Latinos who were understood to be a growing electorate that would vote solidly Democratic, if it voted. Among Florida Latinos, Bush concentrated on rural voters and Miami Cubans (as did, to a limited degree, Lieberman). This focus on small electorates in competitive states led to an interesting and previously unseen phenomenon in national Latino campaigns. Small Latino electorates in some of the most competitive states, particularly Wisconsin and Pennsylvania, got more attention from both campaigns than much larger Latino electorates in noncompetitive states. In Wisconsin, for example, both Bush and Gore had fully staffed and funded Latino campaigns to win what could amount to no more than 30,000 Latino votes (many of whom were reliable Democrats or Republicans). This outreach came at the expense of efforts to mobilize more Latino voters in noncompetitive states; the *Ganamos con Gore!* Illinois's staff, for example, was moved en masse to Wisconsin.

This pattern of candidate neglect in most states with large Latino populations changed somewhat in the last weeks of the campaign. Governor Bush renewed his campaign efforts in several states where he had initially seemed to have given up, including two states with significant Latino populations: California and Illinois (Tapper 2000). Analysts were divided on the purpose of this strategy. Some saw a desire for a landslide (and the mandate that it would supply). More cynical observers saw the move into the previously noncompetitive states as more strategic: by competing in perceived Gore strongholds, Bush presented himself as the front-runner with a solid lead. Whatever the purpose of this last-minute strategy, it reinforced the broader pattern of the campaign. Most of the candidates' energies and resources were focused on a handful of states and, for the most part, these states did not have sizeable Latino populations.

The parties also put some money into these noncompetitive states at the presidential level (or regions within those states). In the last weeks of the campaign, the California Republican Party spent as much as a million dollars to win Latino votes. Both parties—through their coordinated campaigns—invested heavily in three congressional districts in the Los Angeles area and one in California's Central Valley that were competitive (in a year when few races were). Each of these districts had sizeable Latino voter populations.

Our discussion so far has focused primarily on the major parties and particularly on Bush and Gore. The nominees of the other parties did little to no outreach to Latinos. While this is not particularly surprising in the case of Reform Party nominee Buchanan, the Green Party had prior to 2000 reached out to Latinos in some states (New Mexico, in particular). Ralph Nader, on the other hand, did no discernable Latino outreach. His campaign focused primarily on college campuses and in upper-income white communities. This pattern of neglect of Latino communities by third-party candidates is one we have noted in past campaigns, though in the past the third-party candidate has generally been on the conservative end of the political spectrum.

LATINOS ON THE CAMPAIGNS

The lack of Latino influence extended beyond simply the focus of the campaigns. Latinos did not hold prominent roles in the Bush campaign and played a more muted role in the Gore campaign than they had in the 1996 Clinton campaign. It is especially noteworthy that not only were there no Latinos on Bush's general campaign staff, but that they also did not even have major roles in designing the campaign's Latino outreach. The most influential Latino involved with the campaign was Lionel Sosa (see chapter 2 in this volume), a well respected Hispanic media consultant with deep ties to the Republican Party. Within the campaign, the highest ranking Hispanic was Sandra Colin, also a media specialist, who was responsible for media relations. According to Colin, her office distributed campaign materials regularly to Spanish-language newspapers, radio, and television. Beyond that, she noted that the outreach effort had relatively few resources. She also indicated that she saw no evidence that the Republican Hispanic National Committee headed by Leslie Sanchez played a major role in the campaign (Colin 2001).

The Bush campaign had another resource who, though not formally part of the campaign, spoke with a great deal of authority. Bush's nephew, George P. Bush, had been introduced to the nation in the 1988 campaign by then–vice president George H. W. Bush as one of his "little brown" grandchildren. By 2000, George P. had grown into a young, quite self-assured man who spoke before many Latino audiences of his uncle's commitment to the Latino community. Although short on specifics, George P.'s message often emphasized the compassion in the Bush message of compassionate conservatism and the value of diversity, using his own experiences as an example. George P. appeared in several Bush campaign commercials, speaking in both Spanish and English; served as youth chair of the Republican National Convention; marched in New York's Puerto Rican Day parade; and was the public face of Latino outreach during the general election campaign.

The roles Latinos had in the Gore campaign were much more modest than they had been in 1996 but were much more substantial than in the Bush campaign. Headed by Janet Murgia, the deputy campaign manager; Jose Villareal, the campaign treasurer; Dag Vega, the deputy spokesperson for Gore and Lieberman; and Mark Magaña, the overall strategy advisor, approximately ten Latinos had significant positions in the campaign. Latinos were also more prominent in the Democratic Party infrastructure than they were on the Republican side. Lydia Camarillo directed the Democratic Party's Los Angeles convention. Maria Echaveste, who had played a lead role in both

1992 and 1996, served as an influential consultant. Others involved were glamorous personalities such as Jimmy Smits and Esai Morales, who served as candidate "surrogates." The Gore campaign was also able to tap a rich cadre of Latino elected officials as surrogates. These included Henry Cisneros, the former Housing and Urban Development secretary, Federico Peña, the former Transportation secretary, Energy Secretary Bill Richardson, and Representatives Loretta Sanchez (CA) and Robert Menendez (NJ). Gore's daughter, Karenna Gore-Schiff, also did much campaigning on her father's behalf with Latino audiences and was also frequently seen and heard on Spanish-language media.

Although Murgia was the consensus choice of the Hispanic delegation, other Latino leaders were dissatisfied with how the Latino campaign evolved. According to one campaign insider, the most significant problem was the rift between Murgia and Areceli Ruano, who had a key position with the Democratic National Committee. Others expressed concerns that not only did the campaign not have a Latino strategy, but also that none was proposed. *Ganamos con Gore!* was also criticized by staffers for lacking a strategy-making role. Its primary role came to be one of distributing Spanish-language and Hispanic-focused campaign materials.

LATINO ISSUES IN THE NATIONAL CAMPAIGN

Despite this low prominence of Latino voters in the campaign, several Latino issues did come to the fore in the campaign. These were not always central to the candidates' strategies, but nevertheless were part of popular and media discussions of the campaign. These issues included a court decision that, temporarily, granted Puerto Ricans the right to vote in the presidential election and a legislative proposal to extend amnesty to a large number of undocumented Latinos residing in the United States.

Just as the general election was getting underway, a federal district court in Puerto Rico ruled that voting was a fundamental right of citizenship and, consequently, Puerto Ricans residing in Puerto Rico were entitled to vote in presidential elections (*de la Rosa et al. v. The United States of America*, 2000 U.S. Dist. Lexis 13553). On appeal to the circuit court, the district court's ruling was reversed and vacated with instructions that the case be dismissed (*de la Rosa et al. v. The United States of America*, 2000 U.S. App. Lexis 25499). The circuit court held that the U.S. Constitution limits the election of the president to states that have representation in the electoral college (plus the District of Columbia, which received representation in the electoral college by way of a constitutional amendment). As a result, residents of Puerto Rico could only earn the presidential vote by becoming a state or through constitutional amendment.

During the month and a half that the district court's ruling was on appeal, the possibility of a Puerto Rican vote peripherally entered the campaign. Puerto Rico quickly passed enabling legislation to hold a popular vote on the same day as the rest of the country and Bush promised to campaign for its votes. Few expected the district court's ruling to stand, however, and neither campaign dedicated resources to win Puerto Rico's votes.

A second Latino-related issue was more actively discussed throughout the campaign. This was a legislative proposal endorsed by Democrats in the House of Representatives and the White House to legalize approximately 800,000 undocumented immigrants, primarily Central Americans. Democrats demanded that this legislation be attached to the Justice Department appropriation for 2001. Throughout the fall, the White House promised to veto any Justice Department appropriations bill that did not include this legalization provision. It asserted this tactic was a first for a president: never before had an appropriations bill been threatened with a veto for what it did *not* include. After the election, however, the White House relented and accepted a more modest legalization that narrowed its focus to undocumented immigrants who were family members of Immigration Reform and Control Act (IRCA) legalizees and others who should have been eligible for the 1986 IRCA, but were administratively denied legalization. This excluded most Central Americans who had been the original target of the legalization legislation.

Finally, Latino organizational leaders sought to influence the national policy debate by issuing a national "leadership agenda" that represented issues recognized as important by thirty-one national Latino organizations (National Hispanic Leadership Agenda 2000). This model of issuing a document codifying Latino issues in the election year has been followed to varying degrees in each national election since 1988.[6] The agenda identified forty-three issues under five broad categories: education, civil rights, government accountability, economic empowerment, and health. After a day-long conference to publicize the agenda in Washington, D.C., in October, its organizers invited the candidates or their representative to respond. Neither candidate appeared, although Lieberman called in from his campaign plane. His message was largely symbolic, speaking of Democratic support for issues of concern to Latinos and his own family connections to immigration. Representing the candidates at the meeting were Senator Orrin Hatch and Representative Xavier Becerra. Both representatives spoke in very general terms about their candidates' attachments to the Latino community and made promises about Latino appointments to future administrations (they knew their audience), but neither gave much indication of having read the agenda.

The minimal impact the agenda had illustrates the failure of Latino organizational leaders to exploit the interest the major parties had in the Latino vote. Had the document been released earlier, it could have been the core of a national campaign to influence the policy agenda of both candidates and a mechanism for holding candidates and parties accountable. Instead, by coming so late it was essentially irrelevant.

Both Bush and Gore sought to use issues to reach Latino voters. Bush's message to Latinos emphasized the personal: his own connection to Latinos, his family connections to the Latino experience through his sister-in-law, and his ability to and willingness to use Spanish. Aside from this personal connection, the issues he emphasized before Latino audiences were quite similar to those he discussed with Anglo audiences: compassionate conservatism, family values, opportunity, and education reform. Family values, as presented to Latino audiences, also included a proposal to fund additional resources for naturalization processing at the Immigration and Naturalization Service. Looking too carefully at the details of these programs misses the core of the Bush Latino strategy, however, which focused primarily on the more personalistic connections that Bush tried to make.

Gore, as was the case more generally in his campaign (for better and for worse), offered more policy specificity in his outreach to Latinos. The Gore Latino message focused on three themes: education, health care, and immigration reform (particularly the Latino Immigrant Fairness Act, a legalization program debated in Congress during the fall campaign). The particular spin offered by Gore and his campaign was to connect each of these issues to Latino aspirations, showing how Gore's positions more than Bush's would allow Latinos to achieve their goals in life. Gore's staff had an added responsibility: it had to undermine press assumptions that Bush was making unprecedented inroads for a Republican among Latino voters.

THE POSTELECTION

Latinos had their biggest impact on the election after election day. The controversies surrounding the vote count in Florida included Latinos as some of the key players, both at the state level and in Miami-Dade County, which was one of the major targets of the Gore campaign for a hand count of ballots that machines determined had no vote. The "angry mob" that caused Miami-Dade County to suspend its recount included, among others, members of Miami's Cuban American community, but congressional staffers on leave from their Washington jobs made up its majority. Florida Republican Party chair Al Cardenas was a frequent participant on news shows for the month when the result was in doubt. One of the key Gore staffers in the postelection was Marie Therese Dominguez, who had staffed Gore Latino outreach in central Florida in the month before election day. In the legal battle that ultimately decided the election, however, Latinos were not active participants.

In the end, Florida Latino votes certainly contributed to Bush's 537 vote certified victory margin. Without the state's Latino vote, Gore would have won an uncontested victory. However, as we discuss later, Florida Latinos were *less* likely to vote Republican than they had in the past. So, while they were part of the winning coalition, they made no new contribution to it. To the contrary, they may have contributed less than was expected of them.

The close Florida result, and its huge significance to the final outcome of the election, spurs a careful dissection of all decisions made in Florida campaigning and voter decision making. A tangible example of this phenomenon is the outrage over Palm Beach County's butterfly ballot and the likelihood that at least 3,000 intended Gore votes went to Buchanan. Another "what if" scenario specifically involves Florida Latino voters, especially Cuban Americans. In this what if, the question is: What if Elián's mother had never set out for the United States in November 1999? A Tomás Rivera Policy Institute poll conducted in the weeks before the election asked Florida Latinos whether the federal government's decision to seize Elián from his Miami relatives made them more likely to support Bush or Gore, or had no effect (2000a). For six in ten, the decision made no difference. Among the remainder, however, Bush was the overwhelming beneficiary. More than four in five said the decision made them more likely to support Bush. In a race as close as Florida's in 2000, this Bush advantage among Florida Latinos is decisive.

In the final electoral step, more Latinos than ever before were elected to the electoral college (see table 1.6), a completely honorific position with no substantive dimension. Election, of course, somewhat misstates how these delegates earned their posts. Instead, they were appointed by their state parties based on their anticipated loyalty and, in many cases, their long service to the party and then elected by voters who in most states are unaware of who they are voting for. The 2000 electoral college was approximately 7 percent Latino. This was an increase from the 6 percent in 1996 and 5 percent in 1992. As has been the pattern in past elections, Democrats were more likely to appoint Latino electoral college delegates than were Republicans. In 2000, 9 percent of Democratic delegates and 5 percent of Republican delegates were Latino. Depending on one's perspective, Latinos are *over*represented in the electoral college, at least relative to their share of the electorate. According to the CPS, Latinos made up 5.3 percent of the 2000 electorate.

OPINION SURVEYS

The unclear outcome of the 2000 race is particularly ironic since opinion polling reached unprecedented levels throughout the campaign. This explosion of surveys and polls extended to Latinos who were the subject of at least four national opinion surveys beginning in July and ending in October. These national surveys were supplemented by polls, particularly focusing on the presidential horse race. Often, these horse race–focused polls are of limited value because they offer so little information on their sample.

It should be noted that this plethora of polls focused primarily

Table 1.6   Latino Electoral College Delegates, by Party, 1992, 1996, and 2000

	1992		1996		2000	
	Dem.	Rep.	Dem.	Rep.	Dem.	Rep.
Latino	21 (5.7%)	8 (4.8%)	24 (6.3%)	6 (3.8%)	24 (9.0%)	13 (5.0%)
Non-Latino	349	160	355	153	243	258
Total	370	168	379	159	267	271

Note: Latino surname lists underestimate the true Latino population by approximately 20 percent.

Source: Authors' calculations using standard sources of Latino surnames.

or exclusively on Latino vote choice in the presidential race fueled press debates about the depth of Latino support for Bush. The polls that had the weakest methodological statements tended to show the highest levels of support for Bush. Some of these were released by polling firms with ties to the Republican Party. Although undiscussed by Cottle (2000) in her notion of the ricochet pander, these polls could also play a role. By giving the ultimately inaccurate notion that Bush could do well among Hispanics, the polls reassured moderate whites that Bush was a bridge builder and that his compassionate conservatism resonated with some minorities.

The four national Latino surveys were conducted by the *San Jose Mercury News*, the Public Broadcasting Service, the Tomás Rivera Policy Institute, and the Willie C. Velásquez Research Institute. Although the focus of each survey was slightly different, they paint a remarkably similar picture of the Latino electorate ("Special Report" 2000; Public Broadcasting Service 2000; Tomás Rivera Policy Institute 2000b; Willie C. Velásquez Research Institute 2000a, 2000e, 2000f). They found that Latinos were Democrats and most planned to vote for Gore. These patterns were even stronger among registered voters or those who were likely to vote (based on previous voting patterns). The exception to these patterns were Florida Latinos who were more likely to be Republicans than Democrats and planned to vote for Bush. These results were consistent with previous voting patterns. Each showed somewhat weaker Hispanic support for Gore than Clinton had earned in 1996.

Latino policy concerns identified in these surveys reflected their partisan preferences (see table 1.7). The issues that are most relevant to Latino communities focus on domestic politics and particularly

Table 1.7   Most Important Issue Facing the Nation and the Latino Community, 2000 (among Registered Voters) (%)

	Most Important Problem Facing the Nation	Most Important Problem Facing Latinos
The economy	12.5	7.4
Unemployment/jobs	6.0	12.0
Education/public schools	15.0	23.3
Crime	10.0	5.4
Drugs	9.1	3.8
Health care	4.9	1.6
Race relations	3.4	12.2
Values/family values/morality	5.0	2.4
Budget deficit	0.8	0.2
Social security/care for elderly	4.1	0.9
Illegal immigration	2.3	6.0
Affirmative action	0.4	0.9
Welfare/welfare reform	0.8	0.8
Environment	0.5	0.4
Political system/corruption/scandal	2.3	1.3
Foreign policy/international concerns/defense	3.7	0.6
Abortion	0.5	0.3
Other	18.6	20.4

Note: This survey like all other "national" Latino surveys in 2000 was not truly national. This survey was of registered voters in the five states with the largest Latino populations: California, Texas, New York, Florida, and Illinois.

Source: Tomás Rivera Policy Institute (2000a)

on education. More than in previous years, Latino concerns focused on the economy, but even here, their economic interests tended to focus more on jobs and unemployment issues than on the deficit (the economic issue most discussed by the candidates was what to do with the federal budget surplus that existed at the time). Foreign policy continues to not be a relevant concern among Latinos. As has been the case in previous studies of Latino policy preferences, there is relatively little variation in either the most important issue facing the nation or the Latino community among different Latino national

Table 1.8   Latino Vote, 1996 and 2000, National and Selected States

	1996 Vote	2000 Vote	Change (%)
Arizona	163,479	247,000	+51.1
California	1,290,914	1,597,000	+23.7
Colorado	128,629	158,000	+22.8
Florida	509,984	678,000	+32.9
Illinois	127,232	218,000	+71.3
New Jersey	248,416	179,000	−27.9
New Mexico	206,468	191,000	−7.5
New York	512,935	502,000	−2.1
Texas	1,059,647	1,300,000	+22.7
Other	680,296	864,000	+27.0
Total	4,928,000	5,934,000	+20.4

Note: Current Population Survey data are collected monthly through a household survey of approximately 50,000 households and rely on self-reporting of voting and voter eligibility in the weeks after the election. These data likely overestimate actual voting levels, perhaps by a significant amount.

Sources: de la Garza and DeSipio (1999: table 1.3); authors' calculations based on U.S. Bureau of the Census (2002c: table 4a)

origin groups. Thus, while there are some differences in Latino partisanship based on national origin, these differences do not extend to policy concerns.

LATINOS AND 2000 ELECTORAL OUTCOMES

The Latino vote increased by approximately 20 percent over 1996 levels. According to self-reporting in the CPS, 5.9 million Latinos turned out in 2000,[7] up from the 4.9 million who had turned out four years before (see table 1.8). Most of the states with large Latino populations also saw increases, some quite dramatic. Illinois, for example, saw an increase from 127,232 voters in 1996 to 218,000 in 2000, an increase of over 71 percent. It is unlikely that these data accurately portray the change in Latino turnout between these two elections. The CPS is a national survey of approximately 80,000 respondents, so the sampling error at the state level for a subpopulation such as Latinos can be quite large and most likely explains much of this gap (the 1996 estimate could have been low—it did reflect a decline from 1992—and the 2000 could be high). The two states that showed a decline in Latino turnout—New Mexico and New York—saw very small declines.

Although the data are considerably weaker, the candidates' decisions to focus on Latino electorates in small, nontraditionally Latino states appear to have had some impact on turnout. Latino turnout in Pennsylvania may have doubled. Turnout in Wisconsin increased by a more moderate one-third.

The Latino vote went overwhelmingly for Democrat Gore (see table 1.9). National exit polls showed support for Gore by between 62 and 67 percent of Latinos. Bush earned between 29 and 38 percent of the Latino vote. Neither Nader nor Buchanan received many Latino votes.

Latino presidential voting at the state level showed more variation than it had in past elections. Gore received over 80 percent of New York Latino votes (a state where Bush made no effort to campaign). Bush won the votes of between 40 and 43 percent of Texas Latino votes (a state where Gore did not campaign). The exit polls indicate that Florida Latino votes split their votes nearly evenly (with a slight advantage to Bush). Scholars of Florida Latino politics, including Kevin A. Hill and Dario Moreno in this volume, contend that the exit poll estimates of an evenly divided Florida Latino electorate are the result of a faulty sample that overrepresents central Florida Latinos who are more likely to be Democrats. While this is likely true (Florida exit polling was shown to have many weaknesses on election night), it also seems fair to note that Florida Latinos will probably not be giving 70 or more percent of their votes to the Republicans in future elections.

Nationally, Gore did less well among Latinos than did Clinton in 1996 and Bush did better than Dole. The comparison is weakened by the fact that Ross Perot earned approximately 6 percent of the Latino vote in 1996. Clinton won approximately 72 percent of Latino votes and Dole won 21 percent in 1996. Clearly, though, Bush gained ground over 1996 Republican Latino support levels. While he did not do as well as some on his staff predicted that he would, he did win approximately 33 percent of the votes that went to either Gore or Bush. This accomplishment, however, may be less dramatic than it initially appears to be. The Bush campaign succeeded in returning the Republican share of the Latino vote to the levels earned in the 1980s. In 1980, Ronald Reagan earned 33 percent

Table 1.9   Exit Polls of Latino Presidential Candidate Choice (%)

	Gore	Bush	Nader	Buchanan	Latino Share
Latinos Nationally					
ABC	62	35	—	—	NR
CBS	66	29	—	—	NR
CNN	62	34	2	1	7
Los Angeles Times	61	38	1	—	7
New York Times	67	31	2	—	4
USA Today	64	32	2	—	6
States					
Arizona					
CNN	66	32	2	—	11
ABC	65	34	1	—	10
California					
ABC	68	29	3	—	14
CNN	67	28	4	1	14
Los Angeles Times	75	23	2	—	13
Colorado					
ABC	68	25	6	—	14
CNN	69	24	6	1	14
Florida					
ABC	48	49	1	—	11
CNN	48	50	—	1	11
Illinois	No statistically valid data				4
New Jersey					
ABC	58	35	6	1	5
CNN	56	34	7	3	5
New Mexico					
CNN & ABC	66	32	1	—	32
New York					
ABC	80	18	1	1	8
CNN	81	16	2	1	8
Texas					
ABC	54	43	3	0	10
CNN	57	40	3	—	10

Note: Most exit polls rely on the same data, which are collected by the Voter News Service consortium. Each news agency, however, develops its own analysis methodology and weighting. NR: Not reported.

Source: Authors' compilation of published exit polls.

of the Latino vote (and 36 percent of the vote that went to Reagan or Jimmy Carter). In his 1984 reelection, Reagan won 37 percent of the Latino vote. George H. W. Bush won 30 percent in 1988 ("Who Voted" 2000).

Turnout, even dramatically increased turnouts, does not guarantee influence. Earlier in our discussion, we identified four forms of Latino electoral influence. In the 2000 race, we only saw one of these—very close state races in which Latinos voted with the winning candidate and, consequently, are partially responsible for his victory (see table 1.10). Because the races were so close in New Mexico and Florida, other groups can make this claim as well, but Florida Latinos (at levels that are likely much stronger than the exit polls show) and New Mexico Latinos were cohesive voters on the winning candidates' sides and ensured Bush's and Gore's narrow victories.

In the other seven states, Latinos cannot be said to have had much direct influence on the state outcome. In four states (Illinois, New Jersey, New York, and Texas), the winner's margin was larger

Table 1.10   Latino Influence on Award of Electoral College Votes

	Electoral College Winner	Popular Vote Margin	Latino Vote	Estimated Latino Vote for Winner	Result Had No Latino Voted
Arizona	Bush	96,311	247,000	81,510	No change
California	Gore	1,293,774	1,597,000	1,117,900	No change
Colorado	Bush	145,521	158,000	38,710	No change
Florida	Bush	537	678,000	335,610	Gore victory
Illinois	Gore	569,605	218,000	NA	No change
New Jersey	Gore	504,677	179,000	102,030	No change
New Mexico	Gore	366	191,000	126,060	Bush victory
New York	Gore	1,704,323	502,000	404,110	No change
Texas	Bush	1,365,893	1,300,000	539,500	No change

Notes: "Estimated Latino Vote for Winner" is calculated by multiplying major state exit poll data for the state's winning candidate.

Scholars of Florida Latino politics, including Dario Moreno and Kevin A. Hill in this volume, contend that the exit poll estimates of an evenly divided Florida Latino electorate (50 percent for Bush and 48 percent for Gore) are the result of a faulty sample that overrepresents central Florida Latinos who are more likely to be Democrats. Even with these lower estimates of Latino votes for Bush, Gore would have won had *no* Latino voted.

Voter News Service did not release data for the Latino vote in Illinois.

Sources: Exit polls: authors' compilations based on published sources; turnout data: authors' calculations based on U.S. Bureau of the Census (2002c: table 4a).

than the Latino vote. In two other states (Arizona and Colorado), strong majorities of the Latino vote went to Gore while the non-Latino votes went to Bush. In these states, even if all Latinos had voted for Gore, Bush still would have won. Finally, in California, Latinos provided a large share of Gore's margin of victory. If no California Latino had voted, however, the result would have remained the same, but the partisan picture might have been quite different. Without solid Latino support for the Democrats, California would have been a very competitive state.

The standards that we set for accepting the assertion that Latinos influenced the outcome of the election are admittedly high. Quite clearly, the strongly Democratic nature of these Latino voters mean that they made Gore competitive in several states and, more broadly, are central to any Democratic victory coalition (Reich 1997: 330). Were Latinos not a part of the electorate, the solid Gore lead in California, for example, would have largely dissipated. While acknowledging the importance of this core Latino vote, however, we do not want to overstate its importance. Since it is impossible to imagine the disappearance of the Latino electorate, we cannot say that Latinos particularly influenced the election's outcome by just doing what they always do.

Preelection polling indicates that seven in ten Latinos were likely to vote for Democratic congressional candidates (Tomás Rivera Policy Institute 2000a; William C. Velásquez Institute 2000a, 2000e, 2000f). In practice, Latinos may have voted for the Democrats at somewhat lower levels, not for lack of support but for lack of competition. Approximately two-thirds of Latinos lived in noncompetitive districts where little mobilization occurred.

LATINOS AND NONPRESIDENTIAL RACES

The number of Latinos in Congress did not increase as a result of the 2000 general elections. That said, Latino incumbents did very well indeed, raising large sums of money and facing little serious opposition. In many ways, the 2000 elections can be viewed as a lull before a storm, that storm being the redistricting that takes place in the two years that follow the election or when a seat in a high-concentration Latino area becomes vacant due to a death or retirement.[8] Only three serious Latino candidates opposed incumbents and in each case the challenger faced daunting odds. None of these three candidates (Republican Rich Rodríguez in California, Democrat Michael Montoya in New Mexico, and Democrat Regina Montoya-Coggins in Texas) prevailed.

With one exception, congressional Latino incumbents did quite well. None faced serious opposition in the general election and all raised significantly more money than their opponents (strengthening their chances in subsequent elections). Their money advantage was particularly striking when compared to previous years (see table 1.11). Although Latino incumbents did not raise quite as

Table 1.11   Congressional Fund-Raising, 1995–1996 and 1999–2000: Latino Candidates, Challengers to Latino Incumbents, Election to Open Seats

	1995–1996	*1999–2000*	*% Change*
Incumbents			
Average for:			
Latino incumbents	$368,758	$762,881	+106.8
Latino incumbents facing major party opponents	$339,215	$1,057,283	+211.7
All incumbents	$725,677	$900,026	+24.0
General Election Challengers to Incumbents			
Average for:			
Major party challengers to Latino incumbents (all ethnicities)	$57,143	$108,688	+90.2
Latino challengers to Latino incumbents	$28,026	$135,848	+384.7
Latino challengers to non-Latino incumbents	NA	$528,024	—
All challengers to incumbents	$262,813	$364,944	+38.9
General Election to Open Seats			
Average for:			
Latino candidates	$480,545	$78,017	−83.8
All candidates	$640,000	$1,080,944	+68.9

Note: In 2000, one Latino incumbent (California's Matthew Martinez) lost in a party primary and, consequently, did not run the general election. If he is excluded from the average, the amount raised by Latino incumbents increases to $794,521.

Sources: 1995–1996 data from de la Garza and DeSipio (1999: table 1.5); 1999–2000 data: authors' calculations of Federal Election Commission data available at http://herndon1.sdrdc.com/fecimg/srssea.html (accessed January 28, 2003).

much as did incumbents in general, they significantly closed what had been a much bigger gap with all incumbents in a previous election cycle (1995–1996, the last presidential election cycle). The fifteen Democratic incumbents had raised an average of $762,881 between January 1, 1999, and December 31, 2000. This represented an increase of over 106 percent from 1995 to 1996. The average for all incumbents was $900,026, a 24 percent increase from 1995 to 1996.

Latino incumbents had a greater fund-raising advantage over their opponents than did incumbents in general. The average major party general election challenger to Latino incumbents raised $108,688. Major party general election challengers to all incumbents raised more than three times as much as challengers to Latinos, $364,944.

Of the three Latinos who challenged incumbent Anglos, two raised significant sums. Montoya-Coggins tapped connections she had made while serving in the White House to raise $1.64 million for her campaign, close to the $2 million raised by incumbent Pete Sessions. In California, Rodríguez raised nearly $1.2 million in his loss to Cal Dooley, who had raised about $1.8 million.

The exception to the pattern of safe Latino seats was California's Matthew Martinez, who lost to state senator Hilda Solis in the Democratic primary. Solis received support from a number of prominent California Hispanics, including Representative Loretta Sanchez. Angered by his defeat and the lack of loyalty of his traditional Democratic supporters, Martinez served out the final months of his term as a Republican.

Several competitive California congressional districts, however, targeted Latino voters. Of these, perhaps the most interesting was Republican Rodríguez's challenge of incumbent Calvin Dooley in a majority Latino (though not majority Latino voter) district. Rodríguez did not face many of the barriers usually experienced by Republican Latinos outside Florida. He was well known in the district. Rodríguez's strategy was, in part, to tap ethnicity to draw traditionally Democratic Latinos to the Republican fold. Exit polling indicates that this strategy failed. Rodríguez drew about 33 percent of the Latino vote, or roughly the level that Republicans can expect in most elections (J. García 2000; Michelson and Leon 2001).

Three other California races did not have Latino candidates, but Latino votes were actively sought. These three congressional seats—

the Twenty-seventh, Thirty-sixth, and Forty-ninth District seats—were all won by Democratic challengers by margins of between 2 and 8 percent. Latinos made up between 7 and 12 percent of the districts' voters (Bunis 2000). The natural increases in the size of the Latino population set the stage for these districts to go Democratic and they would not have elected Democrats without Latino votes. So, each of these Los Angeles–area districts could be an example of the first form of Latino influence that we identified (an electoral outcome resulting from a change in the Latino vote) and are certainly a form of the second form (the outcome being different if no Latino had voted).

The number of Latinos in state legislatures increased from 139 to 147 (National Association of Latino Elected and Appointed Officials Educational Fund 2000). Half of this gain occurred in California. Despite these gains, one senior Latino legislative leader lost, though to another Latino. New Mexico speaker of the house Ray Sanchez, a Democrat, lost in a close race to Republican John A. Sanchez. Nationally, the number of Latinos in state senate seats declined by one.

CONCLUSION

The 2000 elections saw significant changes related to the Latino electorate. Because of population increases, the Latino vote was more explicitly and emphatically courted than ever before. For Democrats, this meant building on a well-developed foundation. For Republicans, it signaled a dramatic shift in strategy.

The most obvious and significant result of this development was that the tone with which Latinos and their issues were discussed changed. Not only were they not targets to be attacked, they were a community to be respected and won over. This sets a new threshold for how national campaigns will address Hispanics in the future.

This campaign also legitimated Spanish in presidential campaigns for Latinos and the nation. Historically, Hispanics had been segregated and demeaned for speaking Spanish. Such behavior would be much more difficult in the face of presidential candidates who openly used Spanish to woo Latino voters and welcome the nation's Hispanics into American society.

Relatedly, this was the first campaign to witness extensive campaigning in Spanish. This went beyond a few sentences at national Hispanic meetings; it involved well-designed and orchestrated campaigns implemented through the Spanish media. With this, Spanish-language television and radio were thrust onto the political stage to an extent that had been unimagined even as recently as 1996.

Substantively, however, little changed. That is, despite their numbers, the Latino vote had no significant impact on the results of the election. Even in Florida, where they are one of many groups that can take credit for Bush's victory, their support for Bush was less than what Republican presidential candidates normally count on. In other words, rather than credit Florida's Latinos with Bush's victory, it may be more accurate to state that he won the state, and the national election, in spite of lower-than-expected levels of Latino support.

Finally, as has been true since 1988, Latinos remain marginal in terms of national electoral influence. To the extent that they have become more visible participants, it is more because of the importance others attach to them than because of any initiatives of their own. Now that they are well ensconced on the national stage, it is up to elected leaders and the heads of organizations to find ways to make real the political potential that Latino demographics promise. Until that is accomplished, Latino political voices will continue to be muted.

FORMAT OF THE BOOK

We broadly follow the format of our three previous volumes on Latinos and national election cycles (de la Garza and DeSipio 1992, 1996, 1999). We present state-level analyses of the role of Latino electorates in shaping outcome in eight states with large Latino electorates. Our state-level analyses evaluate campaign strategies, the course of the campaign, the roles of the major candidates and their campaigns in organizing the conduct of politics, and the degree to which Latinos mobilized, participated, and shaped the outcome of the election in each of the eight states. We precede these state-level analyses with two thematic chapters that assess unique circumstances in the 2000 campaign.

The two thematic chapters are Robert G. Marbut Jr.'s "¡*Un Nuevo Dia?* Republican Outreach to the Latino Community in the 2000 Campaign" (chapter 2) and Harry P. Pachon, Matt A. Barreto, and Frances Marquez's "Latino Politics Comes of Age: Lessons from the Golden State" (chapter 3). "¡*Un Nuevo Dia!*" analyzes what was probably the most unique feature of the 2000 race: the unprecedented Republican and Bush campaign outreach to Latinos. Marbut analyzes the Republican understandings of how to reach Latino voters and how they structured their outreach campaign. Chapter 3 analyzes changes in California politics over the past decade and what they portend for Latino electoral politics nationally. Over the past decade, California Latinos have been able to achieve a new prominence, not solely as voters, but as a voting bloc that can influence state government and public policy. This chapter explores the 2000 race as the consequence of a decade of political and demographic change in the state. These two thematic chapters analyze the changing nature of the Latino vote with an eye beyond the 2000 elections.

The heart of this volume is state-level analysis of how the campaigns to reach Latino votes were conducted and how Latinos responded to these campaigns. The nature of the campaign varied dramatically in 2000 from state to state and this variation appears in our analysis. In some states, such as New Mexico, there was an active campaign by both parties in both the primaries and the general election. Other states saw less campaigning or, in some cases, virtually none, such as in Texas or Arizona. As a result, we limit analysis of the campaign in these states with low competition for Latino votes to allow for a more thorough discussion of the states where the campaign for the Latino vote was most active.

The state-level analyses are organized into three sections. First, we examine three small southwestern states with long-standing Mexican American populations who have long had influence at the local level. These chapters include F. Chris Garcia and Christine Marie Sierra's "New Mexico Hispanos in the 2000 General Elections" (chapter 4), Rodney Hero and Patricia Jaramillo's "Latinos and the 2000 Elections in Colorado: More Real than Apparent, More Apparent than Real?" (chapter 5), and Manuel Avalos's "Will More (Votes) Continue to Equal Less (Influence)? Arizona Latinos in the 2000 Elections" (chapter 6).

These are followed by chapters on Texas and California, states that we identify as must-wins if Latino votes are to be influential in shaping the outcome of the presidential race. Lisa J. Montoya analyzes Texas in "Still Waiting in the Wings: Latinos in the 2000 Texas Elections" (chapter 7). California is the focus of Luis Ricardo Fraga, Ricardo Ramírez, Gary M. Segura's "Unquestioned Influence: Latinos and the 2000 Elections in California" (chapter 8). The focus of Fraga, Ramírez, and Segura differs from chapter 3's discussion of California in that its primary focus is the conduct of the 2000 campaign, though it too takes notice of the significant changes in California and California Latino politics over the past decade.

Finally, three chapters measure Latino contributions to electoral outcomes in states where Latinos are newer contributors to state politics: Angelo Falcón's "'Pues, At Least We Had Hillary': Latino New York City, the 2000 Elections, and the Limits of Party Loyalty" (chapter 9), Kevin A. Hill and Dario Moreno's "Battleground Florida" (chapter 10), and Louis DeSipio's "Electoral College Dropouts: Illinois Latinos in the 2000 Presidential Election" (chapter 11).

NOTES

We would like to thank Fernando Guerra and Loyola Marymount University's Center for the Study of Los Angeles for hosting a meeting of the project research team.

1. This was the difference in the Florida vote certified by Florida secretary of state Katherine Harris. The gap on election night was 1,725 votes and narrowed to as little as 193 votes before the U.S. Supreme Court terminated recounts and hand counts of undervotes.

2. We use the terms "Latino" and "Hispanic" interchangeably to refer to residents of the United States who trace their origin or ancestry to the Spanish-speaking countries of Latin America or the Caribbean.

3. These data, and all data reported here from the Census Bureau and the Current Population Survey (CPS), overreport actual turnout levels for all populations. They rely on self-reporting in the weeks after the elections and are likely to include as voters people who did not vote, but reported that they did. There is no definitive estimate of this overreporting, but it is estimated to be between 10 and 40 percent (Shaw, de la Garza, and Lee 2000). The citizenship data derived from the CPS are also based on self-

reporting and, so, may mischaracterize the share of the Latino adult population made up of U.S. citizens.

4. Although children can naturalize, it is much easier for them to follow a different path, one that Immigration and Naturalization Service itself recommends to parents seeking naturalization. Once the parent naturalizes, he or she can apply for passport in the name of the child who is eligible based on the parent's U.S. citizenship. This strategy is significantly cheaper for the parent and extends to the child a de facto U.S. citizenship and the evidence needed to prove it.

5. Ironically, McCain's claim was probably more sound than Bush's that he had won a near majority of Latino votes in the most recent Texas gubernatorial race (de la Garza, Shaw, and Lu 1999). Bush's claim was based on exit polls that do not stand up to more rigorous analysis of Texas electoral results. McCain, on the other hand, had traditionally done well among Arizona Latinos. Both benefited from weak, underfunded Democrats who had no resources to mobilize Latino voters.

6. Although the National Hispanic Agenda has succeeded at bringing press attention to "Latino issues," it is not clear that it has ever had any impact on candidates or campaigns. Strategies have changed from issuing the document as much as a year before the election (1988) to after the election (1996). Relative to previous years' efforts, 2000 was the second most extensive in our observation with a well-funded day-long conference in Washington to publicize the document. That said, it received little press attention and several of the leaders of the Latino organizations that sponsored the document did not attend the event.

7. Many pundits seized on the Latino share of exit poll respondent pools as a measure to estimate the Latino vote (Werner 2000). By multiplying the 100 million voters nationwide by the 7 percent Latino respondents reported in one exit poll, pundits asserted that 7 million Latinos voted. Exit polls, however, are not designed to measure the size of components of the electorate. Three exit polls reported the Latino share of their samples, but reported three widely different Latino shares: 4, 6, and 7 percent. Each of these reflect the weighting assigned in the exit polls to Latino respondents.

8. In the 2002 congressional elections, as many as five new Hispanic members of Congress were elected, though there is some debate about this number. The new members included Dennis Cardoza (D-CA), Mario Diaz-Balart (R-FL), Raúl Grijalva (D-AZ), Devin Nunes (R-CA), and Linda Sánchez (D-CA). Cardoza and Nunes are of Azorian (Portuguese) ancestry and are not Latino by some definitions. A long-term member of Congress, Richard Pombo (R-CA), who was first elected in 1992, has recently begun to identify himself as Hispanic. Representative Pombo is of Portuguese ancestry.

2

¿Un Nuevo Dia?

Republican Outreach to the Latino Community in the 2000 Campaign

ROBERT G. MARBUT JR.

THE LATINO ELECTORATE HAS RECENTLY EMERGED AS A MAJOR POLITical force in American presidential elections. With the exception of Cuban Americans in Florida, Latinos have traditionally registered and voted Democratic. Historically, most Republican Party presidential candidates have ignored Latinos and not directly addressed issues relevant to the Latino community in either the primary or general elections of presidential campaigns. The campaign of Bob Dole in 1996 is a classical example of this neglectful approach used by many Republicans. Other Republican candidates, such as California governor and unsuccessful Republican presidential aspirant Pete Wilson, have been openly antagonistic to Latinos and have used hostile Latino and immigration issues as wedge issues to gain support of white conservatives. An alternative to the traditional Republican approaches of neglect and antagonism emerged in the 1990s in the presidential campaign of Texas governor George W. Bush, who made unprecedented attempts to attract Hispanic voters in 2000. No Republican presidential candidate has ever given so much thought, put in so much effort, or spent so much time and money trying to attract Hispanic voters as Bush did in 2000.

LATINO DEMOGRAPHY AND U.S. POLITICAL CHANGE

Since 1980, political strategists have focused on a series of demographic groups as potential swing groups. First, it was the Reagan Democrats, then angry white males, then soccer moms, and more recently married women. For some political leaders, Hispanics are the new group that must be won, if not in the next election in future ones. This presents a challenge for Republicans since most Hispanics identify as Democrats.

Five demographic, political trends, and factors account for the emergence of Hispanics as one of the sought-after voting blocs by candidates and parties: the overall size of the Latino community, its current and projected growth rates, the increasing size of the pool of Hispanic registered voters, the concentration of likely Latino votes in a handful of states with large numbers of electoral votes, and a growing recognition among some Republican leaders that any gain among white voters to be had from attacking Latinos is more than compensated for by the loss of Latino and moderate white votes to the Democrats. The first four of these trends have been extensively analyzed elsewhere and do not need discussion here (DeSipio 1996a; de la Garza and DeSipio 1999; see also chapter 1 in this volume). The final factor, however, deserves some discussion.

Latino Republicans and Republican supporters of Latino outreach have tried to alert their party to the rising Hispanic voting strength for the better part of three decades. Many longtime strategists like Lionel Sosa, Sam Barshop, and Stuart Spencer have encouraged the GOP to actively target and pursue the Latino vote. Strategists like Sosa and Spencer have argued that Latinos should feel at home in a Republican Party standing for self-reliance, hard work, support of small businesses, family values, and antiabortion issues (Purdum 1997).

More recently, Frank Guerra, the Republican National Committee's (RNC) lead Hispanic advertising consultant in the 2000 elections, reported that Hispanics are a natural constituency group for the Republican Party in that "Hispanic values line up with the values of middle America" and the values of the Republican Party (Sylvester 2000). Sosa, Guerra, and others believe that Hispanics could become a natural ally to Republican presidential candidates in about thirteen states, many of which are rich with electoral votes. Furthermore, they contend that if Republicans attempt to appeal to Hispanics, Hispanics could become a significant support group for the GOP.

To tap into the emerging Latino voting community success-fully, Republican and nonpartisan strategists generally argue that the Republican Party needs to make symbolic, sensitive, and sub-stantive appeals to Latinos. This is the approach successfully used by Republicans like John McCain, Reagan, and Bush.

As importantly, these strategists assert that Republicans must *not* offend Latinos by running on anti-immigrant and antiminority issues, even if these attacks might gain non-Hispanic white votes in a close election. Governor Wilson's focus on these issues led many Latinos to conclude that he and his party were hostile and an-tagonistic toward Latinos. The long-term deleterious effects of such a strategy are seen most dramatically in California (with a moder-ate spillover effect to other states, especially those in the western part of United States). Most political observers attribute the growth in Hispanic registration and turnout in the mid- and late 1990s to Republican-led attacks on Latinos and immigrants—such as Propo-sitions 187, 209, and 227 and the Contract with America—and the rhetoric of some Republican leaders—such as Pat Buchanan and Wilson (Smith 1998; Purdum 1997). Most of these new Latino vot-ers registered as Democrats and voted for Democratic candidates. Lance Tarrance, a GOP pollster and a key Republican strategist in 2000, described Wilson's behavior and actions as "a case history of what not to do" when trying to appeal to Latinos (Marinucci 2000). Wilson remains politically unrepentant, saying in a feature newspa-per interview, "People who refer to wedge issues are generally liber-als who want to duck the issue. Wedge issues are real issues. They are problems calling out for attention" (Marelius 1998).

LATINOS AND THE REPUBLICAN PARTY

With the exception of Cuban Americans, the Democrats have been the party of most Hispanics. Democratic presidential candidates have consistently supported favorable policy positions on issues important to most Hispanic voters. Republican candidates, on the other hand, have either ignored or antagonized Latinos. Neglect is the most common Republican behavior and, arguably, is not unexpected since most Republican candidates can expect little support from Latinos. Some Republican candidates, however, have found that they can use Hispanics to win non-Hispanic votes. Wilson and, perhaps, the framers of the 1994 Republican Contract with America used anti-immigrant positions as wedge issues to win white votes. The *styles* of Republican presidential candidates have varied, yet most have favored neglect or antagonism in their dealings with Hispanics. Only recently has a new Republican outreach strategy appeared as a central component of a Republican candidate's campaign: pursuit.

Traditionally, most Republican presidential campaigns have been neglecters. The presidential campaign of Bob Dole in 1996 is the most recent example of this approach (DeSipio, de la Garza, and Setzler 1999). Dole rarely reached out to Latinos and did not address issues of importance to them. He did not want to antagonize the conservative right, especially in the key battleground state of California. Many of his advisors felt that Dole could not win the presidency unless he won California. Because of this must-win California strategy, Dole became a politically expedient supporter of California Proposition 187. Republican neglecters, like Dole, tend to hail from places where Hispanics are not a significant factor in local politics and they tend to concentrate their energies on traditional Republican constituencies.

The antagonists are composed of politicians like presidential candidates Wilson and Buchanan, who have used anti-Hispanic policies as wedge issues in their campaigns. The roots of the use of Hispanics to win non-Hispanic support can be found in a much earlier Republican leader. Herbert Hoover blamed the Great Depression, at least in part, on Mexican and Mexican American laborers.

The pursuers are made up of candidates like 2000 presidential candidate George W. Bush who feel that the future viability of the Republican Party is integrally tied to successfully attracting a significant number of Hispanic voters. In his campaign, Bush aggressively tried to attract Hispanic voters and often described himself as a "different kind of Republican" (Sosa 2002).

While Bush took the pursuer strategy to new levels, he is not the first Republican to follow such a strategy. In the 1952, Dwight D. Eisenhower made some tentative efforts to speak to Latino audiences (Sosa 2002). In 1976, during the presidential Republican primary campaign against Reagan, Gerald Ford made a concerted effort to attract Hispanic voters in the critical swing state of Texas, though with mixed success.[1] Reagan was more successful than any previous Republican presidential candidate in attracting Hispanic voters and was especially successful in attracting Cuban Latinos. Reagan made television appeals to Hispanics in the southwestern United States, emphasizing the policy themes of profamily, anticommunism, promilitary, and individual responsibility. Despite this success, non-Cuban Latino voters were never central to Reagan's victory strategy. This pursuit of Latino votes that had appeared intermittently in Republican presidential politics reached a new level in 2000.

GEORGE W. BUSH AND HISPANIC OUTREACH

Bush aggressively pursued Hispanic voters both as governor and as presidential candidate. In part, this outreach reflected Bush's Texas roots. His experience with "minority" groups was primarily with Mexican immigrants and Mexican Americans. His outreach to Latinos, however, also reflected a strategic calculation that he could distinguish himself from other Republican contenders by making a concerted effort to win Latino votes. His pursuit of Latino support for his gubernatorial and presidential campaigns, rooted though it was in his Texas origins, challenged the Republican Party to broaden its base.

Governor Bush

Bush did not face citizen-initiated propositions while governor of Texas, but he did make his concerns and uneasiness about these issues publicly known. Bush openly spoke out against these propositions, calling them "divisive" (Smith 1998). Unlike Wilson, he refused to support the cutting of social services that benefited illegal immigrants (Mayes 1999). Before he was even inaugurated to his first term, Bush lobbied the Texas legislature to rally support against Proposition 187–like initiatives. In November 1994, Bush argued that he supported providing education and health benefits to undocumented immigrants, "I'm for educating the children of illegal immigrants" (Stutz 1994). Bush said later, "I was against the spirit of Prop 187 for my state. . . . I felt like every child ought to be educated regardless of the status of their parents" (Schneider 1999).

As governor, Bush promoted bilingual education and embraced bilingualism. He often talked of the advantages of learning both English and Spanish, and regularly conducted interviews in Spanish.

Beyond these issues, Bush worked very hard to develop relations with Mexican officials. He met with President Ernesto Zedillo four times in his first four years as governor of Texas and vigorously supported the North American Free Trade Agreement as well as the certification of Mexico's antidrug efforts. During his governorship, Bush met regularly with his elected counterparts from Mexico and even celebrated Cinco de Mayo with Mexican border governors and officials.

In his gubernatorial campaigns, Bush worked hard to create a pro-Hispanic style and to pursue Hispanic voters. At campaign events, Hispanic elected officials, including some Democrats, introduced Bush. He frequently spoke some Spanish from the stump and strategically used Spanish-language advertising to reach out to the Hispanic community. Observers like Domencio Maceri (1999) assert that showing interest in the Hispanic community, openly speaking Spanish, and generally being sensitive to the issues of the Hispanic community is critical in order to gain an "emotional entree to voters minds." *Substance* is what matters over the long term, but *style* is what opens the communication channels. The combination of Bush's 1998 gubernatorial campaign outreach to the Hispanic community and a weak Democratic candidate led to Bush receiving record levels of support for a Texas Republican from the Hispanic community.

Hispanic Outreach by Bush during the 2000 Presidential Campaign

The senior campaign staff tasked with developing a Hispanic outreach strategy—Lionel Sosa, Frank Guerra, and Lance Tarrance—

proposed a five-step process to win Hispanic votes (Sosa 2002; Guerra 2001). First, the Latino community had to feel that both the Bush campaign and Bush the candidate were sensitive toward and welcoming of Latinos. Second, the campaign through advertising and appearances had to address issues relevant to the Latino community. Third, because of the past history of Republican insensitivities toward Latinos, the 2000 Bush campaign would have to spend unprecedented levels of funds on a highly integrated Latino outreach program. Fourth, the advertising and outreach had to focus on Bush the individual candidate and not on Bush the Republican Party nominee. Finally, to be successful beyond the 2000 campaign, if he won the election, the Bush administration would have to follow through on the campaign rhetoric to show this was not just a one time, politically expedient outreach effort.

Sosa, Guerra, and Tarrance saw this five-step Republican Latino outreach program as a first step in a ten- to twenty-year initiative that would ultimately yield a majority of Latino voters for Republican candidates. They felt that it would be important to be patient, yet vigilant and steady when reaching out to Latino voters. Because of the actions and positions taken by the antagonist Republicans during the 1990s, they believed that it would be unlikely that Bush could regain the Republican advances of the 1980s in the short term. Thus, to regularly attract Hispanic voters, Republicans would have to develop a long-term strategy of attack.

The first step of the Sosa, Guerra, and Tarrance plan required that Bush create an "emotional entree to voters minds" (Maceri 1999) and to foster a welcoming atmosphere through symbolism, style, and policy positioning. From speaking some Spanish at almost every rally, to often using Hispanic elected officials to introduce him at campaign events, to addressing some of the issues important to Hispanics, Bush actively tried to present a very pro-Latino image of himself, his campaign, and a Bush administration. Additionally, the Bush campaign produced several television advertisements in English and Spanish that featured George P. Bush, a nephew of George W. Bush whose mother is a Mexican immigrant. In one of these spots, George P. said his uncle believed in "opportunity for every American, for every Latino" (Meckler 2000a; Sosa 2002). Bush often spoke at rallies and in interviews of the need to reach out to the Hispanic community and the need to be sensitive to Hispanic issues. At a speech in Los Angeles on April 7, 2000, to the National Hispanic Women's Conferences, Bush said, "It's so important to have leadership that tears down barriers, leadership that offers a future hopeful for everybody, leaders that reject the politics of pitting one group of people against each other" (Orlov 2000).

Unlike past Republican outreach efforts that were limited narrowly to the Cuban American community and that were often sub rosa, the Bush campaign was very open and conspicuous with its Latino outreach efforts. Michael Madrid, a GOP consultant in California, said the Republican Party "genuinely believes that Hispanics will be a conspicuous part of the new majority [the Bush winning coalition]" (Marinucci 2000).

This *welcoming* approach was also evident at the Republican convention in Philadelphia when several Hispanics were showcased and when a California delegate gave a prime-time speech entirely in Spanish. Arturo Vargas, the executive director of the National Association of Latino Elected Officials in Los Angeles, felt that Bush's Latino outreach efforts "should not go unnoticed" and that Bush was helped by the fact that Hispanics were "all over the stage" in Philadelphia (Green 2000).

Many within the Bush campaign felt it was imperative to create an opening with Hispanics early in the campaign in order to provide credibility before the general election. To this end, the Bush campaign kicked off its Hispanic advertising campaign with a Spanish radio advertisement in Iowa on October 26, 1999. Then, for the first time ever in a presidential primary contest, the Bush campaign ran a Spanish-language television advertisement starting on February 7, 2000, which aired in Arizona. Overall, the advertising outreach to Hispanic voters during the 2000 Bush campaign was unprecedented for a Republican presidential candidate. Beyond paid advertising activities, the Bush campaign worked hard to receive pro-Latino earned media exposures. To that end, the Bush campaign made an unprecedented number of campaign appearances targeting Latinos. Sosa noted that these campaign appearances were more effective than ever in moving polling numbers (2002).

The second step in the Sosa, Guerra, and Tarrance strategy was to speak to issues of importance to Hispanics. Bush appealed to Hispanics with "middle-class family issues" such as education reform, a senior citizen prescription drug program, a commitment to fami-

lies, Social Security reform, middle-class tax cuts, planks supporting the military, small business, and self-reliance. Many within the
RNC and the Bush campaign felt that an overall package of middle-
class Republican issues would appeal to independent and conservative Hispanic voters. During the early stages of the campaign, Bush
presented these middle-class issues at campaign appearances,
through Hispanic surrogates and in the general market English-
language advertising. Additionally, regarding Latino specific issues
such as immigration and U.S.-Mexican border policy issues, Bush
tried to be very Latino friendly. Bush frequently said that he em-
pathized with undocumented workers entering United States from
Mexico, often saying in speeches that "[f]amily values don't stop at
the Rio Grande." During the campaign, Bush often said if elected he
would "look to the South, not as an afterthought" but as a key component of America's foreign policy.

The third element of the Bush Hispanic outreach program was
to develop a well-funded, highly integrated Latino advertising
campaign. Bush's Latino advertising outreach program included
English-language television and radio commercials, Spanish-
language television and radio commercials, and print advertising.
It is commonly accepted in political advertising circles that most
Hispanic voters receive the majority of their news and political information from English-language television. To capitalize on this
understanding, the Bush campaign made a conscious and concerted effort to include Hispanic images in their general market
English-language television advertising (Meckler 2000a, 2000b;
Sosa 2002). Additionally, the Bush campaign created Hispanic-
targeted, English-language advertisements that used Hispanic mo-
tifs featuring Hispanics within group and family settings. According to Hector Orci, a corporate Latino advertising executive, this is
important since "the center of the universe in Latino culture is the
family" as compared to non-Latino families where the "individual" is the focal point, therefore, it is critical to produce Hispanic-
targeted advertisements with family and group images ("Bush
Campaign Begins to Air Spanish-Language Ad" 2000). During the
general election phase, the Bush team ran almost all of the English-
language Hispanic motif television spots in Florida and New
Mexico. These spots were put into rotation with the general market English-language advertisements. This rotation schedule was

approximately proportionate to the percentage of Hispanic population within each state.

Beyond English-language advertisements, the Bush campaign and the RNC actively produced and placed Spanish radio and television spots. Radio advertising began with an October 1999 commercial in Iowa. It starts with an announcer saying in Spanish, "Once again, the spotlight is on Iowa . . . and for the first time, it's shining on the Latino community. . . . We're voters too and George W. Bush believes that all Iowans should help elect a president." The advertisement goes on with the announcer saying that "in this presidential campaign, you will see a fresh start, the beginning of a new day for Latinos. . . . [George W. Bush] believes that the American dream belongs to everyone." The spot ends with Bush saying in Spanish, "This is George W. Bush . . . it's a new day" (David 1999; Cross 1999).

Bush's Spanish-language television campaign next appeared in Arizona before the Republican primary on February 22, 2000. This was the first time a Spanish-language television advertisement and dedicated Latino media campaign had ever been used in a presidential primary campaign ("Bush Campaign Begins to Air Spanish-Language Ad" 2000; Marinucci 2000). The television spot opens with a male voice-over saying in Spanish, "In our country, a new day has arrived." The spot focuses on Bush's family values and ends with Bush saying in Spanish, "Es un nuevo dia." This tag line—it is a new day—was used for two reasons. First, the Bush campaign wanted to subtly tie Al Gore to Bill Clinton and promote the idea that a Bush administration would be different from the Clinton-Gore administration. Second, the Bush campaign wanted conservative and independent Latino voters to see Bush as "a new kind of Republican" who was different from past Republican presidential candidates. The theme of "a new day" and "a fresh start" were often used in advertisements and campaign speeches (Bruni 1999; Sosa 2002; Guerra 2001).

Why did the Bush campaign start its Hispanic-targeted advertising so early in the campaign compared to other presidential campaigns? The simple answer is that it was part of an overall campaign strategy to attract Hispanic voters. One might argue that buying Spanish-language radio in Iowa is neither tactical nor strategically significant since there are so few Hispanics living in the state and the cost of Spanish-language radio in Iowa is so inexpensive. The Bush campaign made a strategic decision to send a message to all Latinos across the nation that Bush was serious about his desire to attract Hispanic voters both in the primary and general election phases of the campaign. The tactic worked. The campaign received extensive news media coverage about this decision to place Spanish-language advertisements so early in Iowa. The placement of Spanish-language spots by the Bush campaign in Arizona was also strategic in that it was part of a comprehensive attempt to knock McCain out of the presidential Republican nomination race by beating him in his own state. The Bush team developed this plan after Arizona senator John McCain beat Bush in the New Hampshire primary. In his Senate campaigns, McCain had become very successful in attracting Latino voters, drawing around 55 percent of the Arizona Latino voters in 1998. During his 1998 senate reelection campaign, McCain used advertisements that dubbed Spanish over his general market English spots. It was felt that including Spanish-language advertising as part of the overall strategic effort against McCain was important.

The bulk of the RNC's advertising campaign was placed in the final month of the campaign. Polling in the final weeks of the campaign determined that the best two issues for Republicans to focus on were education and health care reform. This was true for both undecided general market voters and for conservative and moderate Latino voters. In the final ten days of the campaign, the RNC produced and placed two Spanish-language television advertisements that addressed education and prescription drugs/health care, respectively (Guerra 2001). In California, these spots appeared in the Los Angeles, San Diego, Sacramento, Fresno, and Bakersfield television markets. In Florida, they appeared in the major markets of Miami, Orlando, and Tampa. Additionally, these spots appeared in Nevada and New Mexico. They also appeared in unexpected markets such as Philadelphia, Washington state, Alaska, Oregon, and Georgia. The Bush campaign and the RNC also produced and placed a limited amount of Spanish-language print advertising. Without counting the English-language Hispanic motif television advertisements that ran in proportionate rotation in Florida and New Mexico, the RNC and the Bush campaign spent at least $11 million on Hispanic outreach. The Bush campaign spent $3.5 million on Spanish-language television and radio and the RNC spent an additional $3.5 million on Spanish-language television. The RNC and Bush campaign also spent around $4 million on Latino grassroots outreach programs (Guerra 2001; Sosa 2002). By any measure, the Bush campaign spent more time strategically thinking about Hispanic advertising outreach, spent more money on Hispanic advertising, and spent more time trying to woo Hispanic voters than previous Republican candidates.

The fourth step in the overall strategic Hispanic outreach program was to focus on Bush the individual, rather than Bush the *Republican* presidential nominee. Many strategists within the Bush campaign believed that the best way to reach out to Latinos was to emphasize that Bush was a different kind of candidate compared to past Republican presidential candidates. They felt that Bush had to send a message that he was going to make a fresh start with the Latino community by being more inclusive of Latinos than any prior Republican candidate and to distance himself from the Wilson philosophy of negative wedge issues. Gary Mendoza, a former deputy mayor of Los Angeles and a California Republican activist, said he hoped Latinos "don't think of George W. Bush as having an 'R' after his name" (Booth 2000). This was similar to the approach Bush used in his 1998 gubernatorial reelection campaign. During his 1998 reelection campaign, Bush ran two advertisements, one in English and one in Spanish, featuring a testimonial of a Hispanic woman saying "who cares if [Bush] is not a Democrat."

This theme of independence was extensively showcased at the Republican convention in Philadelphia. During the night that featured cultural diversity, the Bush campaign showed a long feature spot that Sosa produced. In it, a Hispanic woman says, "It kind of reminds me of the days when the Kennedy's used to go to the Latino neighborhoods, to our neighborhoods. . . . [T]hey loved everybody and everybody loved them . . . that's how I feel about George W. Bush" (Sosa 2002). During other spots, Bush said that "I am proud of the Latino blood that flows in the Bush family." Bush was never described nor identified as a Republican in any of the Latino English- or Spanish-language advertisements. Instead of focusing on Bush's party identification, Sosa designed all the Latino outreach advertisements to focus on four critical traits that make up the *inner core* of a candidate: optimism, empathy, strength, and leadership. Sosa asserted that every president elected since 1952 beat his opponent on a composite basis in these four areas. He also said that whichever candidate could convince more voters that he was more optimistic, more empathetic, stronger, and a better leader would win the presidency in 2000. Sosa felt that exposing Latinos to Bush's *inner core* was critical, and if done correctly, many Latinos would vote for Bush.

Beyond these four themes, Sosa also added the theme of inclusiveness to all of the Latino-targeted English- and Spanish-language advertising. This approach made a lot of sense when one considers that polling research found only 16 to 25 percent of Hispanics self-identified as Republicans, yet 34 percent of all Hispanics self-identified as conservatives. A *Washington Post* poll found that Latinos *trusted* Democrats by thirty-three percentage points more than the Republicans to do a better job in dealing with the main problems of the nation. Although 68 percent of Latinos self-identified as conservative or independent, the Republican Party had a major obstacle to overcome: trust.

The final component of the five-part strategic Latino campaign laid out by Sosa, Guerra, and Tarrance was for Bush, if elected, to follow through on the pro-Hispanic campaign rhetoric. Many within the campaign believe that Bush stands a good chance of attracting more than 40 percent of the Latino voters in 2004 *if* he remains inclusive of the Hispanic community, empathetic to Hispanic issues, and *delivers* on the promises made during the campaign. On the contrary, if Bush does not deliver, he will be open to strong attacks by the Democrats. As Joseph Andrew, the former DNC chair, said, "The Republican party cannot, with one ad campaign, erase the bad feelings that their anti-Hispanic record and exclusionary rhetoric has left within the [Latino] community" (Andrew 2000).

It is important to note what this five-step Republican Latino outreach program did not include. There were no full-time, in-house Hispanic senior advisors within the daily functioning of the Bush campaign structure. This is surprising, especially since Bush headquarters was located in Austin, Texas. Sosa was not only the most influential Hispanic advisor to the Bush campaign, but he was also a consultant to the campaign.

Expectations and Goals

Republican leaders hoped Bush would match or exceed Reagan's 37 percent support among Latinos in 1980. During the 2000 elections, Jim Nicholson, the chair of the RNC, said "The Latino community is in play in this election like never before" (Perez 2000). Many Democrats within the Gore campaign echoed Nicholson's view. Los Angeles County supervisor Gloria Molina said, "These people [Latinos] are not automatic anything. . . . They are certainly not automatic Republicans and they are not automatic Democrats, either" (Booth 2000). Nicholson hosted several top-level campaign meetings to develop a strategic plan to target Hispanic voters. Beyond the Bush campaign placement of Hispanic English- and Spanish-language targeted advertisements, the RNC produced and placed Spanish-language television advertisements in targeted metro markets within battleground states.

The Republican objective was to focus on media markets that contained high concentrations of conservative and independent Hispanic voters within targeted battleground states. Down the stretch, the Bush campaign became very focused on the mathematics of the electoral college and thus targeted media markets in Florida, Nevada, and New Mexico that had high concentrations of conservative and independent Hispanic voters. It should be noted that the Republicans took a serious look at targeting California about eight weeks out when polling indicated that Bush had pulled to within nine percentage points of Gore. However, once a cost-benefit analysis was conducted, the Bush campaign chose not to target California.

The Republicans had two goals regarding Hispanic voters: first, to attract enough Hispanic voters in targeted battleground states to help Bush win the presidency, second, for Bush to match or exceed Reagan's 37 percent Hispanic voter support. Many Republican strategists felt that attracting a moderate number of traditionally pro-Democratic Latino voters to Bush would be enough to dilute the support for Gore in key battleground states, and thus swing these states to Bush. They also felt that Bush could successfully attract Latino voters since Gore, at least in the beginning of the campaign, tended to target Latino voters through the broad prism of *minority issues.*

Did Bush achieve his goal of attracting a higher percentage of Hispanic voters than Reagan? No, but he came close to Reagan's 37 percent. Exit polls reported by ABC News, the *Los Angeles Times*, and the *New York Times* placed Bush's share of the Latino vote in the 31 to 38 percent range (see table 1.9). The Voter News Service reported that Bush received 35 percent of the Hispanic vote and Republican strategists claim he received 36 percent. In percentage terms, Governor Bush did better than Dole in 1996 and George H. W. Bush in 1988 or 1992. In terms of actual Hispanic votes, Bush received more than any prior Republican presidential candidate.

Testing the Impact of Republican Outreach

Since Bush was the sitting governor of Texas and had faced state voters twice in addition to his 2000 residential run, analyzing Texas results offers insights into Bush's success with Hispanics. There is no single test that can be utilized to accurately and confidently measure Hispanic voting patterns without bias. I use three different measurements to analyze how successful Governor Bush was in attracting Hispanic voters in Texas compared to the 1992 and 1996 presidential campaigns.

First, I measure down ballot defection rates in 1992, 1996, and 2000. My hypothesis is that the less loyal Hispanic voters are to the Democratic Party, the less cohesive they will be in voting for Democratic candidates in the future, resulting in a higher ticket splitting rate between candidates from different parties on the same ballot. This measurement is obtained by calculating the percentage difference between the share of the vote received by the Democratic presidential candidate and the share of the vote received by the Democratic candidate with the highest difference from the presidential candidate in each county. For example, if the Democratic presidential candidate received 56 percent of the Hispanic vote in Gordon County and the Democratic candidate with the highest percentage difference, the attorney general candidate, received 44 percent of the Hispanic vote, the percentage point differential for Gordon County is –12 percent. I limit my analysis to Texas counties with Latino concentrations above 50 percent. The closer the differential is to 0 percent, the more cohesive and loyal a county is to the Democratic Party in a particular election. The advantage of this measurement is that it will detect party splitters and party defectors by providing a relative measure of loyalty toward the Democratic and Republican Parties: the closer to 0 percent, the relatively more loyal they are to Democratic candidates. The limitation to this measure is that Hispanics who are loyal and unified for the Republican Party will get masked.

The analysis of Democratic down ballot defection rates is inconclusive on whether the 2000 Bush campaign did better in regards to attracting Hispanics than the Republican presidential campaigns in 1992 and 1996. The lack of clarity regarding this data set may be caused by variables tied to the Ross Perot campaigns of 1992 and 1996. It is clear from the data that the higher the concentration of Latino voters in a county, the more likely it is that the county will be more loyal to the Democratic Party. This trend holds true for all three elections in this study in that the regression slopes for 1992, 1996, and 2000 all converge toward 0 percent, thus indicating significantly higher levels of Democratic loyalty and cohesiveness as the percent concentration of Hispanics within a county increases. If the Republican Party is to be successful in realigning Latino voters, the Republicans will initially need to break Hispanic voters' loyalty to the Democratic Party.

The second measure uses linear regression analysis to determine the correlation between the percentage of Hispanics living in a county and the percentage of votes for the Democratic presidential candidate in the respective county. Again, I limit my analysis to counties with Latino population concentrations exceeding 50 percent. I use linear regression to determine the relationship between the Hispanic population percentage and the percent who voted for the Democratic presidential candidate. The more robust the correlation between the percentage of Hispanic population and the percentage county vote for the Democrat presidential candidate, the larger the B coefficient and the steeper the regression slope. A smaller B coefficient indicates that the Republican presidential candidate did relatively better in predominantly Hispanic counties. Simplified, relatively steeper lines indicate Hispanics voted more for the Democratic candidate, while relatively shallower lines indicate that Hispanics voted more Republican.

The advantage of using this measurement is that it deals with aggregate real votes and does not suffer from self-report biases of voting and sampling technique errors. Additionally, using county-level data matches up closely with market advertising units strategically used by campaigns in that most media markets are just one county or are a small number of counties. The weakness of this measurement is that there may be omitted variables so that the estimated effect of ethnicity is overstated. This may be especially true for lower Hispanic percentage counties, but is much less a factor for the higher Hispanic percentage counties.

The regression slope for the Gore 2000 campaign is shallower and never crosses the regression slopes of the Democratic campaigns of 1992 and 1996. This means that the Gore campaign was much less effective in attracting votes from highly concentrated Hispanic counties than the Clinton presidential campaigns of 1992 and 1996. It is thus very significant that the 2000 Bush campaign did much better in gaining relatively more votes in highly concentrated Latino voting counties relative to the Republican campaigns of 1992 and 1996. In fact, a dramatic finding in this study is that the 2000 Bush campaign outperformed the Republican and Perot campaigns combined in attracting voters from highly concentrated Hispanic Texas counties in both 1992 and 1996.

The final measurement used by this study of Texas is exit polling data from the 1992, 1996, and 2000 general elections. In 1992, the Southwest Voter Research Institute exit poll reported that George H. W. Bush drew 15 percent of the Hispanic voters and in 1996 it found that Dole drew 17 percent of Hispanic voters. In 2000, the Voter News Service exit poll showed George W. Bush drew 43 percent of Hispanic voters in Texas, while the William C. Velasquez Institute showed that Bush drew 33 percent. The analysis of exit polling indicates that Bush did much better in 2000 than his father did in 1992 or Dole did in 1996.

When taken together, two out of the three measurements indicate an increase in support by Texas Hispanics of Bush compared to that of the 1992 and 1996 Republican candidates.

LESSONS FOR THE FUTURE: RELATIVE SUCCESS OF LATINO OUTREACH IN THE BUSH AND RNC CAMPAIGNS

The goal of the first Republican strategic objective in 2000 was to convince moderate and conservative Latinos that Bush was sensitive to their issues and concerns and that he would openly welcome

Latino voters. In many ways, this was the easiest component of the plan to implement since Bush was comfortable with Hispanic out-reaching. In fact, Bush was the driving force behind the Hispanic outreach strategy. Through family ties and political experience, Bush felt that moderate and conservative Hispanics would fit in well with the coalition he was trying to put together. Because of his commitment to the Hispanic outreach program, as well as his per-sonal style of outreach, the campaign was able successfully to send strong and early messages that the Bush campaign was very wel-coming of Latinos.

The objective of the second component of the Latino outreach program was to address policy issues relevant to the Latino com-munity. Both the Bush campaign and the RNC were successful in the final weeks of the campaign with the positioning of education and health care as relevant Latino issues. This proved to be fortu-itous for Bush in that these two issues also played well with other demographic groups that the Republicans were targeting. This made it very easy to *stay on message* even when targeting different demographic groups. Beyond these two issues targeted in the final weeks of the campaign, polling showed that conservative and mod-erate Latinos generally favored Bush's policy positions on family values, antiabortion, and a strong military defense. Many conserva-tive and moderate Latinos also liked the stances Bush took on im-migration and on language issues and small business initiatives. However, the Latino community differed strongly with Bush on many topics such as gun control, size of government, and the num-ber of federal service programs. In the short term, the Bush cam-paign was smart to focus on a limited package of issues that were relevant to moderate and conservative Hispanics. Many Latinos did feel that Bush was trying, but they did not feel he was going far enough in regards to issues important to the Hispanic community. In 2000, developing a comprehensive and extensive package of is-sues relevant to the Hispanic community would have been hard for the Republicans, without risking a loss in support of other key con-stituencies. As Latinos become more discerning of Republican pol-icy issues, it will become more difficult for future Republican pres-idential candidates to balance diverse policy concerns. No longer will it be good enough to just try. Instead, to be successful Republi-can presidential candidates will have to address a broader spectrum of issues relevant to the Latino community. Future Republican candidates will have to be cognizant of this paradox. If Bush wants to be more successful in attracting Hispanic voters in 2004, he will have to address a more comprehensive set of issues relevant to the Hispanic community.

As for the third step of their comprehensive outreach plan, the Bush campaign and the RNC were quite successful in developing and carrying out a well-funded, strategic advertising program. By all measures, the advertising programs developed by the Bush campaign and the RNC in 2000 were the best Latino advertising outreach programs ever developed and implemented by Republicans. The funding level of the Republican Latino outreach program in 2000 was unprecedented and may prove to be the most well-funded Latino outreach campaign ever by either a Republican or a Democratic candidate. However, the ultimate measures of success for any political advertising campaign is not how much was spent on placements or how creative it was, but *how effective and efficient was the campaign in attracting votes for the candidate?* For a Republican, Bush was quite effective in attracting Latino voters. It is too early to develop a definitive answer to the cost efficiency question. The Republicans did spend extensively on Latino outreach and it may have made the difference in Florida. If Republicans view Latino outreach efforts as a part of a long-term strategy to *solidify* Latino support and to include Latinos in future winning coalitions, the cost efficiency calculation changes considerably. On the other hand, if outreach efforts are infrequent and disjointed, they will probably not be very cost effective. Beyond these questions, one should also ask if Bush's success was a result of his advertising program, his policy positions, or a combination of both. Since much of what Bush did were symbolic *firsts* for a Republican presidential candidate, an accurate assessment is difficult. Additionally, the fact that many believed that the Gore campaign took the Hispanic community for granted in the early stages of the campaign made it much easier for Bush to make significant inroads into the Hispanic community early in the campaign.

The campaign was quite disciplined in implementing the fourth strategic objective of focusing on Bush the individual rather than Bush the Republican nominee. As for the fifth part of the plan, to follow through on campaign promises, it is too early to ascertain success or failure. In symbolic terms, Bush has started well with the nomination of an inclusive cabinet and key staff members. Additionally, he did take his first foreign policy trip to Mexico. As the Latino community becomes more politically sophisticated, Latinos will become more discerning between symbolic issue stances and substantive policy positions. Bush was able to attract Latino voters in Texas because his issue positions were sensitive, symbolic, and substantive. On a national level, he symbolically opened the Republican door to the Latino community in 2000. Bush will now need to create a political home that is as relevant to Latinos on the inside, as it is welcoming from the outside. The ultimate determination of success of the fifth component of the strategic plan is very much interconnected with the success or failure of step two, the development of meaningful issue positions relevant to the Latino community.

For Sosa, Guerra, and Tarrance, the five-part Hispanic outreach program was more strategically intuitive than it was politically tactical, in that it was based on lessons they all had learned over decades of Republican campaign work. In many ways, they could have set up this plan for any *willing* Republican presidential candidate. Clearly, the success of their plan is due in large part to the commitment and support of Bush the candidate.

Measuring Republican Latino Outreach Programs

Madrid, the Republican Hispanic strategist in California, asserts that "we don't need to get a majority, but we need to begin to choose battlegrounds. . . . [I]f we get 25 to 30 percent, that's coalition-building. . . . [I]f we get 35 to 40 percent, that's the White House and three-quarters of the governors' offices" (Marinucci 2000). Because of the size and growth rate of the Hispanic voting community, Republicans must become routinely competitive with the Democrats, or else the Republican Party will, for the foreseeable future, become the political party out of power. In the short term, for the Republicans to be successful with Hispanic voters, the Republicans only need to make moderate inroads with Hispanics in key battleground states. If Republicans continue to present a welcoming image, develop a broader package of issues relevant to the Latino community, and then deliver on campaign promises, Republicans could foreseeably attract more than 50 percent of Latino voters. To do this, Republicans must remain vigilant with, and true to,

Latino outreach programs. Additionally, Republicans must be patient and realize that, just as with the realignment of the South, the political benefits do not come overnight. If the Republicans handle this correctly over the long run, Republicans could permanently realign a majority of Hispanics into the Republican Party. On the other hand, if Wilson-type Republicans take control of the Republican message and political apparatus, they will doom the Republican Party as the party out of power. As the Republican strategist Stuart Spencer asserts, if the Republican Party wants to remain competitive with the Democratic Party, the Republican Party can no longer afford to lose market share in the fastest growing segment of voters.

Potential Impediments to Successful Republican Outreach Programs

The most obvious impediment to success would be if Wilson-type Republicans took over the political apparatus of the Republican Party and resumed the overt attacks on the Hispanic community. The second biggest potential impediment to success would be if Dole-type Republicans took control of the party and stopped or made intermittent the comprehensive Latino outreach efforts. Beyond these two potential macro impediments, there are several smaller potential obstacles that, if handled improperly, could cause major damage. Both the RNC and Republican presidential candidates must start to run real grassroots initiatives that extend beyond business and upper-class Hispanic elites. In the short term, running air war campaigns that skim moderate and conservative Hispanic voters may be cost effective. However, to get the big gains, air wars will have to be coupled with ground wars.

When it comes to issue positioning, Republicans must address key issues relevant to the Hispanic community, such as gun control, affirmative action, immigration, government service programs, and bilingualism. It is true that there is some overlap of issue affinity between core Republican issues and Hispanic relevant issues. However, this overlap is not significant enough to sustain extensive Latino outreach. This may explain in part why Bush started well in the polls with Latinos, but as the campaign went on, his Latino support eroded. The initially large bounce in support of

Bush by Hispanics is characteristically similar to traditional post-convention *bounce effects* and may be explained in part because he was the only candidate emitting a pro-Latino message to Latino voters during the early stages of the campaign.

In terms of high-level administrative appointments, Republicans need to be cautious not to try to serve two masters at the same time: moderate Latinos on one side and hard-line conservative Republicans on the other. In some circles in the Republican Party, it has become fashionable to suggest the appointment of "twofers"—that is, minorities who have conservative views. The problem is that extreme far-right conservative Hispanics do not represent moderate and conservative Hispanics, nor do they represent the mainstream of the Hispanic community. To reach out to moderate Hispanics effectively, a Republican administration must appoint both moderate and conservative Hispanics.

There are two final areas of concern about which Republicans should be cognizant. First, Republicans must understand that Latinos have emigrated from more than twenty different countries. Rodolfo O. de la Garza asserts that "[the Latino] experience in the United States is much less uniform then African-Americans. . . . [T]he interests of Mexicans and their descendants in California, for example, tend to be very different than the interests of Cuban Americans and their descendants in Florida" (Pitts 2000). Whether targeting advertising or developing policy positions, Republicans must be aware of the intra-Latino differences and understand what they mean politically. Finally, Republicans must realize what it takes for a presidential Latino outreach campaign to be successful. When one carefully compares the successful outreach programs of Kennedy in 1960, Clinton in 1996, and Bush in 2000, one will notice a common alignment of role players that catalyzes successful Latino outreach programs. For each of these campaigns the presidential candidate himself strongly championed the Latino outreach program, there were key high-level supporters within the campaign apparatus that supported the outreach efforts, and there was at least one highly skilled Hispanic political operative. In the 1996 Democratic campaign, Clinton strongly supported Latino outreach and Henry Cisneros and Federico Peña forcefully advocated for the Latino outreach program within the campaign structure. Additionally, Andy Hernandez, Maria Echaveste, and others were extremely effective political operatives. In the 2000 Republican campaign, Bush strongly supported the Hispanic outreach efforts and Karl Rove and Mark McKinnon actively supported the Hispanic outreach programs within the campaign structure, while Sosa and Guerra were outstanding political operatives. It clearly takes planning, persistence, funding, and support to put together successful outreach programs. Great outreach programs do not just happen.

If Republicans continue their outreach programs and develop a better package of Latino relevant issues, the Democrats will have to fight back with a strong counter effort to keep Latinos in the Democratic Party or risk losing a major constituency. For too long, the Democratic Party has taken Latinos for granted while the Republican Party has flipped back and forth between ignoring Latinos and bashing Latinos. A competitive political climate, where both Republicans and Democrats actively seek the support of the Latino community, would greatly benefit Latinos. Finally, the Latino community can help itself by developing successful voter turnout programs. As for the future, the 2004 presidential campaign may prove to be the political turning point in the interaction between Latino voters and Republican presidential candidates.

NOTE

1. While at a campaign rally in front of the Alamo, President Ford was handed a tamale to eat as part of a photo-op, at which time Ford proceeded "with gusto" to bite through the corn husk, rather than taking it off first. Ford's gaffe was so embarrassing that it was printed on the front page of the *New York Times*. In response to a press conference question after his loss to Jimmy Carter to name the single most important lesson he had learned from the campaign, Ford responded that he learned how to shuck a tamale (Popkin 1994).

3

Latino Politics Comes of Age

Lessons from the Golden State

HARRY P. PACHON, MATT A. BARRETO,
and FRANCES MARQUEZ

〰〰〰〰〰〰〰〰〰〰〰〰〰〰〰〰〰〰〰〰〰〰〰〰〰〰

AS THE TWENTY-FIRST CENTURY BEGINS, CALIFORNIA LATINO POLITICS has reshaped the lens through which Latino politics nationally is viewed. This new image has three characteristics: Latinos are an active ethnic electorate, California Latino elected officials have achieved the critical mass to influence policy outcomes, and both political parties compete for Latino loyalty. This image is a marked contrast to the traditional view, which held that Latinos were present in the state in large numbers but were not an electoral force, that Latinos were unable to win statewide offices, and that both political parties (but more distinctly the Republicans) could ignore Latino policy preferences.

As the Latino population disperses, several other states face a similar demographic and political environment to California's in the 1990s. The Latino electorate nationally, and not just the Latino population, are growing and this Latino electorate is influenced, in part, by the anti-immigrant and anti-Latino sentiment that swelled in California in the mid-1990s. English-only laws and anti-immigrant organizations have surfaced in much of the Midwest and Southwest.

Latinos are the largest minority group in twenty-three states. Recent mayoral elections in three of the largest cities in the United States (Los Angeles, Houston, and New York) demonstrate that Latinos can be players, if not yet regular winners, in the urban areas where they reside. The lessons learned in California are precursors for what other states will experience in the early decades of the twenty-first century. This chapter examines statewide developments in California's Latino community that brought about this change. In addition, we examine how these changes and their consequences are perceived by Latino political elites.

THE CHANGING STRUCTURE OF CALIFORNIA'S LATINO COMMUNITY AND ELECTORATE

The Latino electorate has grown from 8 percent of the state's electorate in 1990 to approximately 14 percent in 2000 (see chapter 8). In raw numbers, this reflects a growth from roughly 800,000 Latino voters statewide to 1.6 million Latino voters in 2000 out of a statewide electorate of 10 million. Latinos have increased their share of registered voters in this same period from 10 percent to more than 16 percent (see table 3.1). There has been a corresponding increase in the number of Latinos elected to public office. In 1990, there were 572 Hispanic elected officials statewide. By 2000, the number had increased to 760. The most dramatic change occurred in the state legislature where the number of state representatives and senators increased from six to twenty-seven, an increase of 350 percent (National Association of Latino Elected and Appointed Officials Educa-

Table 3.1   Change in California Registered Voters, by Race and Ethnicity, 1990–2000

	1990	% of total	2000	% of total	Change
White	10,600,000	78.6	10,500,000	71.8	−100,000
Latino	1,350,000	10.0	2,350,000	16.1	+1,000,000
Black	950,000	7.0	900,000	6.2	−50,000
Asian/Other	600,000	4.5	900,000	6.2	+300,000
Total	13,478,000		14,632,000		+1,154,000

Note: Due to rounding, percentages for each year may not equal 100.

Source: Field Institute (2000).

tional Fund 1990, 2001). Political gains, however, were not simply numerical. Statewide elected and political leadership offices, such as the lieutenant governorship, the speakership of the assembly, and the chair of the Democratic Party are now, or have been, held by Latinos during the past decade. Equally significant is that both political parties now publicly acknowledge the importance of the Latino electorate ("They'll Be Back" 2001; Marinucci and Wildermuth 2001). These gains and visible political presence were brought about by a confluence of demographic and political factors, as well as by institutional changes in the government of the state.

Population Growth and an Increasing Electorate

California's Latino population continues to grow at a faster rate than the white non-Hispanic population. As table 3.2 illustrates, the number of California Latinos increased by 38 percent between 1990 and 2000 and the non-Latino white population increased by only 2 percent during the same time period. Much of this growth was concentrated in Los Angeles County, where four out of ten Latinos in the state reside. Los Angeles County's Latino population grew from 3,351,238 to 4,242,213; Latinos account for 45 percent of county residents.

The growth of the Latino electorate, however, is not simply a function of population growth that includes minors under eighteen and immigrants ineligible to vote. The electorate, however, builds as young people age, immigrants naturalize as U.S. citizens, and adult citizens register and vote.

Table 3.2   California Population Growth, by Race and Ethnicity, 1990–2000

	1990	% of total	2000	% of total	% Growth
White	17,131,831	57.2	17,421,511	50.3	1.7
Latino	7,774,789	26.0	10,688,752	30.8	37.5
Black	2,105,207	7.0	2,337,935	6.7	11.1
Asian	2,745,781	9.2	3,999,427	11.5	45.7
Other	184,789	0.6	205,770	0.6	11.4
Total	29,942,397		34,653,395		15.7

Note: Due to rounding, percentages for each year may not total 100.

Source: Authors' compilations based on U.S. Bureau of the Census 2002d.

California saw unprecedented numbers of Latino permanent residents naturalize as U.S. citizens in the 1990s. Nearly 600,000 Latinos naturalized between 1990 and 1999 (out of a total 1.6 million new naturalizees). No other decade saw such an increase in naturalized citizens in the Golden State. There were several reasons for this new level of naturalization, some of which may not reappear in the future (DeSipio 1996b). Proposition 187 and the corresponding anti-immigration rhetoric that culminated in the passage of the national welfare reform bill in 1996 was probably the most important factor (Johnson, Farrell, and Guinn 1997; Segura, Falcón, and Pachon 1997; Pachon 1998). In addition, 3 million formerly undocumented immigrants who became legal permanent residents under the Immigration Reform and Control Act of 1986 became eligible for U.S. citizenship in the mid-1990s. More than one-third lived in California. Third, new Immigration and Naturalization Service (INS) policies, specifically a requirement that legal permanent residents renew their Alien Registration ("green") cards, prodded some to seek naturalization. Fourth, the Mexican government's decision to liberalize its property ownership policies and move toward a policy allowing dual nationality for Mexican émigrés encouraged others. Fifth, the Clinton administration changed longstanding INS policies and promoted naturalization among immigrants, at least briefly. Finally, and perhaps least recognized, was a recognition among Latino civic organizations, political leaders, and the Spanish-language media in California that naturalization was the missing link in Latino political empowerment strategies. It is not an exaggeration to say that the major barrios in East Los Angeles, Santa Ana, and the San Fernando Valley all experienced U.S. citizenship drives led by Latino organizations in the 1990s. The pro–U.S. citizenship message of these drives was reinforced on Univision and Telemundo. The combination of these factors resulted in new citizens becoming a large segment of the growing California Latino electorate.

Real or Perceived Growth in the Latino Vote?

Some scholars have posited that increases in Latino voting are the result of population growth and not actual increases in voting and turnout (de la Garza, Haynes, and Ryu 2001; Shaw, de la Garza, and Lee 2000). Examination of the Los Angeles County Latino electorate demonstrates that Latino registration and voter turnout is growing rapidly (Barreto and Woods 2001). Between 1994 and 1998, turnout among registered Latinos increased, which largely benefited the Democratic Party. Examination of Los Angeles County voter registration records from 1994 and 1998 demonstrates that Latino registration and turnout grew more rapidly than non-Latino registration and turnout. These results are derived from the universe of registrants in Los Angeles County (n = 3.9 million) and are not susceptible to confidence interval problems that a random sample of registered voters would be.

In 1994, 600,127 Latinos were registered to vote and in the general election that year 241,364 Latinos voted, a 40.2 percent turnout rate (see table 3.3). Four years later, the number of Latinos registered grew to 841,442 and the number of Latinos who voted increased to 358,826. The net increase of 241,315 Latino registrants between 1994 and 1998 was a 40.2 percent jump in registration, while the addition of 117,462 Latino voters was a 48.7 percent increase, exceeding the growth rate for registration. As a result, the 1998 Latino turnout rate grew to 42.6 percent (Barreto and Woods 2001). The non-Latino vote increased by only 10.3 percent in this same period and non-Latino registration declined.

While most voting studies find that Anglos vote at higher rates than minorities, we find that Latino-registered voters in Los Angeles County turned out to vote at higher rates than non-Latino voters in 1998. We should note that turnout rates reported here are for reg-

Table 3.3   Latino and Non-Latino Registration and Voting, Los Angeles County, 1994–1998

	1994	1998	Change	% Change
Latino				
Registration	600,127	841,442	+241,315	+40.2
Voting	241,364	358,826	+117,462	+48.7
Turnout	40.2%	42.6%	+2.4	
Non-Latino				
Registration	3,064,212	3,043,499	−20,713	−0.7
Voting	1,142,197	1,259,517	+117,320	+10.3
Turnout	37.3%	41.4%	+4.1	

Source: Barreto and Woods (2001: table 1).

istered voters, not for all U.S. citizen adults. When citizen adults are considered, Latinos have lower rates of turnout than non-Latinos.

There are also important partisan implications to the increases in registration and turnout. Previous scholarly research finds that Republicans vote at higher rates than Democrats (Verba, Schlozman, and Brady 1995; Arvizu and Garcia 1996; Calvo and Rosenstone 1989; Wolfinger and Rosenstone 1980). We find that in Los Angeles County in 1998 Latino Democrats turned out at the highest rates (46 percent). Non-Latino Republicans and non-Latino Democrats turned out at 44 percent and Latino Republicans at 41 percent.

New Latino registrants in Los Angeles County affiliate with the Republican Party at very low levels. Matt A. Barreto and Nathan D. Woods introduce the concept of "GOP detachment" to explain "the extent to which new Latino registrants fail to register with the GOP at rates consistent with Latino GOP registration in 1994" (2001). In Los Angeles County as a whole, both the Democratic and Republican Parties lost registration to third parties, but the GOP loss was five times greater than that of the Democrats. In 1994, 19.9 percent of all Latinos were registered with the Republican Party. Among Latinos who registered to vote in the four years between 1994 and 1998, only 10.3 percent registered Republican.

Party registration of the new Latino voters in 1998 provides additional evidence of Democratic dominance among Los Angeles County Latino voters. Of the 117,462 new Latino voters, 88,000 were registered as Democrats, compared to only 8,221 as Republicans (and 21,241 as Independents or with third parties), a ten-to-one advantage for the Democrats.

POLITICAL FACTORS AND LATINO VOTER MOBILIZATION

This growth in the Latino vote and detachment from the GOP must be seen, in part, as an outgrowth of the conservative statewide ballot measures seemingly targeted at the Latino community. Other studies at both the aggregate and individual level support the claim that the Republican Party's support of such divisive initiatives as Propositions 187, 209, and 227 contributed to higher voter turnout rates as well as attachment to the Democratic Party during the late

1990s (Segura, Falcón, and Pachon 1997; Pantoja, Ramírez, and Segura 2001; Barreto and Woods 2001).

California Latinos not only saw 187 as an anti-illegal alien measure, but also as an anti-Latino measure. The rhetoric of the campaign, the xenophobic statements by 187 proponents, and the advertisements associating illegal aliens with Latinos more generally all had the impact of polarizing and mobilizing the community. As one Republican analyst noted:

> 187 was the catalyst for bringing all Latinos together. It was the Republicans who woke them up . . . they [Latinos] felt a common threat; they felt the community was under attack. What they felt was somebody saying "We don't want you here, regardless of the fact that you and your family have been here for 400 years." It was a personal attack; it was a cultural attack. And that has finally brought all these voters together in one group, a community united against a common threat, a common enemy.[1]

Evidence of a newly mobilized Latino electorate can been seen in 1994 election results. The number of Latinos voting in 1994 equaled the number of Latinos voting in the preceding presidential election. No other state with a large Latino population exhibited this phenomenon.

Further impetus for Latino political mobilization came in 1996 and 1998 with two other statewide initiatives: Proposition 209, which eliminated racial and ethnic preferences in state and local government programs, and Proposition 227, which largely eliminated bilingual education. Latino activists and political leaders saw both initiatives as antiminority. These propositions did not resonate as strongly among the Latino electorate as had Proposition 187. Three out of four Latino voters voted against 209 and two out of three voted against 227. In all three cases, the Latino vote contrasted markedly with the majority of Californians who overwhelmingly supported the propositions (187 passed with 60 percent of the vote, 209 with 55 percent, and 227 with 61 percent).

The three consecutive initiatives placing the Latino electorate at odds with the majority electorate polarized Latinos in a way not previously seen in California. The traditional basis of ethnic politics has been the common identification with a group on the basis of race, religion, or nationality (Hawkins and Lorinskas 1970). Unintentionally perhaps, during three elections the solidarity of Latino voters in California statewide elections was reinforced.

Can this unity continue? Some would say that without the impetus of a hot-button issue, Latino voter participation would decline. As one political leader stated:

> You saw in March of 2000 for the first time since November of 1994, the Latino share of the electorate actually dropped; and the reason is because there was no emotional wedge issue . . . no overarching enemy. And so the question then becomes one of sustainability, and I think that is one of the biggest questions facing the community going forward. It was easy when you were being attacked. The question is: Can anybody present a positive cohesive agenda for this growing electorate? And my answer is no.

Term Limits

Proposition 140, passed by California voters in 1990, restricted state legislative officeholders in the assembly to three two-year terms (six years total) and to two four-year terms in the state senate (eight years total). With this, "the California state legislature became the first modern American legislature to have a complete term limit mandated membership turnover in one of its chambers" (Caress 1998: 263). Prior to the 1990s, longevity in office characterized the California state legislature. At the local level, turnover rates were higher as office competed for offices up the political ladder, but at the state legislative level turnover was absent. During the 1980s—a period that spanned 400 separate state legislative elections—only 5 of the 120 incumbent legislators in the California Assembly and Senate were defeated (Heslop 1990). Term limits benefited Latino candidates by opening up additional seats when current members "termed out" or left their seats early to pursue a higher office (Block and Zeiger 1990; Caress 1998; Hero et al. 2000). Coupled with the effect of state propositions, term limits opened the door to Latino representation and subsequently produced a greater role for Latino legislators for the state of California as a whole.

Senior legislators left office in 1996, when many state assembly members termed out and in 1998 when a similar limit applied to state senators. This triggered a phenomenon of more special elections being held for the state legislature than ever before. As legislative incumbents sought new positions, they left their current offices, which in turn became open seats. In twenty-four of the twenty-six legislative seats held by Latino members in 2000, the incumbent won the seat the first time in an open race without an incumbent running. Only two defeated incumbents.

With shorter legislative careers, rotation of top leadership positions in the legislature as a whole and in committees also occurred. Prior to 1995, for example, Willie Brown held the assembly speakership for fifteen years. Since 1995, there have been six speakers, including two Latinos. As of March 2001, Latinos held thirty-one of the key committee positions in the assembly, serving as chairs or vice chairs, fourteen committee leadership positions in the senate, and on five joint committees. Latino members serve in leadership capacities on powerful committees such as budget, judiciary, labor, transportation, health and human services, and water and parks, as well as select committees on California-Mexico affairs, agricultural imports and exports, school safety, health access, and many more.

Geographic Dispersion

While important, term limits are not the only factor that has expanded opportunities for Latinos seeking public office. Although the California Latino community is still concentrated in southern California, the population has dispersed across the state. Twenty-nine congressional districts in California now have 100,000 or more Latino constituents. In a state where one out of three residents is Latino, this figure should not be surprising. What may be counterintuitive is that twelve of these twenty-nine congressional districts are outside the southern California counties of Los Angeles, Orange, Riverside, and San Bernardino. There are now sizeable Latino communities in the central region of California and the Bay area. Congressional districts in Fresno, Santa Barbara, San Luis Obispo, Sacramento, Alameda, and Santa Clara also have large Latino constituencies.

These Latino communities outside of southern California have seen voter mobilization and have elected Latinos to school boards and to municipal and county levels. Many of these elected officials are "cross-over candidates"—that is, officials whose ethnic constituency is not the majority of the electorate in their district. As one Democratic Party official stated:

Prior to 1992, there weren't any Latinos in the state legislature out-side of Los Angeles City. And in 1992 you got somebody from the In-land Empire [Riverside and San Bernardino Counties] in the assembly. And in the next year Cruz Bustamante from the Central Valley. And the following, you had Liz Figueroa from Alameda. And Denise Ducheny from San Diego. Latino politicians began to emerge outside of traditional ethnic-hyphenated districts. The new immigrant voter was the backbone of that surge in new Latino voices in California.

New Campaign Strategies

In addition to the dispersion of the Latino electorate and the impact of term limits, new campaign techniques also aided the emergence of Latino elected officials throughout the state. One of the tradi-tional images associated with the Latino electorate has been the low turnout of Latinos on election day. In an earlier analysis of the Latino vote, one of the authors of this chapter noted that Latino elected officials were often told by majority party officials of the low turnout figures in their districts and how this affected cost-benefit decisions in allocating party resources (Pachon and Arguelles 1994). One of the significant changes in the 1990s was the intro-duction of new campaign techniques specifically designed to mo-bilize Latino immigrant and working-class electorates. As one Latino officeholder stated:

> Old political consultants devalue mobilization as an effective part of the political campaign budget and promote heavy mail programs. And while your message is an important part of the campaign, Latino elected officials rely more heavily on mobilizing people to vote.... The fact is that people don't vote if you don't reach out to them. If you shake more hands than your opponent you will win. The reason the Latino voting percentages were less historically, I believe, is because nobody reached out to them.

Latino elected officials credit the resources devoted to field cam-paigns—where there is direct voter contact by volunteers or cam-paign staff—as being the key to victory of many Latinos in the 1990s. Two other factors were also present. First, under the leadership of state senator Richard Polanco, party leaders raised money to finance intensive field operations. Second, unions provided funds and volun-teers for field operations. With all of these factors converging in the

1990s, the Latino electorate has mobilized to a previously unprecedented degree and is playing a more important role than ever before in California's state politics.

INTERPRETING LATINO POLITICAL GAINS IN THE STATE

What difference has it made for the Latino community in the state that Latinos have made such significant political gains? How do Latino civic leaders view these changes? What difference has it made on public policy issues? In order to address these questions, we interviewed fourteen high-ranking Democratic and Republican Latino elected officials at the federal, state, and local levels. We promised confidentiality in regards to attribution in order to ensure candid responses. While such a small set of interviews cannot be representative of all California Hispanic elected officials, these interviews offer substantive insight into the political meanings of increasing Latino electoral turnout and the growing numbers of Latinos elected to office in California.

How do Latino political leaders view the changes in Latino politics in the state? These leaders predominantly give two answers. Perhaps not surprisingly, the first change that Latino political leaders cite is the rise in the numbers in their ranks. For example, as one leader stated:

> The fact that there's been a growth in representation at the state level specifically. Also at the local levels, there's been a large turn over, some of the more traditional smaller cities . . . some of the smaller cities that have been more traditionally represented by Anglo elected officials even though they have large Latino populations have started to change, you know the Cudahys, the Huntington Parks, and so. I mean throughout the state, for instance, you go to Gilroy or Watsonville and you start seeing those changes.

In the state legislature, the increased presence of Latinos is the most obvious. As one of our respondents observed, "There is isn't one piece of major legislation that doesn't have to have a Latino on it somewhere at some committee level, at the chairmanship level, at the leadership level. . . . It's sort of standard now, with the number of Latino legislators." Relatedly, a Latino Democrat observed:

With the build up of Latino voters and the new leadership, the infra-structure has blossomed in a way where Latinos are throughout the leadership and throughout the ranks, both in terms of the infrastruc-ture of the party, within the donor base, within the advocacy base, within just about every facet, including having the chairman of the party be a Latino, and having major representation at the state and na-tional level, as members of the executive board.

The second most common observation is on the growth of the Latino electorate. Typical of the responses included:

Registration of new immigrant citizens. Over the last I'd say eight years, all the growth in enrollment as voters in California is the result of Latino new immigrant citizen voters. And significant within that is not just the number, but also the participation of those voters. Their participation was greater than any other demographic group. But when you segregated the new immigrant voter, that voter who voted after 1994 or registered after 1994. That voter was a very motivated voter, a new immigrant voter who had gone through quite a bit of bashing and big issue politics being played out on both a state and national stage. So if I'd say the one most significant thing.

Yet, another political leader saw the growth of the Latino elec-torate in larger terms:

[Latinos have] emerged from a small niche segment of the electorate into a true member of the governing coalition. And beyond that, I think the next ten years [are] going to take us from a member of the governing coalition to the central core of who governs California.

In 1990, again you exist more as an exotic niche, where you can get away—both Democrats and Republicans could get away with kind of the "viva" campaigns and the quick photo ops down on Olvera Street. Now as we've certainly more than doubled our share of the electorate in those ten years, and in many ways have been overrepresented in terms of political weight and our political weight is needed, whether it's to win elections or to move legislation, or to sway public opinion to win elections, to move legislation or to sway public opinion. And for that to occur in a ten-year period is really virtually unprecedented in American history in the size and scope of a place like California.

Our respondents also noted other changes. The professionaliza-tion of political campaigns, the increasing sophistication of Latinos who are running for office, and the emergence of "cross-over" can-didates are seen as factors that are different now than a decade ago.

What are the differences in policy outcomes resulting from the presence of Latino elected officials in larger numbers? The presence of minority elected officials has an impact on the bureaucracy and on the legitimacy of ethnic group issues. In response to the question "What difference in public policy has it made that Latino elected officials are now present in visible numbers?" the literature suggests that the presence of minority elected officials has a corresponding impact on the bureaucracy and the legitimacy of ethnic group issues. Once again, our respondents agree with these findings. In response to the question "What difference has it made to have more Latinos in elected office?" respondents identified the following issues:

> First of all, within the city bureaucracy, there was an outreach, so the bureaucracy reacted to my presence. And some of the managers came and offered specific programs. Others were responsive when I called; certainly, there were some who tried to avoid doing anything, [even though] that's typical . . . there seemed to be a real hope. But our perspective is still a perspective that comes from our base. Our base is generally [a poor and working-poor community]. It is a small business community. It is a community that is short on all services from health care to education. And so our impact is reflected on our push for more services in all of those areas that are basically driven from a perspective of those who want to improve conditions for poor and working poor in our community—the disenfranchised. I don't think that the advances, the amount of money that has been invested in health care, the amount of money that has been invested in education, and the amount of money in affordable housing last year would have been possible without Latino elected officials being present.

Furthermore, on the issue of policy legitimacy the following observation was made:

> The obvious thing is when you have more people who share the same experience on the decision-making body, it really elevates the consciousness of the remaining members in terms of that experience. When you have more people who share the same experience, it really raises the consciousness of the other members of that building body. When three people talk with [a] similar background about an issue and give a similar perspective, it really raises the issue to a different level of understanding from that person's viewpoint whether he or she is Latino, African American, or any other ethnic group.

The political leaders interviewed for this study were adamant that on issues such as food stamps for immigrants, funding for affordable housing, and English-language instruction, the presence of Latino elected officials has made a difference. Moreover, their presence has also put their respective jurisdictional bureaucracies in a position of having to respond to Latino constituents.

Yet, curiously most Latino leaders interviewed for this study rejected the idea that it was a unique "Latino agenda." According to the respondents, the issues are similar for Latinos and non-Latinos: health care, quality education, and safe neighborhoods. While there are hot-button issues, such as immigration, bilingual education, and affirmative action, of particular interest to the Hispanic community, these are the exceptions and not the rule. Yet, within the issues of common concerns between Latinos and non-Latinos, there are differences in emphasis. For example, as one respondent stated:

> Take affordable housing, a huge issue; it's going to get bigger. And it's going to get bigger. And its become a much more intrinsic problem, a specific problem to the Hispanic community. Why? Because again, we're younger. We have young families and we're less affluent. We're also in our first home-buying years, and there's not enough housing stock for Latinos to buy our first houses. I mean you can't expect Latinos to go up to Ventura or San Bernardino County and buy a $300,000 home three years out of school. And the fact that we're not building enough homes means that our community is going to be disproportionately affected by issues like that. Education: the state legislature is going to come out with a report, if they haven't already, showing this clustering problem that Senator Deborah Ortiz has basically identified, showing that upward of 70 percent of Latino children are clustered in the bottom 30 percent of underperforming schools. While education affects all, it affects our community much differently.

Other respondents also noted a different emphasis when they identified health care as an issue affecting everyone in California, yet affecting Latinos in a slightly different way. For most Californians, according to the respondents, health care issues center around HMO reform; for Latinos, health care reform is a matter of *access* to affordable health care. Thus, in a way a possible contradiction exists. While there may not be a specific self-identified

Latino agenda, there may well be a Latino dimension to some of the major issues affecting all Californians. This Latino dimension is driven in part by the average lower socioeconomic status of the community.

What issues do the respondents envision gaining in importance in the future? The respondents identify a self-awareness of a new role of Latino leaders and the Latino electorate. One leader stated the following:

> And I would . . . tell you that probably the greatest fear I have about our growth, is that as we're starting to wield power and starting to grow. And we're starting to acquire positions of influence in government and in other places, that we don't forget that as we were starting to acquire positions of influence in government and in other places, that we don't forget that we were marginalized, [and] that we don't forget about the other people who are still marginalized and are being marginalized at all times in the process. . . . I know there's a lot of discussion about how Latinos are going to take over the African American seats. I know that's something that takes place in terms of the inner workings in some of the political inner circles. Yet, there hasn't been one case where a Latino has run against an African American candidate and beaten [him or her] out of a seat. That can't be said for other groups.

The concern about Latinos being pitted against African Americans is also mentioned in the context that Latino versus black scenarios are always mentioned, but little corresponding attention has been paid to the fact that black legislators who have lost their seats have lost them to white non-Hispanic candidates.

An additional dimension of the future of Latino politics that is mentioned by respondents is the impact of Latino policy preferences that do not fall neatly into traditional liberal and conservative categories. One respondent focused on this issue in particular:

> [The impact] of the electorate and the increased number of Latinos has moved . . . a more progressive agenda that is aimed at helping a population who has economic concerns first and foremost. Yet, in macro terms it has had the affect of buffering some of the excesses of both parties and you don't see that as much in [the] Republican Part[y] quite as clearly as you do in the Democratic Party. You have to remind yourself that there's a very corollary side between the emergence of

Latino power in the Democratic Party and its moderation. It's no longer the party of Jerry Brown. It's no longer the party of Willie Brown. It's more a party of Cruz Bustamante. . . . That's not a coincidence. . . . You're also going to see that begin to occur among Republicans over the course of the next ten years. The presence of Latino activists in the Republican Party will tend to present a more moderate, a more tempered and more tolerant approach to policy. I don't think you're going to see the emotional rhetoric coming from the Republican Party that you saw.

If this perspective is correct, then one may expect major changes to occur in both parties. Already in 2001, there were four Republican Latino state legislators in office who had established a Hispanic Caucus of their own and hoped to recruit other Latinos to run under the Republican banner. If they prove successful, these new Latino candidates may end up challenging white Republicans for elective office. In 2004, the Republican leadership rejected endorsing a Proposition 187–like initiative and a Republican governor, after signing a bill denying unauthorized migrants driver's licenses, pledged to Latino state legislators that he was "open to compromise." At the same time, the policy positions of Latino Democrats on key issues will not coincide in all cases with traditional liberal positions within the Democratic Party. For example, Latinos may have conservative viewpoints on issues such as gay rights, welfare, and criminal justice.

A mobilized electorate, the dramatic growth of Latino political elites at all levels of California government, and an awareness of Latino political strength by the major parties captures the new political environment confronting California's Latinos and all Californians. Major questions still remain unanswered. Will new Latino voters continue to participate at the levels that they did in the past? Now that Latino naturalization numbers have declined from their highs of the late 1990s, will the presence of a growing number of noncitizens affect the politics of the group? Finally, with both political parties acknowledging the presence of Latinos, what impact will this have on ethnic bloc voting for the future? While these questions call for further inquiry, there is little doubt that the 1990s irrevocably changed Latino politics in the Golden State.

NOTE

1. We conducted interviews with fourteen senior Democratic and Republican California Hispanic elected officials. We selected interviewees based on their knowledge of California politics. Interviewees include federal, state, and local officials. We promised each anonymity in order to ensure candor.

4

New Mexico Hispanos in the 2000 General Elections

F. CHRIS GARCIA and CHRISTINE MARIE SIERRA

A BURGEONING LATINO POPULATION IN THE 1990s SPURRED MEDIA commentators, pundits, politicians, and political activists to speculate that the 2000 presidential election might turn on the Latino vote. The rapid growth of the Latino population meant that campaign strategists at the minimum had to pay more attention to Hispanic voters in 2000. Purportedly, the Hispanic vote was up for grabs and, most notably, Republicans were making overtures to Hispanics as they never had before. This was true even in New Mexico, with its several-decades-long history of Hispanos voting disproportionately for the Democratic Party.

Heightened attention to the Latino vote nationwide necessarily drew attention to New Mexico, where Hispanics constitute the largest proportion (36 percent) of any state electorate. In addition to their electoral size, Hispanos (the identity term used most commonly by people of Spanish/Mexican ancestry in New Mexico) in New Mexico have established long-standing patterns of political participation in all aspects of the electoral process. They have voted at levels comparable to those of Anglos in the state and significantly

higher than those of Latinos in other states. In part, the high proportion (88 percent) of U.S.-born—and New Mexican–born—citizens
among the state's Hispanic adult population contributes to their relatively higher rates of political participation. Prominent among the
state's elected leadership, Hispanos also play an integral role in state
politics as policy makers.

Given Hispanics' rather unique history and status in state politics, scholars have characterized *nuevomexicano* politics as "excep-
tional" or distinctive from Hispanic politics in other states (Garcia
1996; Garcia and Sapien 1999; Sierra 1992; Vigil 1985). At the same
time, it was the prominence of Hispanic politics in the state that led
political pundits and analysts to consider New Mexico when specu-
lating on how the Latino vote nationwide might behave.

LESSONS FROM RECENT ELECTIONS

The 1996 presidential election in New Mexico drove home how pivotal the Hispanic vote could be. New Mexico Hispanos voted heavily for Democratic presidential candidate Bill Clinton, while non-
Hispanic white voters preferred the Republican presidential
candidate Bob Dole (Garcia and Sapien 1999). The heavy vote by Hispanics for Clinton made a significant impact on the outcome of the
election. In fact, New Mexico was one of only two states in which
the Hispanic vote actually made a difference in which candidate received the state's electoral votes (de la Garza and DeSipio 1999).

Although Hispanos in New Mexico have shown themselves to
be "old reliables" in voting fairly consistently for Democratic Party
candidates (de la Garza and DeSipio 1999: 73), a 1997 congressional
race suggested that Hispanos voting more Republican was not out
of the question. For the first time in thirty years, New Mexican Hispanos did not have a Hispano representing them in the U.S. Congress. In a special election held in the late spring of 1997, heavily
Hispanic northern New Mexico had sent Bill Redmond to Washington, D.C., a representative who was white, Protestant, Republican,
and born in Chicago. Mayor Debbie Jaramillo of Santa Fe observed,
"Hispanics have controlled the politics of northern New Mexico
for so many years—what the heck happened?" (Brooke 1997).

Redmond's victory was a surprise to most, but it was also part of a demographic shift that had been occurring in New Mexico, as wealthy "whites" moved in and changed the character of the area (Sierra, Rodriguez, and Gonzales 1999). In 1970, 65 percent of the surnames in Santa Fe were Spanish, but by 1990 that number was down to 49 percent. As wealthy Anglos moved in, rising real estate prices and taxes had forced old Hispanic families to trade their adobe houses in the city for trailers on the outskirts. As Mayor Jaramillo stated, "The white people moved in, painted the town brown and moved the brown people out" (Brooke 1997). Moreover, growth in the high technology sector in New Mexico revealed itself in the state's demographics, as an increasing number of voters were evenly split between Republicans and Democrats.

Contributing to Redmond's victory was New Mexico's Green Party. The Greens ran a credible candidate for Congress, Carol Miller, who capitalized on the disaffection many voters felt with the Democratic nominee, Eric Serna. Miller drew 17 percent of the vote, a good proportion coming from traditional Democrats, including Native Americans. The role of the Green Party and its future impact on state politics and traditional voting patterns added to speculation that the upcoming 2000 presidential election might yield some surprises. Republicans in particular found reasons for optimism: a larger proportion of the population was Republican, more so than had been the case for almost seventy years; the rise of third-party politics could play to their advantage; and under the right conditions, Hispanos might be successfully courted by the party.

The 1998 midterm elections featured an unprecedented number of Hispanic candidates seeking high elective office throughout the country and voters in key states such as California mobilized around "Hispanic issues," such as immigration and bilingual education. Although New Mexico featured its own share of Hispanic candidates for state and local level office, not much was being made of "the ethnic factor." That is, neither the (Hispanic) ethnicity of candidates nor "ethnic issues" were being openly discussed in the state. As one newspaper headline put it, the ethnic factor was "only a whisper" in New Mexico campaigns (Glover 1998).

F. Chris Garcia and Bianca Sapien note that "ethnicity is and always has been an important factor in the politics of the state," but they acknowledge its enigmatic qualities—an apparent but subtle overlay to New Mexico politics (1999: 76). Hispanics have long run for and won elective office at all levels. In that sense, Hispanic ethnicity is no big deal as Hispanics enjoy a level of parity, for example, in the representation of their numbers in the state legislature. A "politeness" often attaches itself to electoral competition under the mask of multicultural harmony. Electoral contests thus may reflect the more covert and complex nature of ethnic politics, as they did in the 1998 elections.

New Mexico's 1998 gubernatorial race pitted Hispanic Democrat Martin Chavez against incumbent Republican Gary Johnson. Candidate Chavez was quoted as saying, "I don't play ethnic politics. I don't engage in it, and I don't approve of it. I think it divides people. I am immensely proud of my heritage, but I am an American" (Glover 1998). Republican incumbent candidate Gary Johnson agreed that ethnicity was not a factor in the gubernatorial campaign and said he would like to think that it is because New Mexico is truly a tricultural state and has moved beyond ethnic distinctions.

Even as these statements were being made, polling data suggested ethnic patterns of support for the gubernatorial candidates. Chavez was running more strongly among Hispanic voters, with 58 percent of their support, than was Johnson, with only 22 percent of Hispanic support. In the end, Johnson won reelection with 55 percent of the vote.

At the congressional level, two races carried important implications for Hispanic politics in the state. In the southern congressional district, former state representative E. Shirley Baca of Las Cruces ran an unsuccessful race that would have reinstated Hispanic congressional representation in the state. In the Third Congressional District, Democrat Tom Udall successfully defeated the short-term incumbent Bill Redmond, who had won the seat in the special election of the preceding year. Udall's victory restored Democratic control of the northern New Mexico seat, but not Hispanic control.

While the ethnic factor was being tempered or erased in some electoral contests, other New Mexico politicians launched initiatives that underscored the importance of the Hispanic vote. New Mexico senior senator Pete Domenici, the state's leading Republican politician, announced in August 1999 that he was forming Pete's PAC, a political action committee designed to help finance Hispanic

Republicans' campaigns for national, state, and local offices in 2000. Domenici noted that Hispanics across the country were becoming much more active politically and felt that one way the Republican Party could reach out to Hispanics was by fielding good qualified Hispanic candidates. He observed that the Republican Party had historically given "lip service" to the importance of recruiting good Hispanic candidates, "but has failed to put its money where its mouth is" (Coleman 1999).

THE 2000 ELECTIONS

In anticipation of the early 2000 presidential primaries, a December 1999 survey of New Mexico voters gave some indications of how New Mexico voters and Latinos in particular might act in selecting the respective parties' presidential nominees. The poll indicated that either of the Republican candidates, George W. Bush or John McCain, would handily defeat a Democratic opponent. At the time, it was noted that in a tight race in the general election, New Mexico's five electoral votes could become very important. Moreover, the state would attract additional attention because of its bellwether status—the fact that the state's voting results had, with one exception, been the same as that of the nation in every presidential election since statehood in 1912. At the start of the presidential election year, then, considerable attention focused on the role New Mexico could conceivably play in the upcoming elections. Given Hispanics' prominence in the voting electorate, some flux in state politics and traditional voting alignments, and more vigorous Hispanic outreach by Republicans, *nuevomexicano* politics appeared to be in play at both the national and state levels.

The Primaries: Too Late to Matter

Primary season in New Mexico drew little attention. New Mexico insisted on holding its presidential primary on June 6, the last date on which a presidential primary was held. Furthermore, there were no open seats for the U.S. Congress or Senate or a gubernatorial contest to capture voter attention. Thus, New Mexico's primary seemed to be of more interest outside the state than within it. Nevertheless, the presidential candidates put New Mexico on their spring calendar as they looked toward the fall election. Ari Fleischer, a spokesman for Republican presidential candidate George W. Bush, stated, "New Mexico is an extremely important battleground state. It can swing any direction this election. The governor [Bush] looks forward to campaigning in New Mexico" (Coleman 2000a).

Interest in the New Mexico primary campaigns first stirred with the results of a statewide survey released in mid-March. The poll asked registered voters which party would they support for the state legislature. All 112 state legislative seats were up for election in 2000. Among Hispanics, 52 percent said they would be more likely to vote for Democrats. Only 19 percent were likely to cast votes for Republicans. Hispanic support for Democratic Party candidates appeared to be somewhat lower than the 60 to 70 percent scholars had estimated Hispanic Democratic affiliation to be. In contrast to the Hispanic numbers, poll results showed 42 percent of Anglos were likely to vote for Republicans, while 25 percent were more likely to vote for Democrats (Fecteau 2000a).

This poll portended some major changes in Hispanic political leadership in the state. Voters were also asked to assign grades to the governor and to the leaders of the state legislature, both of whom were Hispanic. Governor Johnson, a conservative Republican, had been embroiled in a public standoff with the liberal Democratic legislators over the state budget and other issues. Voters assigned average grades of C− to the governor and Raymond Sanchez, the state house leader. Senate pro tem leader Manny Aragon received an even lower grade of C−/D+ (Fecteau 2000b). Observers noted that the political season's most interesting battle might be the one focused on these two Hispanic legislative leaders. The state Republican Party was planning to go all out to defeat Speaker Sanchez in particular.

With regard to the presidential election, the March poll again mirrored the national poll results, as is typically the case. New Mexico voters were split evenly, 41 percent for Bush, 41 percent for Al Gore. Hispanic voters gave 55 percent of their support to Gore and 26 percent to Bush. Among Anglo respondents, 49 percent preferred Bush, and 34 percent chose Gore (Fecteau 2000c).

In spite of these results, many analysts thought that the Hispanic vote included enough independent or swing voters that could be attracted to Bush by the time of the general election, thereby giving the state's five electoral votes to Bush. In fact, Bush's campaign manager in New Mexico, Colin McMillan, said that Hispanics would like what they saw in Bush, "A lot of Democrats, particularly a lot of Hispanic voters in rural New Mexico, identify with Governor Bush's message" (Gallegos 2000a).

New Mexico's battleground status appears in a review of campaign visits made by the candidates for president and vice president as well as those made by politicians and celebrities campaigning on their behalf. Between March and November, Bush and Gore each visited the state four times. Dick Cheney visited four times and Joe Lieberman three times. Bush appeared with Cheney once. Senior Republican surrogates (including former president George H. W. Bush) visited ten times; senior Democratic surrogates (including President Clinton) visited eight times. Four of these visits occurred before the June primary. Overall, there were thirty-one candidate or surrogate visits; sixteen included events with Hispanic emphasis.

Vice President Gore was the first major party presidential candidate to come to New Mexico, arriving on April 28. The vice president met at a local middle school with 350 "mostly undecided" voters in a question-and-answer format. Although the town meeting did not target Hispanics, Gore's comments related to Hispanic concerns. Gore stated that Hispanic and American Indian students presented special problems because of their elevated dropout rates. He held that "we should dramatically reduce dropout." He also touched on other issues related to Hispanics' primary policy concern, education, including a call for more charter schools, smaller class sizes, greater family involvement, and bonuses for highly qualified teachers. Gore said, "I'm asking you to give me a mandate to make this the number one crusade," referring to educational reform. Gore also noted that the great diversity of New Mexico is an example of how the nation could be stronger by celebrating our differences (Roberts 2000; Gallegos 2000b).

Reform Party candidate Patrick Buchanan next visited the state. He held a rally at the University of New Mexico, which drew a small group of about eighty supporters, and spent the day touring Albuquerque, meeting with supporters, and raising money. He made no special appeal to Hispanics. In fact, he was wary of the importance of Hispanic support in New Mexico, as he noted that his views on immigration would probably damage his appeal with Hispanics. He said that America should "do what it takes" to secure its borders from illegal immigrants, including putting up security fences in areas where illegal immigrants flood into the United States. "I believe we have a duty and an obligation to protect our borders from what is an invasion of illegal immigration," Buchanan said. However, Buchanan tried to balance the impact of this statement by stating that he was Catholic and conservative, which he said were traits shared by many Hispanics (Coleman 2000b).

A month after Gore's visit, Governor Bush came to Albuquerque. Bush said he had a plan for winning the Hispanic vote, duplicating his alleged success in Texas with Hispanic voters. Bush said:

> I think I can make great inroads in the Hispanic community when I talk about my passion for educating every child. I've got a record in Texas of working with Republicans and Democrats, and the [school] test scores prove that we really are making great progress with our Hispanic youngsters. I am an entrepreneur. I was a small business owner. There are 600,000 Latino-owned small businesses in California, and it shows there is a common ground. I've got to make clear my support for NAFTA and tout my relations with Mexico. I've got great relations with President [Ernesto] Zedillo [of Mexico]. (Coleman 2000c)

With reference to crime, Bush stated, "I think the Latino community understands my strong desire to enforce laws on the books. I'll be aggressive about pursuing folks who break the law." When asked his position on border control, Governor Bush said, "We've got to enforce the border. We need more border patrol agents. We need to modernize the crossing points. I support Operation 'Hold the Line.' I'm very mindful of why people are coming. They are coming to find work. I view border policy this way. For the short term, it's border enforcement, more agents, more focus. Long term, it's NAFTA and trade" (2000c).

In addition to these strategic statements on policy issues, Governor Bush had a meeting with a small but influential group of Republican Hispanic leaders. The group reportedly intended to "remind the Texas Governor that he must do more than just talk about compassionate conservatism." They also wanted Bush to look to Hispanics as an important constituency, including seeking Hispanics for key positions in his presidential campaign and to lead his administration if he were elected in November (Gallegos 2000c).

The primary election was held on Tuesday, June 6. As expected, Bush easily won the Republican nomination, as did Gore with the Democratic nomination. None of the congressional and legislative incumbents, including the leaders of the state legislature, were seriously challenged in the primary. Turnout was quite low.

New Mexico Hispanos and the Vice Presidency

Late in the primary season, speculation turned to the selection of vice presidents for each ticket. Since both parties were campaigning for the Hispanic vote, there was some speculation as to whether a Hispanic vice president would seriously add strength to a ticket. Prominent among the names suggested as a nominee on the Gore ticket was New Mexico's Bill Richardson.

Richardson was born in California to a Boston banker father and a Mexican mother and spent most of his childhood in Mexico City. He grew up bicultural and bilingual. Richardson had the support of prominent Hispanics. His backers contended that having Richardson on the ticket could help Gore in heavily populated Latino states like California, Illinois, and even Texas.

Richardson had served several terms as the U.S. congressional representative from heavily Hispanic northern New Mexico before President Clinton appointed him as U.S. ambassador to the United Nations in 1997. He was notably successful in several international diplomatic missions. In 1998, the president asked him to take over as secretary of the Department of Energy, making him the only Hispanic member of the cabinet during Clinton's second term. But Richardson's political capital began to sink with unforeseen events that became headline stories across the country. Controversy swelled around events that involved the Los Alamos National Laboratories (LANL), which were under the supervision of the Department of Energy. A disastrous fire burned a considerable portion of the laboratories and generated public outcry as to the cause of the fire (the result of a prescribed or "controlled burn" by the National Park Service) and the government's responsibility to ensure the safety of the national labs and the communities that surround them—concerns to which Secretary Richardson had to respond.

Additionally, as secretary of energy, Richardson's tenure coincided with a number of alleged security breaches at the national labs and included the ill-fated prosecution of LANL scientist Wen Ho Lee. Richardson was sharply criticized by Republicans, especially in appearances before Republican-led congressional committees. Within a few weeks, Richardson went from being a very likely vice presidential candidate to one not likely to be chosen. Efforts on the part of the National Hispanic Leadership Agenda, an association of Hispanic organizations, to defend Richardson and demand an apology from the U.S. Senate for its "unwarranted" criticism of the secretary could not turn the tide of negativity surrounding the secretary. And so the door closed on the possibility of a Hispano becoming a vice president of the United States in 2000.

The Republicans: Conventional Problems

On June 10, a few days after the low-key primary, the Republican Party held its state party convention in Albuquerque. Prior to the convention, an internal battle had been brewing within the state Republican Party for the prestigious position of Republican National Committeeman. The position had been held for the previous four years by New Mexico Hispano Manuel Lujan Jr. Lujan, a moderate, had served as secretary of the U.S. Department of the Interior from 1989 through 1992 under President Bush and had also served as U.S. representative for the First Congressional District (Albuquerque) for twenty years. He was being challenged by Mickey Barnett, a former state senator and long-time conservative activist. At the convention, Barnett defeated Lujan by a delegate vote of 453 to 330. Some prominent members of the party viewed this as a tactical mistake by the Republican Party in their effort to attract Hispanic voters.

As it turns out, there was another tactical error made by the Republican convention with regards to Hispanos. The convention chose twenty-one delegates to the Republican National Convention in Philadelphia. Of the twenty-one delegates, two were Hispanic. This caused some Hispanic Republicans to question the New Mexico party's commitment to diversity. Outspoken former governor David Cargo joined Hispanic party members in criticizing the delegate selection saying, "It looked like ethnic cleansing to me. It's not good news for the Republican Party" (Coleman 2000d).

In an *Albuquerque Journal* editorial, the state's largest newspaper, the GOP was criticized for its failure to take actions in the convention that would fulfill the party rhetoric of inclusiveness, stating that "the party's big tent of inclusiveness isn't quite as roomy as the GOP would have voters believe." The editorial elaborated that "what the GOP's state convention results show is that the party simply has yet to catch up to New Mexico's demographics or its own rhetoric when it comes to Hispanic membership" ("GOP 'Big Tent' Still Short on Hispanics" 2000).

This tactical error probably helped spur New Mexico Republicans to greater efforts to recruit more Hispanics into their ranks. In late June, largely under the auspices of a new group called Viva Bush, Republicans prepared fact sheets to distribute to Hispanic Democrats, mostly in northern New Mexico.

The Republicans also relied on surrogates to win Hispanic votes. In July, George P. Bush, the twenty-four-year-old nephew of George W. Bush, brought his personable style and a message of inclusion to Belen, New Mexico, in a campaign stop for his uncle. During his speech, George P. said he wanted to encourage younger people to vote and wanted to convince Hispanics that they have a home in the Republican Party. He said, "This year, Election 2000, will be known for one thing—that the Republican Party starts to represent the emerging diversity of our society, namely Latinos." He commended the Viva Bush organization for its recruitment of Hispanics and other minorities and urged membership in Viva Bush because "the future of this party lies with the Latino community." David Alire-Garcia, the executive director of the New Mexico Democratic Party, was critical, saying that Bush's remarks rang hollow; rhetoric was one thing but the record of Republicans with regard to Hispanics was a poor one (Coleman 2000e).

The National Conventions

At the Republican Party National Convention in Philadelphia, Bush advisors reportedly met with New Mexico's two voting Hispanic delegates. One said that Bush's success would be based on latching onto issues that both Hispanics and non-Hispanics hold dear to their hearts. He said that "Bush's emphasis on children and education regardless of what language they speak is important, whether you are Hispanic or not, and predicted that message's success in New Mexico" (Gallegos 2000d).

Members of the national campaign's Hispanic caucus met with the New Mexico delegates to the Republican National Convention to devise a strategy appealing to Hispanics. Conservative commentator, Linda Chavez (originally from Albuquerque), urged the New Mexico delegates to be aggressive in trying to bring Hispanics into the Bush camp. She said supporters of the Texas governor should use their e-mail and contacts in church and civic groups to win Bush support. Some of the New Mexico delegates in turn urged the Bush campaign to bring the candidate into the heavily Hispanic communities of northern New Mexico, saying that this would create a major opportunity to help independent voters and Democrats to vote for Governor Bush if he came there personally. Nothing was reported about strategy in the southern and eastern ("Little Texas") regions of the state.

Prior to the Democratic Party's national convention, Lydia Camarillo, the convention's chief executive officer, visited New Mexico. She stated that this Democratic convention would be the most diverse convention in American history. She remained confident that most Hispanic Americans would vote for Gore in November. She claimed that the Clinton-Gore administration had appointed more minorities to federal office than any presidential team in history and that Gore had long championed bilingual education, affirmative action, and higher minimum wages, all issues deemed important to Hispanics.

Over half of New Mexico's thirty-five delegates to the Democratic convention were Hispanic, making it the only state delegation with a Hispanic majority. Some delegates thought that being Hispanic and Democratic were just about synonymous. Delegate Gloria Nieto said, "My grandfather took me to see President Kennedy when I was in the first grade. If you look at any Latino household, you'll see pictures of the Pope and pictures of the Kennedys. My relatives all say the same thing—the Republicans have never done anything for us." The Democratic delegates reportedly did not trust GOP outreach efforts to Hispanics. E. Shirley Baca, a former state lawmaker from Las Cruces, said, "I believe the Republicans want the Hispanic vote, but they don't want our issues" (Kelley 2000).

At least two New Mexicans, both Hispanic, enjoyed prominent roles at the Democratic convention. State Attorney General Patricia Madrid served as sergeant-at-arms and state House Speaker Raymond Sanchez gave a speech to the convention. In addition to the twenty Hispanic delegates (57 percent), the thirty-five-member New Mexico delegation included three Native Americans and two African Americans. Republican state Chairman John Dendahl accused Democratic leaders of "engineering" the makeup of their delegation to appear politically correct. Noting that less than a dozen of the Democratic Party's delegates were Anglo, an amount that did not reflect the state's roughly 37 percent Anglo population, he stated, "For those who care about counting noses by ethnicity, there are only 11 Anglos in the entire [New Mexico] Democratic delegation" (Coleman 2000f).

THE GENERAL ELECTION

Between late August and October, the candidates or their surrogates visited New Mexico nineteen times, frequently directing special appeals to Hispanics. Bush and Cheney made the first postconvention visit to the state on August 19, reaching out to Hispanic voters in southern New Mexico with a message of inclusiveness and unity. In Mesilla, on the outskirts of metropolitan Las Cruces, Bush addressed several thousand supporters. At one point, he spoke in Spanish, telling Hispanics that the American dream included everyone. The plaza in Mesilla reportedly looked like a "fiesta," with many in the crowd (estimated to be as high as 5,000) shouting "Viva Bush" during pauses in the speech.

A few days later, Gore made his second trip to New Mexico. He made two major stops during this visit to Albuquerque. He first appeared at the University of New Mexico campus outdoors before a friendly crowd. The festive nighttime rally featured mariachi music, colorful bunting, and a host of Democratic officeholders and notables, with Hispanics among them. In warm-up speeches before the crowd, Albuquerque mayor Jim Baca underscored his strong support for Gore because of the candidate's stances on environmental protection. Attorney General Patricia Madrid spoke of the importance of choosing a president whose Supreme Court appointments would protect women's rights. She noted that Bush's running mate, Cheney, had voted against affirmative action and the equal rights amendment when he was a Wyoming congressman.

For his part, Gore addressed the rally by invoking a New Mexico version of one of his campaign themes: "Fighting for American families." Pledging to "fight for you," Gore spoke of the importance of protecting the environment, which he linked to New Mexico's economic health. He touted the administration's accomplishments over the past eight years, specifically noting the nation's lowest Hispanic unemployment rate ever measured. He drew applause when he said in Spanish that "education is important in my family and should be in every American family." For its part, the *Albuquerque Journal* reported the Gore rally as a success with the front-page headline "Bilingual Gore Woos UNM Crowd" (Fecteau 2000d).

The following day, Gore pushed his health care agenda at what was called "a neighborhood gathering," by invitation only, in the largely Hispanic South Valley of Albuquerque. At the private affair attended by a few dozen people, Gore responded supportively to Lydia Regino, who argued for more compassion in allowing legal immigrants more flexibility to access health care. He also nodded in approval as Christina Carrillo spoke about the advantages of universal health care. The candidate persuaded some in attendance to tell their stories for the television cameras and other news media at a subsequent gathering at a nearby public park. He stated that the election was not about him or his opponent but that "it's about you. It's about the families of the South Valley" (Gallegos 2000e).

Gore expanded on his ideas for health care insurance, specifically for children. He listened attentively to a Hispanic couple from the South Valley describe their hardships in getting health insurance to cover medical treatment for their two-year-old son's broken leg. Gore would later invite the couple to be among the entourage of "real people" from across the country who would serve as informal advisors as the candidate prepared for a televised presidential debate.

Ralph Nader, the Green Party candidate for president, led off the September visits to New Mexico. Nader's September visit was a two-day affair that included fund-raising, a speech at the Albuquerque Convention Center, and visits to Santa Fe and Farmington's San Juan Community College. The Greens were hopeful that

New Mexico would continue to provide fertile ground for their party-building efforts.

Also in early September, Federico Peña, a former secretary of the Transportation and Energy Departments in the Clinton cabinet and former mayor of Denver, came to New Mexico to tout the economic plans of Vice President Gore. Peña met with about sixty Hispanic business and community leaders from the Albuquerque area at the largely Hispanic West Mesa Community Center. Small business owner Tina Cordova praised the Clinton-Gore administration for helping her Albuquerque construction company flourish. Margy Hernandez, owner of La Mexicana Tortilla Company in Albuquerque, told Peña that her business had grown over the past eight years and that she would be supporting Vice President Gore because he would keep the economy strong.

Alternating visits by presidential candidates continued when Bush returned to Albuquerque on September 15 to push his education agenda and stump for Republican candidates, such as U.S. representative Heather Wilson, who was running for a third term. Appearing before an audience of about 350 people at the University of New Mexico's Continuing Education Center, Bush offered a detailed description of an education plan based on what he claimed was his successful model in Texas. He specifically addressed the challenges of education for ethnic and racial minorities and explicitly gave his support to a school voucher system. During his campaign appearance, he announced the formation of "Hispanics for Bush," to be headed by former representative Manuel Lujan Jr., the national Republican committeeman who had just a few months before been ousted from his position by the Republican state convention. Also named to the group's leadership were Mayor Carlos Ramirez of El Paso, Texas, a Democrat, and Miami music mogul Emilio Estefan, the spouse of Latina pop superstar Gloria Estefan (Keller 2000; Webb 2000, who refers to Hispanics for Bush by another name, the Latino National Committee). Speaking with reporters, Estefan said he liked the governor's message of inclusiveness, which aimed to unite Hispanics as a powerful national constituency. Estefan had recently been named chair of yet another newly formed Hispanic group: the Bush-Cheney 2000 National Latino Coalition. Counted among this group's members were educator Jaime Escalante of *Stand and Deliver* movie fame, Antonia Novello, former U.S. surgeon general, and Lujan.

Only days after Bush's visit, both major party vice presidential candidates came to the state. Lieberman primarily reinforced what Gore had said about health care reform. Lieberman spoke in a heavily Hispanic area of Albuquerque.

By late September, Pete's PAC had contributed $26,000 of $62,000 raised for New Mexico Hispanics running for state legislative and judicial seats. Domenici said his PAC contributions were relatively small, but that they might give "incentives and a little bit of encouragement to Hispanic Republicans." In addition to New Mexico, Pete's PAC had also given campaign money to Hispanic Republican candidates in California, Florida, and Texas (Coleman 2000g).

September saw three independent opinion polls of New Mexico and New Mexico Hispanic voters (see table 4.1). Overall, New Mexico voters were closely split with 42 to 43 percent supporting each candidate. Hispanic voters supported Gore and non-Hispanic voters supported Bush. Although Hispanic support for Bush was considerably lower than GOP partisans had hoped, Republicans apparently thought there was still hope for them to receive 35 to 40 percent of the Latino vote. Heather Wilson, the incumbent Republican representative, expected to receive about one-third of the Hispanic vote, drawing on a common Republican contention, "Hispanics are Democratic by registration, but they also tend to be Catholic, culturally conservative, and family oriented" (Farney and Porter 2000).

Toward the Finish Line

The perception that New Mexico was still a critical prize to be won fueled a continuing rash of visits by candidates and their surrogates. President Clinton visited on September 25, primarily to meet with donors at an afternoon fund-raiser at Santa Fe's historic La Fonda Hotel. One of Clinton's aides stated, "[T]here is a large Hispanic vote down in New Mexico, and we want to make sure they are energized and ready to get out and vote" (Coleman 2000h).

Prior to the first presidential debate on October 3, Gore picked several "average American families" from around the country to help him prepare for the debate and to attend the debate in Boston with him. Gore invited a Hispano from the South Valley of Albuquerque, Joseph Austin, a construction worker, to fly to Florida to help him prepare for the debate and to attend the debate with him.

Table 4.1   New Mexico Presidential Preference Polls, 2000 (%)

	Total Electorate	Hispanic	Non-Hispanic
Poll 1—September 7–13			
Albuquerque Journal/Research and Polling, Inc.			
553 registered voters			
Bush	43.0	25.0	—
Gore	42.0	57.0	—
Nader	2.0	—	—
Undecided	11.0	—	—
Poll 2—September 22–26			
William C. Velásquez Institute			
501 registered voters			
Bush	—	21.4	—
Gore	—	62.1	—
Nader	—	—	—
Undecided	—	15.1	—
Poll 3—September 22–28			
New Mexico State University (José Z. García)			
600 likely voters			
Bush	42.2	29.6	58.6
Gore	42.3	70.4	41.4
Nader	4.7	—	—
Undecided	9.5	—	—
Poll 4—October 30–November 2			
Albuquerque Journal/Research and Polling, Inc.			
769 likely voters			
Bush	44.0	25.0	—
Gore	41.0	54.0	—
Nader	5.0	—	—
Undecided	9.0	14.0	—
Poll 5—November 1–2			
Mason-Dixon Polling and Research, Inc.			
425 likely voters			
Bush	45.0	25.0	56.0
Gore	45.0	64.0	35.0
Nader	4.0	—	—
Undecided	5.0	—	—

Note: Mason-Dixon poll reported "non-Hispanics" as "Anglos." Because of rounding, totals may not add up to 100.

Source: Authors' compilations.

He had met Austin and his family on a campaign visit at the end of August. The selection was given major coverage by the state's largest newspaper, appearing on the front page and featuring two colored pictures.

The weekend of October 21 and 22 found major campaign efforts advanced by both parties in the state. Republican senator Pete Domenici, cochair of Bush's New Mexico campaign, spearheaded several visits to various parts of the state. On October 22, Domenici took some "friends of George Bush" to northern New Mexico to rally support in that traditionally Democratic part of the state. The "Viva Victory Tour" swung through several counties with high concentrations of Hispanic voters. The pro-Bush group of Hispanics included Texas railroad commissioner Tony Garza, San Antonio congressman Henry Bonilla, and El Paso mayor Carlos Ramirez, a Democrat. At each town in the north, Domenici, who was himself very popular among New Mexico Hispanics, introduced the *tejano* officials as "living evidence that George Bush is exactly the kind of man we want to send to Washington because he'll be concerned about us and our concerns in northern New Mexico." Domenici pointed out that Bush's first appointment after being elected Texas governor in 1994 was to name Garza to his cabinet position, adding "you know the Governor cares when his very first appointment is of a Hispanic." Domenici pushed control over natural resources in the north as a policy issue, charging that Gore would favor protecting species such as the Rio Grande silvery minnow over providing water for agriculture and farms. Bonilla, the Republican congressman from Texas, told the rally-goers that Bush shared Hispanic values of hard work, strong families, and individual initiative (Fecteau 2000e).

Democrats grabbed front-page coverage in the *Albuquerque Journal* that weekend with a "nonpolitical" visit by Vice President Gore. Gore came for the grand opening ceremonies of the National Hispanic Cultural Center of New Mexico in Albuquerque. Because Republicans challenged the appropriateness of "politicizing" the event, Gore attempted to make this stop an official vice presidential appearance rather than a campaign one. During his ten-minute speech, he praised the center as a celebration of cultural diversity, "The National Hispanic Cultural Center is a national resource that is in the right place. . . . It is a step forward for diversity and the diverse strands of our history. . . . New Mexico and Albuquerque and the South Valley are now at the center of the world's focus on Hispanic culture" (Coleman 2000i).

Earlier in the day, Henry Cisneros, a former cabinet secretary under President Clinton and former mayor of San Antonio, Texas, met with several dozen Democrats at Garcia's Kitchen, a popular Albuquerque restaurant, and urged them to work at getting out the vote. Cisneros said that Hispanics in swing states like New Mexico could help decide the results of what would be a very close race. In what turned out to be a prescient observation, Cisneros warned that Hispanics didn't seem to be as politically engaged this election as he had hoped. Cisneros said he saw "too much complacency, too much ambiguity about the candidates." Cisneros said, "It's time to engage—now. It's time to pay attention, to rise up and decide that we are going to participate this year and to not sit out what could be an election in which we could be decisive" (Coleman 2000i).

Republican determination to win New Mexico did not let up. Bush had enlisted fellow Republican governors to help boost his presidential campaign by visiting twenty-five states to drum up support for the Republican ticket. Governor Gary Johnson joined GOP governors from Utah, Colorado, and Idaho to campaign for Bush in New Mexico. Beginning in the southern part of the state, the governors spent the morning at a Las Cruces restaurant, making tortillas and meeting with voters. They then flew to Albuquerque, where one of their two stops was the Barelas Senior Center, located in an old and very political Hispanic barrio.

Following the governors' tour were repeat visits by Cheney, Lieberman, and Bush, accompanied by wife, Laura. None of these visits were particularly directed toward the Hispanic vote. Lieberman spoke of prescription drugs and other health concerns at a senior center in a predominantly Anglo part of town. A sign in the audience that read "Viva Chutzpah," though, caught the candidate's attention, spurring him to comment that his candidacy as the first Orthodox Jew on a presidential ticket could open doors to Hispanics and other groups.

But as the election season headed into the homestretch, the Hispanic vote loomed large on Gore's campaign horizon. Although he had made three previous visits to the state, Gore took his campaign for the first time to southern New Mexico to "solidify" his support among Hispanics. The November 2 rally was also to give a last-minute boost to state Treasurer Michael Montoya, who was trying to unseat the ten-term Republican incumbent Joe Skeen in the Second (Southern) Congressional District.

Prior to Gore's speech, the crowd at the Las Cruces Public Schools Sports Complex was treated to music by the Tex-Mex band Little Joe y La Familia and rallying speeches by actors Jimmy Smits and Esai Morales and rock music legend Carlos Santana. The event, touted as a "Hispanic unity celebration," featured a stage with a large sign proclaiming, "Prosperidad para todos." Many in the crowd of 6,000 waved signs saying, "Ganamos con Gore-Lieberman." As had all the candidates, Gore sprinkled his speech with Spanish phrases, in this case, punctuating the speech with the question, "¿Están con migo?" His daughter, Karenna Gore-Schiff, introduced her father in Spanish.

The campaign season in New Mexico came to a close with additional visits for the Republican ticket by former president George H. W. Bush and for the Democrats by Energy Secretary Richardson. Each of the vice presidential candidates, Cheney and Lieberman, made one final visit to the state. By election day, Bush, Cheney, and Gore had made four personal visits to New Mexico in the period since the conventions and Lieberman had made three. Surrogates had also contributed plenty to the competitive pace of visits to the state, showering New Mexico with unprecedented national attention.

Preelection Polls

An *Albuquerque Journal* poll, conducted from October 30 to November 2, showed that statewide, 44 percent of New Mexico's likely voters supported Bush, 41 percent supported Gore, 5 percent supported Nader, and 9 percent were undecided. Hispanic voters' preferences differed significantly from non-Hispanic voters in New Mexico. Fifty-four percent of Hispanic voters supported Gore, while only one in four Hispanics preferred Bush. Fourteen percent were undecided. Another statewide poll conducted from November 1–2 found Bush and Gore tied at 45 percent. This survey by Mason-Dixon Polling and Research showed 64 percent of Hispanics supporting Gore, and 25 percent preferring Bush (see table 4.1).

Projections of voter turnout were mixed. Some pundits thought that the close presidential race, a record number of registered voters, and a record for early voting predicted high turnout. Others were more circumspect. In 1996, only 45 percent of New Mexico's voting-age population had voted, down from 52 percent in 1992, 47 percent in 1988, and 51 percent in 1984 and 1980. All incumbent federal officeholders had solid leads, only one Latino was on the ballot for federal office, there were no controversial issues on the ballot, and only a few localities featured important or contested elections.

THE RESULTS, EVENTUALLY

By election day, New Mexicans, particularly New Mexico Hispanos, had been courted by the presidential candidates as never before. Even with the unprecedented levels of publicity, personal visits, and campaign appeals, only about 47 percent of the voting-age population turned out to vote, a voter turnout rate that improved only two percentage points over the abysmally low 1996 voter turnout rate. Of the state's 973,533 registered voters, 615,607 cast a ballot—a 63.2 percent participation rate. This was down from the 69.2 percent of the state's registered voters who participated in 1996.

In the hours after the polls closed, Gore took an early lead at 49 to 47 percent. Nader was projected to have won 4 percent of the votes. According to exit polls, Hispanic voters had cast 66 percent of their votes for Gore and 32 percent for Bush. Non-Hispanic whites had cast 58 percent of their votes for Bush and 37 percent for Gore.

All the federal officeholding incumbents had won. The only federal race in which a Hispanic was running was in the Second (Southern) Congressional District. There, long-time incumbent Joe Skeen won with 58 percent of the vote over Michael Montoya. The only close state race involved Speaker of the House Raymond Sanchez and his Republican challenger, John Sanchez. Only a few hundred votes separated the two as election night reports came in, with the candidates exchanging the lead as the votes were counted. The final results would not be known for several days.

The closeness of the presidential contest brought to light numerous problems throughout the country with the administration of the voting process, and New Mexico certainly had its share. Final vote tallies for president were held in abeyance as tabulations from

Bernalillo County, the state's largest county with about one-third of New Mexico's registered voters, were plagued by computer programming blunders and a series of other administrative missteps. Among the errors: a software programming glitch that left 67,000 ballots untallied on election day; ballots cast early with a straight party vote that were not tabulated properly; and several hundred ballots that were "misplaced," according to county officials. In spite of the incomplete tally, Gore had been declared the winner, and he remained the apparent winner for three days, as Bernalillo County sorted through its tabulation woes (Cart 2000).

As of the Friday following the election, November 10, Gore's 10,000-plus election night margin (as reported at that time) had evaporated. An Associated Press county-by-county tally had Bush leading Gore by seventeen votes. The secretary of state's unofficial count had Bush ahead by four votes (Li 2000). This slim margin made the presidential race in New Mexico the closest in the nation and one of the closest on record anywhere (Cart 2000).

Tensions among election officials over the election irregularities, more the norm than the exception for Bernalillo County (Albuquerque), spilled into public view. Secretary of State Rebecca Vigil-Giron grumbled, "What can I tell you? It's Bernalillo County. This is not the first or second or even third time this has happened. It's embarrassing to the county because they still can't get it right. They haven't been able to solve these problems in 20 years." Denise Lamb, the director of the State Bureau of Elections, charged that Bernalillo's county clerk was "incompetent." Lamb said, "If I had my way, I'd hang her out the window of [the state capitol]. They've never gotten anything right in that county. [The county clerk] doesn't feel like she wants to waste her time with the pesky election laws of the state" (Cart 2000).

On the Monday following the election, ten of the state's thirty-three counties reported new numbers. The changes were blamed on everything from human error to computer and machine problems. After the Bernalillo County ballots had finally been tallied, Bush had taken the lead. Shortly after that, it was announced that there had been an oversight in Doña Ana County (Las Cruces), where election workers had misread a total of 620 absentee ballots for Gore as 120 votes. With the additional 500 votes, Gore had regained the lead in the state. Gore then picked up extra votes when Rio Arriba County completed its official vote canvass, giving him a 375-vote lead over Bush. The morning of Tuesday, November 14, a week after the election, Gore had an unofficial vote tally of 286,390, and Bush, 286,015 votes. On that day, state police impounded all the ballots across the state as directed by a court order sought by the Republican Party to protect the ballots in case of a recount or a challenge ("Election Flip-Flops" 2000). New Mexico has no provision for an automatic recount in closely contested races.

On November 18, the Associated Press announced that Gore had apparently won in New Mexico. Based on unofficial results sent to the secretary of state, the Associated Press reported that Gore carried the state by a mere 481 votes ("Gore Finally Claims New Mexico" 2000). At that time, New Mexico was the only state in the Union other than Florida that had not yet officially declared a winner. But one more hurdle had to be overcome before the State Canvassing Board would certify the election results and an official vote count would be released. A Republican challenge to the votes in Roosevelt County led to hand counting of votes there. The recount added 324 votes to Bush's total and 209 to Gore's, cutting Gore's lead statewide to 368 votes from the previous 481 (or 483, several tallies each had slightly different counts). But, these votes were not enough to carry the election for Bush.

After all the mistakes, flip-flopping vote totals, and changes in leads, the state Canvassing Board announced Gore the winner and certified the election results on November 30. The official vote in the 2000 presidential contest was: Gore-Lieberman, 286,783, or 47.9 percent; Bush-Cheney, 286,417, or 47.8 percent; Nader-Winona LaDuke, 21,251, or 3.6 percent. The margin between Gore and Bush was 366 votes or .0006 percent—six ten-thousandths of 1 percent (State of New Mexico 2000).

Voting Patterns

The unprecedented amount of campaigning by Republicans apparently had little effect on New Mexico Hispanos. Gore received 66 percent of the Hispanic vote and Bush 32 percent. Non-Hispanic whites accounted for almost 60 percent of the vote in New Mexico; one-third was Hispanic. New Mexicans cast a total of 598,605 votes for major and minor party presidential candidates. Based on exit poll results, this means that Gore received approximately 126,426 Hispano votes and Bush 61,297—a 65,129-vote margin for Gore from Hispanos. Among non-Hispanic whites, Bush received 74,167 votes more than did Gore—130,676 for Gore, 204,843 for Bush. So from the two largest groups—Anglos and Hispanos—who comprised about 92 percent of the New Mexico electorate, Bush ran ahead by 9,038 votes.

Arguably, Gore drew his winning margin from the remaining 8 percent of the electorate: African Americans (3 percent) and "others" (5 percent), predominantly Native American Indians. Both of these groups traditionally have voted heavily Democratic. On the African American vote alone, Gore could have made up his statewide deficit. If African Americans in New Mexico followed national voting patterns in this presidential election, then about 90 percent of their votes likely went for the Democratic candidate, providing more than enough votes (over 16,000) for Gore to carry the state. Although data is unavailable to estimate Native American voting patterns, Gore did win in the state's most heavily American Indian county by 5,000 votes. Hence, the Hispanic vote was a necessary element in Gore's victory in New Mexico; but it alone was not sufficient to carry the state for him. New Mexico's other racial minorities had to kick in their votes to produce the winning margin.

The candidates and their surrogates had paid a great deal of extra attention to Hispanic voters throughout the campaign. Bush and Gore had peppered their speeches with Spanish phrases, concentrated their major festive rallies in Hispanic communities, sent out thousands of messages using Spanish-language flyers and radio advertisements, and visited parts of the state that were generally overlooked in national campaigns. In particular, Bush emphasized a "southern strategy" among the less deeply partisan Hispanics in southern New Mexico. His wife, Laura Bush, also had family ties to the area (the Mesilla Valley between Las Cruces and El Paso) and was no stranger to many locals. Bush and Cheney visited Old Mesilla near Las Cruces early in the fall campaign, Cheney returned to Las Cruces just days before the election, and Republican surrogates campaigned in the area as well.

In some respects, the Bush strategy in the South worked fairly well. Although Bush ultimately lost in Doña Ana County (Las Cruces/Mesilla), he made the race there more competitive than had

been the case in 1996. In the state's second largest county, Gore gar-
nered 51 percent of the vote, compared to Bush's 46 percent, a difference of only 2,649 votes in a county that is heavily Democratic
in registration and over 63 percent Hispanic in population.

A number of Republicans had thought that Bush could generate
among Hispanic New Mexicans the levels of support he had enjoyed with Mexican Americans as governor of Texas. The Republicans' southern strategy aimed at winning by substantial margins
the southern and eastern counties of New Mexico, which are more
similar in some respects to west Texas and are very unlike the old
Hispano communities of northern New Mexico, which have had a
historically distrustful relationship with Texas Anglos. In the Democratic stronghold of the north, the Republicans simply wanted
to hold down the Democrat's margin of support.

Although he also campaigned in the South, Gore spent more of
his resources wooing the traditionally Democratic voting areas in
the northern and central part of the state—appealing mainly to Hispanics in Albuquerque. In the end, Gore fared better in northern
New Mexico than he did in southern New Mexico, where his campaign made some tactical errors: for example, the last-minute appearance and a less than optimal setting for attracting a greater
number of Hispanics from the area and neighboring El Paso (Texas).

But it is not exaggeration to note that with a difference of only
366 votes statewide, anything could have changed the outcome. For
example, the weather may have been a factor. On election day, the
weather in the north and central part of the state was pleasant, but
on the more conservative, Republican-voting eastside, the weather
was cold, windy, and snowy.

Congressional and State Election Outcomes

As mentioned previously, the only Hispanic to run in a congressional race, Democrat Michael Montoya, lost to long-time Republican incumbent Joe Skeen in New Mexico's Second (Southern)
Congressional District. In the First Congressional District (Albuquerque), Republican incumbent Heather Wilson beat challenger
John Kelly (50 percent to 43 percent) in a three-person race (the
Green candidate took 6 percent). The Democratic Party establishment had campaigned for Kelly, and the state party had distributed

bilingual political ads to Latino voters, urging them to vote against Wilson and the Republicans. Important to note, because of its negative racial (though not Hispanic) implications, was Kelly's visible role as the U.S. attorney who initiated the ill-fated prosecution of Los Alamos scientist Wen Ho Lee. Wilson, a protégé of Pete Domenici, the state's senior senator, received endorsements from local Hispanic business owners and the Hispanic Business Roundtable, a national group of (Republican) Hispanic business professionals. In the Third Congressional District, Democrat incumbent Tom Udall easily defeated his Republican rival (67 percent to 33 percent) to remain the federal representative of heavily Hispanic northern New Mexico.

Whatever disappointment Republicans experienced in the election was countered by the euphoria they felt over a state legislative victory. Republican newcomer John Sanchez, a thirty-seven-year-old Albuquerque roofing company owner, defeated Democrat Raymond Sanchez, who had served in the New Mexico House of Representatives for thirty years and had been its speaker for the last sixteen. John Sanchez beat Raymond Sanchez by 206 votes out of a total of 9,960 cast.

The Republican Party also unsuccessfully targeted Manny Aragon, president pro tem of the state senate. Indeed, in this election, the state party circulated campaign literature featuring an unflattering photo of Aragon (showing a dark man smoking a cigar) and deriding his leadership and record in the legislature. Diane Denish, the Democratic state party chair, publicly denounced what she claimed were the "race-baiting tactics" of the Republican Party. Aragon won reelection.

Overall, the Democratic Party maintained control of both the upper and lower houses of the state legislature. The Democrats actually gained two seats in the lower house, and Hispanic representation increased by two. In the senate, Republicans picked up one seat while Hispanic numbers stayed the same. Speaker Sanchez would later be replaced by another Hispanic, Ben Lujan, the former majority floor leader. In the senate, Aragon would not survive a challenge to his leadership position by Democrat senator Richard Romero from Albuquerque. And in John Sanchez, the successful challenger to the former speaker, Republicans found a rising star for the party, and a Hispanic to boot.

CONCLUSION

New Mexico Hispanos continued their traditional Democratic voting patterns. While Hispanos were flattered by the attention paid to them by both parties, they continued to vote largely on the basis of which party had been most supportive of them in tangible ways over the last several decades. Low-level patronizing, cultural clichés, and even Spanish-language campaign materials are neither novel nor effective among old-line Hispano families.

As they have for many decades, Hispanos in New Mexico played their usual reliable role—being very active in many aspects of politics, particularly Democratic Party politics. Even though the state's electorate has changed somewhat, the final results of the 2000 general election did not show much change. This continuity persisted despite extraordinary outreach by Democrats and Republicans. Voter turnout rates for 2000, when compared to presidential elections over two decades, however, do raise a question about the long-standing Hispanic pattern of voting in levels comparable to Anglos in the state.

Table 4.2 compares Hispanic and Anglo voter registration and turnout rates in presidential elections from 1980 to 2000. What

Table 4.2 Reported Registration and Voting in New Mexico Presidential Elections 1980–2000, by Race and National Origin (%)

	White	Hispanic	Difference
Registration			
1980	68.3	65.1	3.2
1984	70.7	62.1	8.6
1988	66.6	57.9	8.7
1992	68.0	56.8	11.2
1996	62.7	52.9	9.8
2000	62.9	49.4	13.5
Voting			
1980	60.4	56.3	4.1
1984	62.9	51.1	11.8
1988	57.1	47.4	9.7
1992	63.8	51.3	12.5
1996	53.3	43.4	9.9
2000	54.6	39.5	15.1

Sources: Sierra (1992); Garcia (1996); Garcia and Sapien (1999); U.S. Bureau of the Census (1998, 2002c).

emerges from the data is a widening gap between Hispanics and Anglos in rates of registration and, especially, voting over the long term. Overall, however, the significant decline in voter turnout for Anglos and Hispanics in presidential elections since 1980 shows that New Mexico has not been immune to the general pattern of American disengagement from the electoral process that has been apparent for quite some time.

Table 4.3 presents registration and voting data across New Mexican counties where Anglos or Hispanics account for a majority or more of the county population. A similar county-level analysis of average turnout rates among registered voters was conducted for the 1988 elections (Sierra 1992). In 1998, turnout of registered voters in heavily Hispanic counties lagged behind turnout in predominantly Anglo counties by 5.4 percent. In 2000, the gap closed somewhat to 5.1 percent. What is striking, however, is that turnout rates for registered voters decreased significantly in both heavily Hispanic and heavily Anglo counties from 1998 to 2000. In 1998, turnout among registered voters ranged from a low of 76.2 in predominantly Hispanic counties to a high of 81.6 percent in the predominantly Anglo counties. This range is markedly lower in the 2000 elections. Turnout among the voting-age population shows a mixed picture: heavily Hispanic counties lagged behind predominantly Anglo counties by 12.2 percent. Yet, majority Hispanic counties held a slight edge over majority Anglo counties in their turnout rates among the age-eligible electorate.

The controversial outcome of the 2000 presidential election prevented New Mexico from repeating its bellwether status among states, that is, voting consistently for the winner in national presidential contests. To be sure, Gore won the national popular vote,

Table 4.3   New Mexico Voter Turnout in the 2000 Elections by Ethnic Composition of County

	% of Registered Voters	% of Voting-Age Population
Predominantly Hispano (>60%)	58.6	41.9
Majority Hispano (50–60%)	63.5	46.1
Majority Anglo (50–60%)	62.0	44.1
Predominantly Anglo (>60%)	63.7	54.1
New Mexico	63.2	47.0

Sources: U.S. Bureau of the Census (2000b); State of New Mexico (2000).

and New Mexico voted for Gore. But history will record Bush as the winner in 2000 and New Mexico voting for the losing candidate. With regard to state dynamics, *nuevomexicanos* continued to vote heavily Democratic, and they remained a major factor in New Mexico's electoral outcomes. But unlike 1996, when the Hispanic vote proved pivotal to Clinton's election, it took the votes of New Mexico's other cultural minorities added to those of the Hispanos to give the state narrowly to Gore. One lingering question from the 2000 elections is whether, amid all the hoopla involved in targeting the Hispanic vote, the electoral process will reach new voters as well as engage the old reliables sufficiently to turn them out to vote.

NOTE

We would like to acknowledge David Alire-Garcia, James Fuller, and José Z. Garcia for the insightful comments and information they shared with us. Special thanks go to Gloria Vaquera for her research assistance.

5

Latinos and the 2000 Elections in Colorado

More Real than Apparent, More Apparent than Real?

RODNEY HERO and PATRICIA JARAMILLO

THE LATINO POPULATION IN COLORADO IS SUBSTANTIAL, THOUGH smaller, than in a number of other states and is growing more rapidly than the state's population. These realities, combined with their partisan leanings, typically make Latinos a "necessary" component in electoral coalitions, particularly for Democratic candidates in statewide races. However, this also implies that Latinos are not always "sufficient" to determine outcomes. Latino political cohesion and high turnout are required for it to be "essential" to election outcomes (Hero 1996); but such cohesion and turnout alone do not ensure significant Latino impact. That is, similar behavior by Latinos does not necessarily produce the same results from election to election in Colorado (Hero, Jaramillo, and Halpin 1999). A major issue, then, is to understand how and under what circumstances Latino electoral patterns are most consequential and to recognize that those consequences are seldom clear and simple.

Colorado was largely ignored during the 2000 presidential season, both during the primary and general elections. This may be attributable to the lack of a statewide election for either the U.S.

Senate or governor, *and* the absence of an incumbent president, the first such set of occurrences in Colorado since 1988. On the other hand, state ballot initiatives and the battle for control of the state senate generated political interest among Colorado voters, something that potentially holds broader implications.

Given the outcomes of the 2000 elections, it was difficult to determine the ideological direction the state may be heading. At the top of the ticket, George W. Bush took the state and Colorado's eight electoral votes and Republicans retained control of the Colorado House of Representatives. Countering these developments were the outcomes of the state senate races and ballot initiatives. Although Democrats picked up four seats in the state house, Republicans retained control but the party lost two prominent Republican moderates, moving the GOP in a more conservative direction (Lipsher 2000). In the state senate, Democrats won control after forty years of Republican rule and secured themselves a place at the table in negotiating congressional redistricting. In addition to changes in the state legislature, Colorado passed what may be seen as some modestly progressive ballot initiatives.

Entering the 2000 elections, the potential for Latino influence in any of the ballot races appeared slim. In the presidential races, there was little to no mobilization targeting Colorado Latinos. In fact, there was little reason for Latinos to feel their vote would have any impact on the election outcome given Bush's lead in state polls through most of the campaign season. State legislative races did, however, provide competitive races and opportunities for mobilization of and by Latinos.

Our examination of Latino participation in and impact on Colorado in 2000 confronts a number of barriers, but these are hardly unique to this study. One of these barriers is the small proportion of Latinos in the state, especially when compared to Latino populations in states such as California, Florida, New York, and Texas. The small number makes it difficult to adequately or precisely identify geographically where Latinos reside and, empirically, to generate accurate statistical estimates of Latino behavior with acceptable levels of certainty. An additional barrier exists in the limited availability of data captured at smaller units of analysis than counties and the timeliness and availability of data. These problems are not unique to researchers; they also limit party efforts to target Latinos.

COLORADO'S SHIFTING DEMOGRAPHICS

According to the 2000 census, Colorado's population increased by almost a third in the last decade, making it the third fastest growing state behind Nevada and Arizona and resulting in an additional seat in the House of Representatives after reapportionment (Olinger 2001). The rate of growth among the Latino population is equally remarkable. The Colorado Latino population increased by a little more than 73 percent in the last decade, growing from 424,302 in 1990 to 735,601 in 2000; in 2000, Latinos comprised 17.1 percent of the Colorado population, compared to 12.9 percent in 1990 (U.S. Bureau of the Census 2001; Aguilar 2001). Because Latino electoral participation has corresponded fairly closely with the group's population size in the state, a growth in Latino electoral influence in Colorado can be anticipated.

More than half of Colorado's sixty-three counties experienced greater than a 50 percent increase in the Latino population, and the Latino population in approximately one-third of the counties more than doubled. Counties with substantial increases in the general population do not always correspond perfectly with those counties experiencing substantial increases in the Latino population. However, at the county level the percent of change in the Latino population from 1990 to 2000 does correlate at a statistically moderate level with the percent of change in the general population from 1990 to 2000.[1] Although individual-level data are not available, this evidence suggests that counties experiencing sizable growth also experienced substantial increases of Latinos.

It has been argued that a number of strategic and contextual conditions must be met for Latinos to have an impact on statewide elections (Guerra and Fraga 1996). These conditions include the presence of competitive elections within a state and/or ballot issues relevant to the Latino population; the ability to minimize Anglo backlash against Latino activism; and electoral opportunities created through redistricting, term limits, or open seats. Strategic conditions differ from contextual conditions, in that individuals involved in the electoral system may initiate mobilization efforts in order to motivate interest among Latinos where it might not naturally occur in the electoral context. Latino voters or Latino leaders can engage in activities that increase the possibilities of Latino influence in the process.

A competitive political environment would provide more opportunity for Latino influence. If one or the other of the political parties believes mobilizing the Latino vote would be decisive in any given electoral contest, there would be more likelihood that Latinos would be targeted. It is also important to note that Colorado Latinos tend to be predominantly Mexican American (Aguilar 2001), and Mexican Americans tend to identify with the Democratic Party (de la Garza et al. 1992). Therefore, Democrats would be the more likely party to target Latinos and to do so if the contests appear close in the general election when the group could significantly affect the outcome.

Entering the 2000 election year, Republicans held more than a 150,000-person advantage among registered voters statewide (Colorado Secretary of State 2000b). Compared to 1996, however, both the Republican and Democratic Parties lost slightly in their proportion of registered voters (see table 5.1). In 2000, 35.5 percent of Coloradoans were registered Republicans, compared to 36.1 percent four years before, and registration among Democrats declined from 31.5 percent in 1996 to 30.0 percent in 2000. Although Republicans still have an advantage among registered voters, the growth among unaffiliated voters suggests it is even more essential for the parties to hold their constituents and try to sway the unaffiliated voters in their direction.

State legislative races were extremely important in 2000. With a Republican governor, Republicans would be in a better position to

Table 5.1   Colorado Voter Registration and Party Affiliation, 1980–2000

	1980	1984	1988	1992	1996	2000
Democrat	455,825	514,715	621,624	680,773	719,230	863,740
%	31.8	31.7	30.5	33.9	31.5	30.0
Republican	439,610	514,383	671,100	668,051	824,222	1,022,019
%	30.6	31.7	32.9	33.3	36.1	35.5
Unaffiliated						
	538,822	592,208	744,711	652,768	738,982	989,370
%	37.6	36.5	36.6	32.6	32.3	34.4
Total[a]	1,434,257	1,621,306	2,037,435	2,001,592	2,282,434	2,875,129

[a] The percentages do not total to 100 percent due to rounding.

Sources: Colorado Secretary of State (1980, 1984, 1988, 1992, 1996, 2000b).

maintain control of the state legislature if they could control legislative redistricting. For much of the past twenty years, Democrats could offset a Republican legislature with a Democratic governor, but that is no longer the case. Nineteen senate seats were up in the 2000 elections. Party registration numbers for the nineteen senate districts indicate that the Republicans and unaffiliated each had a higher proportion of registrants in seven of the districts, while Democrats had a higher proportion in only five districts (Colorado Reapportionment Commission 2001). Even in districts where there were greater proportions of those who identified with one party or the other, unaffiliated voters remained a strong presence. This would indicate that any number of senate races could potentially be competitive in the general election.

One final indicator of party competitiveness is the extent to which one party dominates state elected offices. Entering the 2000 elections, Republicans controlled the office of governor, had a forty- to twenty-five-seat advantage over Democrats in the Colorado House of Representatives, and had a twenty- to fifteen-seat advantage in the Colorado Senate. Among Colorado's members of the U.S. House of Representatives, Republicans outnumbered Democrats four to two and both of Colorado's U.S. senators were Republican. At first glance, then, two indicators of party competitiveness suggest that Colorado was dominated by the Republican Party entering the 2000 elections. Republicans held an advantage in statewide registration numbers and controlled major political offices. Party registration numbers from state senate districts indicated the most likely potential area for party competitiveness.

THE 2000 PRESIDENTIAL ELECTION

Throughout the 2000 presidential election, it appeared that Colorado would play little to no role in the final outcome. Although Florida was finally credited with handing Bush the presidency, any number of states appear to have been able to provide the key vote for either candidate. In Colorado, however, the contest did not appear close and it was highly unlikely that Colorado could have swung in Gore's favor. Accordingly, there was only a limited mobilization effort in Colorado targeting Latino voters for the presidential contests.

The results of the 1992 and 1996 presidential elections in Colorado provided little guidance into the potential outcome of the 2000 presidential primary and general election races. In 1992, the Bill Clinton–Al Gore ticket won Colorado, aided in part by the Ross Perot campaign's effect on otherwise likely Republican voters, and became only the second Democratic ticket since 1952 to do so (Hero 1996). In 1996, the race was tighter and Bob Dole squeaked by Clinton and took the state by a slim 4.4 percent of the vote (Hero, Jaramillo, and Halpin 1999). By the 2000 elections, many political pundits were back to declaring Colorado a safe Republican state.

Primaries

The primary system in Colorado is a type of closed system where voters must be registered and affiliated with a party in order to vote in one of the party primaries on election day. Voters affiliated with a party are prevented from switching on primary election day. However, the system permits unaffiliated voters to declare a party affiliation on election day and vote in one of the party contests. The fear among some party officials in Colorado was that large numbers of unaffiliated voters would register on election day and swing the vote away from one of the nominees supported by the party leaders. Turnout in the presidential primaries was amazingly low, however, and the threat of party intrusion never materialized.

Two factors in particular prevented Colorado from having any influence in either of the major party primaries. First, the presidential party nominees were decided only days before Colorado's primary, essentially shutting out Colorado from any role in the decision. Colorado's influence was limited by the timing of its primary as it sat wedged between two dates that carried "much bigger prizes" for the various party candidates. The Tuesday before Colorado's Friday, March 10 primary, California, New York, and twelve other states were scheduled to select their delegates and six more states were scheduled for the following Super Tuesday contests. However, just prior to the Colorado primary date, Bush slowed the momentum John McCain was building, and Gore put an end to Bill Bradley's struggling campaign. Although there were rumors that some of the candidates might make a last-minute appearance in Colorado between the March 7 contests and Colorado's March 10 primaries, much depended on what happened on Tuesday, March 7. Due to the large gains made by Bush and by Gore in the March 7 primaries, Colorado was bypassed by the candidates.

Another contributing factor was a failed attempt to organize a "western primary." The plan was to build a coalition of western state influence by agreeing on a date when all eight inland western states would hold their primaries and caucuses, with the goal of trying to entice candidates running for their party's nomination to visit the states or at least pay closer attention to western issues. However, of the eight possible states, only three states followed through with the plan.

Voters appeared aware of the reduced role Colorado would have in the presidential primaries and stayed home on the day of the Colorado presidential primary. Turnout for the March 10 presidential primaries was extremely low. Only 14.8 percent of registered voters cast ballots in the Democratic primary and 24.1 percent of active registered voters cast ballots in the Republican primary. Some notable figures in the state supported the challengers in the contests. Sol Trujillo, a prominent Republican Latino and the U.S. West chief executive, backed McCain's bid for the Republican Party nomination. Bradley had the support of Colorado's two Democratic members of Congress, Diana Degette (Denver) and Mark Udall (Boulder). In the end, Bush won the Republican primary with almost 65 percent of the Republican vote, compared to McCain with 27 percent of the vote. In the Democratic contest, Gore defeated Bradley, 71 to 23 percent (Colorado Secretary of State 2000c). Polls conducted immediately preceding the primary elections showed Bradley as able to cut into Bush's lead better than Gore (Brown 2000a). Regardless, Colorado voters indicated a preference for Bush over either of the Democratic primary candidates.

Both Bradley and Gore made claims to attracting support of Latino voters. Gore visited the state at the end of February, where he appeared in Denver and Pueblo, occasionally throwing in a phrase in Spanish and vowing to fight for affirmative action, among other things (Brown and Cotten 2000). During the visit, Gore was introduced by Denver city councilwoman Ramona Martinez and Attorney General Ken Salazar, among others, and stated that the Latino and black unemployment rates were at an all-time low since Clinton and Gore were elected in 1992. Bradley's only stop in Colorado was in November 1999. During Bradley's visit, he and his wife focused on poverty issues. Between the end of the nomination season and the August nominating conventions, Gore made one more visit to Colorado to speak to the annual conference for the National Association of Latino Elected Officials.

GENERAL ELECTION

Colorado received only a nod from the two major party candidates during the general election. Although the contest appeared competitive nationwide, Bush seemed the likely winner in Colorado throughout the general election. Neither candidate stopped in the state between the August conventions and the November elections, when the race intensified, although a few surrogates that included friends, family, and running mates did make appearances in symbolic attempts to target the Latino vote. George P. Bush appeared in the state on his uncle's behalf and Bill Richardson did so on the Democratic side. Their appearances were largely ceremonial, however, with mariachi bands and speeches to large crowds. Grassroots mobilization was largely absent.

Denver mayor Wellington Web and Attorney General Salazar were cochairs of the Gore campaign, but leaders in the Gore campaign and the Colorado Democratic Party admitted Colorado was not a high priority. As a result, outreach efforts made to Latinos were more of a state Democratic Party focus than that of the Gore campaign. In fact, coordinators targeting the Latino vote relied largely on Gore television ads being run in New Mexico that spilled over into southern Colorado counties; these counties have large concentrations of Latinos. Due to budget constraints, any free media (i.e., earned media) was considered progress for the campaign. Most earned media time was outside the Denver metro area.

In general, the Republican Party seemed to do very little with regard to targeting the Latino population except to rely on Bush's successful pull of Texas Latinos. According to leaders in the Republican Party, efforts toward the Latino community in Colorado included making literature available in English and Spanish and having a bilingual Colorado Republican Party Web site. However, once the literature left the party headquarters, they were unsure whether the county coordinators distributed the literature or made efforts to target Latino communities. Republicans claimed to have issued bilingual mailings targeted at Latinos, but did not track what those mailings were or from where they received the lists of targeted households.

The lack of attention toward Colorado was largely due to Bush's continuous lead in the state among likely voters. According to polls of Colorado voters, Bush's lead started very early in the campaign season. In early summer, Bush held approximately a ten percentage point lead over Gore. This was not surprising to most observers, given the lead Republicans had over Democrats among registered voters and the tendency of the state's unaffiliated voters to lean toward the Republicans. What was surprising was how quickly the polling numbers changed after the nominating conventions when Gore experienced a bounce. During September, the gap between Bush and Gore closed to within the margin of error. The gap widened again in October, giving Bush a sizable lead, and closed again only days before the election. It is difficult to establish what may have accounted for Gore's late boost, although the timing coincided with the last-minute charges that Bush was concealing DUI charges.

Given that Bush led in the polls much of the election, most Coloradoans were surprised at the delay on election night as polls started closing and states were being declared for one candidate or the other and Colorado was not immediately assigned to the Bush column. Although commentators were certainly apprehensive with calling states after the Florida debacle, it seemed that Colorado was solidly Bush. The early numbers, however, had Gore leading in Colorado and exit polls showed the contest in Colorado to be neck and neck. Not captured in the exit polls, however, was the fact that early voters favored Bush to Gore by a 50 to 35 percent margin (Leib 2000). Bush ended up winning the state with 50.8 percent of the vote or 145,521 votes, very similar to the margin the Republican Party has among registered voters. The final results gave Gore 42.4 percent of the vote and Green Party candidate, Ralph Nader, 5.2 percent of the vote. Some political pundits argued that Nader may have cost Gore the election in some states, but this was not the case in Colorado. Nader drew 91,434 votes in Colorado, not enough to make up the deficit between Gore and Bush even if all of the Nader votes had gone to Gore (Colorado Secretary of State 2000a).

Of the Latino votes, 68 percent went to Gore and 25 percent to Bush (CNN 2000a; ABC News 2000). Compared to 1996, there was a substantial shift in the percentage of Latinos supporting the Republican candidate; in that year, Bob Dole only drew about 12 percent of the Latino vote (Hero, Jaramillo, and Halpin 1999). The Current Population Survey (CPS) reports that Latino voting in Colorado encompassed about 9.7 percent of all Colorado voters. The CPS findings indicate a small increase from 1996, when they reported that Latinos represented approximately 7.7 percent of all voters (U.S. Bureau of the Census 1998). Among Latinos eighteen years and older, approximately 33 percent turned out to vote in 2000, which indicates a 79 percent turnout among registered Latinos (U.S. Bureau of the Census 2002c).

Table 5.2 presents the final vote tallies for the five counties in Colorado with the highest Latino populations, along with the percentage of the county's population that is Latino and the proportion of Latinos eighteen years and older. Gore won three of the five coun-

Table 5.2   Colorado Counties with Highest Percentages of Latino Statewide Votes

	Conejos	Costilla	Las Animas	Rio Grande	Saguache
Latino Population					
Latinos as % of					
Total Population	59.0	68.0	41.0	42.0	45.0
Latinos as % of Voting-					
Age Population	58.4	65.4	39.1	37.4	39.8
President					
George W. Bush (R)	1,772	504	2,569	3,111	1,078
%	48.3	30.6	42.2	61.3	42.6
Al Gore (D)	1,749	1,054	3,243	1,707	1,145
%	47.6	63.9	53.2	33.6	45.3
Total[a]	3,671	1,648	6,094	5,075	2,529
Secretary of State					
Donetta Davidson (R)	1,366	344	2,318	2,970	908
%	37.9	22.8	40.7	60.3	39.9
Anthony Martinez (D)	2,116	1,071	3,039	1,738	1,139
%	58.8	71.1	53.3	35.3	50.1
Total[a]	3,596	1,507	5,700	4,925	2,274

[a]Totals include other candidates in the contests.

Sources: Colorado Secretary of State (2000a); U.S. Bureau of the Census (2002b).

ties and lost one (with a small overall population) by only twenty-three votes. Bush won the fifth county by a substantial margin. Together with results from exit polls, this suggests that Latinos in Colorado were more likely to support Gore than Bush.

Latino representation in the party organizations demonstrated an unevenness similar to that in past campaigns. Examination of Colorado delegates to the national conventions reveals a familiar trend of Democratic dominance in Latinos. Of the sixty-one delegates the Colorado Democratic Party sent to the national convention, fourteen were Latinos, which accounts for approximately 23 percent of the Colorado Democratic delegation (Garcia 2002). In comparison, the Colorado Republican Party reported four Latinos among the forty-four state delegates to the national convention, which is about 9 percent of the delegation; however, both the Colorado Republican National Committeeman and Committeewoman were Latino (Stansberry 2002).

Nevertheless, none of the contextual or strategic conditions delineated by Fernando Guerra and Luis Ricardo Fraga (1996) were met during the presidential elections. Margins of victory were not close in the presidential primary and especially not in the general election. Gore and Bush easily won their respective primary contests in Colorado, and Bush ran ahead of Gore in the polls throughout the general election. There was little perceived need for either candidate to target Latinos in Colorado for mobilization or for Latinos to feel that their vote would make a difference in the outcome of the election. While a small mobilization effort was in place in 2000, the focus was not the presidential race but the state senate contests, with only hopes for spillover to the presidential election.

COLORADO DOWN BALLOT RACES

Primaries

Although there was little room for Latino influence in the presidential election, Latinos had more opportunities for influencing some of the down ballot races in 2000, and more so in the general election than in the primaries. Turnout for the Colorado state primary was, not surprisingly, low, given the lack of Colorado influence in deciding the party nominees: only 6.9 percent of registered voters turned out to vote in the state primaries (Brown 2000b). However, many of the other contests were remarkably competitive.

The primaries themselves proved to be an interesting mix of cakewalks and competitive races. All six of the incumbents to the U.S. House of Representatives from Colorado ran unopposed in their party primaries and the candidates running for their party nominations in the secretary of state race, the only statewide race in 2000, both ran unopposed. Anthony Martinez, from Antonito, located in the southern Colorado county of Conejos, was the Democratic nominee for secretary of state and Donetta Davidson, who was appointed by Governor Bill Owens after the death of the previous secretary of state, was the Republican nominee for secretary of state. If the presence of Latino candidates mobilizes the Latino masses, then this seemed like the most obvious location for Democratic Party mobilization. The secretary of state contest was the only statewide election and the presence of a Latino near the top of the ticket provided a potential for Latino outreach. However, the race was very low profile and mostly overlooked in the press and by the parties.

The low primary turnout notably affected several state legislative races, demonstrating the large influence organized groups can have on the outcome of an election, especially when turnout is light. Many conservative candidates running in the Republican state senate primaries won over their more moderate challengers. The defeat of many of the moderate Republican candidates was somewhat surprising. The *Denver Post* reported that "out of 11 GOP races in which there was identifiable split between right and 'righter' candidates, moderates won only three" (Brown 2000b). Conservative Republicans were declaring a victory and a changing of the guard within the Colorado Republican Party with a strengthened right wing.

The results are most likely due to a combination of the light voter turnout and targeting by independent "educational" groups. When relatively few voters show up at the polls, those who do have a disproportionate impact. Also, these independent groups ran issue ads that tended to make extreme accusations against candidates.[2] Although these groups could not legally coordinate their efforts with a candidate's campaign, many of the candidates on whose behalf the ads were run benefited. Democrats were delighted at the victory of more conservative Republicans, viewing them as easier targets for defeat in the November general election. Races for party nominations to the Colorado House of Representatives were contentious, but did not reach the level of antagonism they did in the state senate primaries.

State General Election and State Legislature

Just as all six congressional incumbents won their party's nominations, all six were also successful in their general election races. Tom Tancredo (R-Littleton) withstood the biggest challenge to be reelected to represent the Sixth District with 53.9 percent of the vote. In the only statewide race, Donetta Davidson easily defeated Anthony Martinez. Davidson entered the contest as a strong incumbent. Although she had only held the office for a brief time, Davidson had a strong record as the county clerk and entered the race with political and professional experience. Martinez had run unsuccessfully for the Third Congressional District in 1998 and was less experienced than Davidson, but other factors also contributed to his defeat. In particular, Martinez did not appear to receive much money or support from the state Democratic Party, as it focused on regaining control of the state senate. In a sense, he became one of many sacrificial lambs. In the counties with the highest Latino percentages, Martinez won all but one with substantial margins.

The nastiest campaigns in Colorado during the 2000 elections were in the fight to control the state senate. Control of the state senate was significant since Colorado picked up an additional congressional seat in the U.S. House of Representatives. Control of the state legislature during 2000–2002 determined control of redistricting in Colorado. The state house seemed set to remain controlled by the Republicans, but Democrats could win control of the state senate with the switching of just three seats to the Democrats. In part because of Colorado's term-limits statute, nineteen senate seats were up for election; of those, nine were considered strongly contested.

Both contextual and strategic variables appear to have contributed to the Democrats winning the state senate. Several of the state senate races were very close. Large amounts of money were raised and spent in the contests by the candidates, the two major political parties, as well as by independent groups. Also, a little-known mobilization effort by the Democratic Party targeted Latino voters in particular districts.

Newspaper and television coverage, as well as interviews with leaders in the parties, indicate that negative campaigning seemed to play a significant role in the senate contests. Analysts have differed about the effects of the negativity on the final outcome of the contests, and some observers suggest that negative campaigning may have had mixed results. In one senate district, a candidate benefited in the primary from attack ads targeting his more moderate opponent, but he may have suffered from attack ads lodged against him in the general election that claimed he "supported the use of the so-called 'date rape' drug and wanted to see guns in schools" (Ames 2000). The candidate, a Republican, lost to the Democratic candidate in this race. An attack mail ad may have backfired in another contest where a Democratic candidate was attacked as a "leader of the radical homosexual agenda" by a group known as Colorado for Family Values. The headline on the brochure read, "The Hollywood-style Radical Homosexual Agenda Is Now Targeting Our Community," and under the headline was a photo of actresses Ellen Degeneres and k. d. lang, both gay activists (Hubbard 2000).

The second factor that may well have contributed to Democrats regaining control of the Colorado Senate can be linked directly to Latino mobilization. Latino leaders recognized the potential impact Latino voters could have in the outcome of various contests. A little-known, but very calculated, effort by a coordinated team of Democratic leaders combined a targeting of the state senate with a push for Latino turnout in eight key districts. Largely the brainchild of Attorney General Salazar, himself elected rather quietly in 1998, but with involvement from Denver city councilwoman Ramona Martinez and former Denver mayor and Clinton administration official Federico Peña, a group of Democrats coordinated an effort that effectively and efficiently used a limited amount of resources to mobilize the Latino vote. Although the focus was on the Colorado state senate, there was some overlap with the Gore campaign, and organizers felt strongly that if they could turnout the vote to benefit Democrats in the state senate, it would also benefit Gore at the top of the ticket (Fagan 2001; Downey 2001).[3]

The group targeted approximately 21,000 Latino households in ten senate races (Fagan 2001). Democrats won seven of the ten. Three of the districts played prominent roles in Democrats regaining control of the state senate in that they switched from Republican to Democratic control.

The plan involved several points of voter contact; some contacts were statewide while others focused on the ten targeted districts. A statewide recorded phone call went out the first day of early voting. However, live contacts focused on the ten targeted state senate races. Soon after the first recorded call, a person-to-person contact was made within the ten districts. A qualitative assessment of the amount of volunteer contact and how effective the coordinators believed they were is presented in table 5.3, along with the number of households in the Democratic voter file for the district (Fagan 2001). Each mobilizing team was given early voting information for that district. The effort involved putting the contact lists together and writing scripts for the contacts. A statewide mailing went out the Thursday before the election in order to arrive on the weekend. A statewide recorded call from Attorney General Salazar went out on Sunday and Monday preceding election day. Salazar also appeared in Telemundo and Univision television commercials and radio commercials were run on Radio Romantica, KCSJ, and a Greeley Latino radio station (2001).

There are some notable features about this particular mobilization effort. It did not target large counties that have the higher proportions of Latinos. Rather, it focused on smaller Latino pockets that could provide useful numbers where the races appeared close. In one state senate district, the Democratic candidate defeated the incumbent Republican candidate by 897 votes. According to the coordinators of the mobilization effort, the Democrats accomplished partial coverage for the 1,900 Latino households targeted. This may have been enough to help the Democrat win the seat. This is the only district in which we have clear empirical evidence that the number of targeted Latino households may have provided the margin of victory for the Democrats, but other state senate races almost certainly benefited from the targeting of Latinos. Since the target was households and not voters, it is difficult to settle on the exact number of votes that were mobilized. Perhaps most striking was that this mobilization effort was not mentioned in any news coverage of the state senate races. The media tended to solely credit the

Table 5.3   Democratic Campaign to Target Latino Voters, 2000 State Senate Races

Senate District	Number of Latino Households Targeted	Latino Voting-Age Population (% of Total VAP in the District)	Degree of Volunteer Phone Contact	Total General Election Vote Count (% of Total Vote)[a]	
				Democratic Candidate	Republican Candidate
8	1,824	13,061 (13)	Best	25,841 47.1	27,002 49.2
13	1,933	4,852 (5)	Partial	36,425 52.2	33,366 47.8
14	2,265	7,617 (8)	Good	27,476 52.3	23,624 45.0
17	2,229	11,972 (12)	Good	29,816 53.7	22,655 40.8
19	1,985	6,380 (8)	Partial	23,482 49.3	22,585 47.5
21	2,858	11,879 (15)	Good	20,709 54.2	17,462 45.7
23	3,435	14,020 (23)	Best	21,718 48.0	22,059 48.8
27	939	4,015 (5)	None	24,026 45.6	27,527 52.2
29	1,809	16,484 (20)	Best	14,726 53.8	11,826 43.2
35	1,677	9,245 (10)	Best	26,077 54.4	20,793 43.4
Total	20,954				

[a] The percentages do not total to 100 percent per senate district due to rounding and third-party candidates.

Sources: Fagan (2001); Colorado Secretary of State (2000a).

actions of the outgoing senate minority (Democrat) leader. Unlike the Democratic effort, the Republican Party did not target Latinos within any of the state senate or house races.

Ballot Initiatives

In contrast to the low level of attention paid to most candidate contests in 2000, a great deal of attention was given to controversial ballot initiatives. Latinos were an early focus of an attempt by One

Nation Indivisible, a Washington-based education reform group led by conservative pundit Linda Chavez, to place a ballot initiative on the November ballot that would have ended bilingual education in Colorado. Colorado U.S. House representative Tom Tancredo (R-Littleton) backed the measure. This initiative would have replaced the existing bilingual education program with a one-year English immersion program for non-English speakers. The wording of the initiative was challenged in court and the Colorado Supreme Court voided the proposition, having found that the wording might mislead voters into thinking that parents would have a choice between bilingual education and one-year immersion. Organizers of the effort had little time to make another attempt before the statutorily prescribed deadline.

Of the ballot initiatives that were on the November ballot, three measures received voter approval. One of those that passed was aimed at closing the "gun-show loophole" (Amendment 22) by requiring a criminal background check on anyone purchasing a gun at a gun show. The former Republican presidential candidate, McCain, appeared in television ads and in person supporting the measure. Closing the gun-show loophole had statewide support early on and maintained that support throughout the campaign, especially given the still fresh memories of the killings in 1999 at Columbine High School in Littleton, Colorado. A *Denver Post* poll in early October showed that 77 percent of Colorado voters either definitely or somewhat supported the initiative. The measure passed with 70 percent of the vote. Exit polls indicate that support among Latinos was equally high, estimating that 77 percent of Latinos going to the polls on election day supported Amendment 22 (CNN 2000b).

Amendment 20, an initiative calling for the legalization of marijuana for medical use also passed. This was the second time around for this particular measure; legal disputes about the collection of signatures nullified the results of the final vote for the measure during the 1998 elections. Amendment 20 would create a registry of seriously ill patients who, with physician approval, would be allowed to use marijuana for medical purposes; however, the amendment did not provide for the distribution of marijuana. A *Denver Post* poll in early October showed that 67 percent supported the initiative, and it passed in November with 54 percent of the vote. Exit polls indicate that Colorado Latino voters were largely split on this measure. An estimated 52 percent of the Latinos going to the polls on election day were said to have supported the measure, compared to 48 percent who opposed it (CNN 2000c).

A third initiative that passed was a constitutional amendment designed to increase funding to the public schools. Written to overcome the limitations imposed by the Taxpayers Bill of Rights Amendment of 1992, this new amendment provided for funding kindergarten through twelfth grade education at a rate of inflation plus 1 percent over the subsequent ten years. The amendment passed with 53 percent of the vote; exit polls on this amendment were not available.

CONCLUSION

The outlook for Latino mobilization in Colorado at the outset of the 2000 elections appeared minimal. Republicans appeared to largely dominate elected office and the statewide race did not appear competitive. The primaries were not competitive and Bush ran ahead in the polls in Colorado throughout the general election campaign and ultimately carried the state rather handily. Requisite conditions for Latino impact did not converge and the potential did not materialize. Thus, Colorado Latinos seem to have played a role similar to what they often have played in years past, that of subtle influence. On the other hand, targeted efforts during the campaign suggest that Latinos may have played a rather important role in the Democrats winning a majority in the state senate. But mobilization efforts of the group and the ostensible role of Latino voters were not widely recognized. Thus, in Colorado the impact of the Latino vote at the state level may have been more significant than has been acknowledged previously.

The shifting demographics of the Latino population in Colorado and their stronger support for Bush than for Republican nominees in years past is likely to send signals to both parties that Latinos are not to be easily ignored in the state. Understanding how the population has changed in the past decade and that Latinos are moving outside of Denver proper and from pockets in southern Colorado is important if the parties intend to attempt additional targeted mobilization efforts similar to what the Democrats implemented in the state senate elections of 2000.

In the past, Latino influence sometimes seemed more apparent than real in Colorado. In the 2000 elections, that influence may have been more real than apparent, at least in some races such as the state senate elections. The typically essential, yet frequently tenuous, nature of Latinos in Colorado politics is thus likely to become increasingly significant. It is possible that Latino influence, when tapped, could slowly reinvigorate the state's Democrats, similar to California in the 1990s or Texas in the early twenty-first century. The work of Democratic Latino leaders in targeting Latinos in the state senate races suggests that Latinos could become a leading presence in the state party. Recent presidential contests suggest Colorado is a state that cannot be taken for granted by either of the major political parties, in no small part because of its considerable and changing Latino population. The results of the 2000 state legislative contests seem to imply an emerging significance of Latino voters as well.

NOTES

1. We collected total and Latino population data for each county. The variables are moderately correlated at .50 and the correlation is statistically significant ($p < .01$ in a two-tailed test) with $N = 63$.

2. Moderate Republican candidate Linda Morton who was running in the state senate Republican primary election against the more conservative Penn Pfiffner appeared to suffer from one of the campaigns waged by a fairly right-wing group known as the Rocky Mountain Gun Owners, led by Dudley Brown. The ads did not advocate voting for Pfiffner or against Morton but were more subtle messages. The text of one ad stated, "Tell Linda Morton that her gun banning agenda is not the answer. And please contact Republican candidate Pen Pfiffner and thank him for his support for our constitutional right to keep and bear arms" (Ewegen 2000).

3. Several funding sources have been suggested for this mobilization effort. The coordinators state that they worked on a shoestring budget. Two particular sources suggested are some of the funds raised during a Bill Richardson fund-raiser held in Denver and funding provided by the American Federation of State, County, and Municipal Employees, although we were not able to verify the second source.

6

Will More (Votes) Continue to Equal Less (Influence)?

Arizona Latinos in the 2000 Elections

MANUEL AVALOS

~~~~~~

LATINOS HAVE SEEN THEIR SHARE OF ARIZONA'S POPULATION GROW over the past decade—from 18.8 percent in 1990 to 25.3 percent in 2000—but their electoral impact during this period has been slight. The Latino share of the Arizona electorate has lagged well behind their share of the population (from 9 percent in 1992 to 15 percent in 2000). Previous analyses of the impact of the Latino electorate in the 1988, 1992, and 1996 on Arizona elections revealed a history of noncompetitive elections in which few Latino candidates have run for statewide office, few ballot initiatives have mobilized Latino voters, and Latino voters have turned out at low rates (Hero 1992; Avalos 1996, 1999).

Arizona Latinos have overwhelmingly registered as Democrats (at rates of 70 to 75 percent throughout the decade) as the state has become increasingly conservative and Republican. Today, registered Republicans outnumber registered Democrats in Arizona by a 42 to 36 percent margin. In only one presidential election (1996) were Arizona Latino voters able to capitalize on their strong Democratic partisanship to contribute to a Democratic victory in a presidential race (DeSipio, de la Garza, and Setzler 1999: 33).

Despite this recent history, many expected that the 2000 elections and the focus both parties placed on courting Latino voters would create new opportunities for Arizona Latinos. Latinos were courted by both presidential candidates during the 2000 campaign in Arizona, but they continued to block vote for the Democratic candidate. This vote, however, was not enough to prevent the continued statewide success for the Republicans; George W. Bush carried the state of Arizona by a comfortable margin.

The inability of Latinos to have a significant impact on the outcome of the presidential election in Arizona was due once again to the absence of three important factors: the continuing noncompetitive nature of statewide elections, the absence of ballot issues of great enough importance to mobilize Latinos to turnout on election day, and the continued low turnout of Latinos in Maricopa and Pima Counties.

THE 2000 CAMPAIGN

Like the 1996 elections, the 2000 race was close throughout. In the final weeks of the election, many pundits believed it was too close to call. As late as mid-October, public opinion polls showed the race dead even at 41 percent. Yet, in the final weeks of the campaign both parties neglected the state almost completely (Gonzalez 2000). Instead, they spent their remaining resources in large, electoral vote-rich states of the Midwest (Michigan, Wisconsin, Illinois, and Pennsylvania) and in Florida. Nevertheless, the Arizona primary and general election provided a number of interesting election procedures and ballot initiatives. Most notable were the introduction of Internet voting in the Democratic primary and Proposition 203, which, if passed, would have ended bilingual education in the state.

The Primaries

The presidential primaries in Arizona were of little consequence to the outcome of either the Bush or Al Gore campaigns. Bush spent little time or money in the Republican presidential primary in Arizona, where Senator John McCain easily won by a margin of 60 to 36 percent. McCain's win coupled with his narrow win in Michigan were key to keeping him in the campaign.

While McCain qualified as Arizona's "favorite son," he did not have unanimous support of the state's Republican leaders. Republican governor Jane Hull surprised many when she endorsed Bush in the fall of 1999. Her endorsement made national news, as did the subsequent *New York Times* story of her description of McCain's temper. While McCain had some previous success in courting Latino voters in his 1998 senatorial race, he did no public courting of the Latino votes in the Arizona primary. Since only a very small percentage of Latinos in Arizona were registered Republican (less than 20 percent) and only one of the twelve members of the Latino legislative caucus was Republican, McCain seemed content to appeal to conservative Anglo Republicans in Arizona's closed primary. There was no organized campaign outreach to Latino voters nor did the rhetoric of his state campaign include specific references to Latinos.[1]

By the time of the Democratic primary, the race for the party presidential nomination had been decided. Nationwide attention was focused on the primary, however, because of the party's plan to use Internet voting. Controversy surrounding the plan arose almost immediately. The party's reason for using Internet voting was a desire to "open up the democratic process not only to the young and technologically advanced, but to everyone. Democrats favor greater participation in our elections and by embracing 21st Century technology. We can assure that more people will cast a ballot on March 11" (Election.com 1999). The Democrats were also able to work out a favorable arrangement with an Internet vendor. Given the unique nature of Internet voting, a number of Internet vendors saw Arizona as a test case and an opportunity to get positive publicity. In essence, they saw Arizona as an opportunity to get in on the ground floor should Internet voting catch on. Votation.com contracted with the Arizona Democratic Party to provide the online voting services free of charge and promised the party that they would pay for all legal fees if a challenge was made to prevent the use of Internet voting.

Under the plan, voters would be allowed to vote via the Internet by mail ballot or at polling places. Voters who chose to use online Internet voting would have a full four days in which to cast their ballot (from March 7–11), while those who chose to vote at the poll would have one day (twelve hours). Originally, the Democratic Party planed to have only forty statewide polling places available. By the time of the March 11 primary, however, 132 statewide polling places were in place, though this was still a fraction of the 2,000 polling places used in normal statewide elections. Of the 132 statewide polling places, about one-third were located in Maricopa and Pima Counties, where 78 percent of all Latinos statewide resided. Five of thirty-three voting locations in Maricopa were located in heavily populated Latino areas. In Pima County, three of the twelve polling places were in heavily populated Latino areas.

While some public online voting sites were established at libraries and community colleges, their availability was not publicized to registered Democrats. The party did send a mailing to registered party members, informing them of the Internet voting process, but it did not include a list of locations for the public Internet voting sites or of polling locations. The party had discussed using phone banks to call registered voters, but did not (Fleisher 2000). For those registered Democrats who requested mail ballots, ballots were sent late so that many voters had less than seventy-two hours to return their ballots. At no time during the planning process for the use of Internet voting were senior Latino party leaders consulted by the Democratic leadership, nor were they approached after the plans for holding the Internet primary were announced. A draft of the Internet plan to be submitted to the Justice Department was sent to seventy-seven members of the Arizona Democratic Party Executive Committee. In a court deposition, Mark Fleisher, the chair of the party, could not recall how many minorities were on this committee (Fleisher 2000).

The Voting Integrity Project, a nonpartisan, nonprofit, public interest organization, filed suit in the federal district court in Phoenix to seek an injunction to block the use of Internet voting in the Democratic primary (*Voting Integrity Project et al. v. Mark Fleisher et al.* 2000). The suit was filed on the grounds that Internet voting would unfairly discriminate against African American, Native American, and Hispanic voters in violation of section 2 of the Voting Rights Act (VRA) of 1965. Relying on a 1999 U.S. Department of Commerce Report, the suit argued that whites were more likely to have Internet access from home than most racial and ethnic minorities from any location, including home, work, school, or library. This phenomenon, referred to as the "digital divide," adversely impacts African American and Hispanic households, which are only 40 percent as likely as white households to have home Internet access nationwide (Wilhelm 2000). Native Americans are even less likely to have home Internet access since it has been estimated that 20 percent of the Navajo and Hopi reservations in northern Arizona have no telephone service and the availability of Internet service providers is substantially less than in large metropolitan areas.

In a deposition, Fleisher admitted that he was aware of federal studies that showed that Anglos had more access to computers on the Internet than minorities, and he believed that Anglo Democrats would be more likely to have access to computers and the Internet than minority Democrats in Arizona (Fleisher 2000). It is clear from his deposition that Fleisher's stated goal of opening up the democratic process was intended for young, white, middle-class Democrats and not for predominately poor and working-class Latinos and other racial minorities.

Other expert testimony provided evidence of historically lower participation rates in heavily concentrated Hispanic precincts in Maricopa and Pima Counties in the presidential elections of 1992 and 1996. It was argued that the introduction of Internet voting would create a dilution (a violation of section 2 of the VRA) of the Hispanic vote, since most of households in these precincts would have little access to Internet voting (Avalos 2000).

Despite the evidence presented in federal court, U.S. District judge Paul G. Rosenblatt ruled that the Democratic Party could go forward with the first binding Internet election. However, Judge Rosenblatt did not dismiss the lawsuit because he suspected that "there is a digital divide that may well result in racial discrimination" (Sherwood 2000).

While record numbers of voters turned out in the Democratic presidential primary, Anglo voters turned out in greater numbers than minority voters, regardless of whether they voted online, by mail, or at the polls. In many minority districts, turnout was about a third of that in predominately Anglo districts. Voters in predominately minority districts used mail-in ballots and voting at the polls, while voters in highly concentrated Anglo districts mostly used online voting and mail-in ballots (Chiu 2000a, 2000b). In the Twenty-second District, a predominately Hispanic and black district in southwest Phoenix, 20 percent of voters cast their ballots on the Internet, 55 percent voted by mail, and 25 percent went to the polls. In contrast, the Twenty-eighth District, a mainly white district in Scottsdale (a suburb of Phoenix), nearly 60 percent voted online, 28 percent voted by mail, and 12 percent went to the polls.

In sum, the primary season in Arizona was relatively uneventful with the exception of the use of Internet voting in the Democratic primary. While this technology had no significant impact on the outcome, the potential impact of this technology nationwide on possible Latino vote dilution remains a serious issue. While nationally the digital divide appears to be narrowing, there are no current comprehensive studies that analyze the impact of this phenomena on Latinos in the most populated Latino states. With the fallout over the various flawed traditional ballot procedures at the polls in the 2000 elections, I would expect that the large-scale use of Internet voting will become a reality in future state and national elections.

General Election

As noted in other chapters in this volume, the 2000 elections generated much press coverage and attention to the Latino vote nationwide. Bush tried to extend his alleged popularity with Texas Latinos to Arizona and Gore attempted to capitalize on and hold the overwhelming Latino support for Bill Clinton in 1996. In the 1996 presidential election, Latinos accounted for 163,000 of the state's 1.5 million votes cast, or nearly 11 percent of the electorate. As can be seen in table 6.1, Arizona Latinos accounted for approximately 21 percent of Arizona's population in 1996. Just 58 percent were registered to vote and 41 percent turned out on election day.

In an attempt to increase Latino voting, the Southwest Voter Registration Education Project, the Southwest Phoenix Action Committee, and the Mesa Association of Hispanic Citizens undertook a statewide registration effort. Armed with volunteers, these groups sought out voters at naturalization swearing-in ceremonies, supermarkets, video stores, and shopping malls and in Latino neighborhoods (Ortiz 2000). According to Census Bureau estimates, Latino voter registration in Arizona grew from 147,000 in 1998 to 247,000 in 2000.

Because the race was so tight nationally in mid-October, both

Table 6.1   Voter Characteristics of Latinos in Arizona, 1992–2000 (%)

	1992	1994	1996	1998	2000
Latino percent of state population	19.0	20.0	21.0	21.0	25.0
U.S. citizen share of Latino adult population	73.8	66.6	55.8	60.6	67.7
Latino share of Arizona electorate	9.0	9.0	10.9	10.6	15.0
Registration rate among Latino U.S. citizens	46.0	45.3	57.9	41.5	49.3
Turnout rate among Latino U.S. citizens	42.9	32.2	41.1	24.2	40.1

Source: U.S. Bureau of the Census (1994, 1996, 1998, 2000c, 2002c).

campaigns actively sought Arizona's eight electoral votes. As late as October, Janet Murguia, Gore's deputy campaign manager for constituency outreach, reported to the press that Arizona and several smaller states with sizeable Latino populations—Nevada, New Mexico, and Oregon among them—were emerging as significant battlegrounds because of the tightness of the race in those states (Gonzales 2000). Both candidates employed Spanish-language radio ads to target Latino voters. Gore's *"Su Voto"* television ad, which was targeted mostly in the Midwest urban centers such as Chicago, Detroit, and Milwaukee, however, never aired in Arizona.

The candidates themselves did not visit the state to win Latino votes. Both campaigns used surrogates to target Latino voters in Arizona. Since there were no visible elected Latino Republicans in the state, most public endorsement of Bush came from Anglo politicians such as Governor Jane Hull and the Republican U.S. congressional contingent led by Representatives J. D. Hayworth and John Shadegg and Senator John McCain. Representative Ed Pastor, the only Arizona Latino in Congress stumped for Gore, but the national Democratic Party spent little on a ground campaign to win Arizona Latino votes.

Unlike 1996 and earlier presidential races, Latinos played a symbolic role in the Arizona presidential race. Local newspapers across the state frequently played up the role Latinos would play in the election and the Bush campaign's courting of Latino voters. The *Arizona Republic,* for example, noted the importance of Arizona Latino voters. In the article, Harry Pachon, the president of the nonpartisan Tomás Rivera Policy Institute, commented on the impact Arizona Latino voters could play in a close race, "All it takes is a 5 percent shift [in Latino votes] to make a 1 [percentage] point shift in the election. So if Gore were to get 40 percent versus 30 percent of the Latino vote, that's a 2 point difference" (Gonzales 2000).

The key, however, to any significant impact of the Arizona Latino vote in 2000 was turnout and the ability of Latinos to vote as a block (Guerra and Fraga 1996). In both the 1992 and 1996 presidential elections, Latino turnout was significantly below the statewide average. In many heavily populated Latino precincts, turnout was 20 to 30 percent below the statewide average. Despite the fact that over 73 percent Latino voters cast their ballot for Clinton, low turnout offset block voting in 1996 (Avalos 1999).

Aside from the presidential race, there were no other competitive candidate races in the state. Reapportionment in Arizona has created very little party competition in U.S. congressional districts. Of the six congressional districts in the 2000 elections, five were heavily Republican and only one (the Second District) had a Democratic majority; it was also the only majority-minority district in the state. This district belonged to Representative Ed Pastor, the only Arizona Latino ever elected to Congress. Because the Second District is so heavily populated by Democrats, the general election in this district has had no serious Republican competition in the 1990s. The 2000 elections followed the historical pattern, as the Republican Party put up only token opposition.[2]

The only other congressional race that involved a Latino candidate was in the First Congressional District, where Democrat David Mendoza ran against Republican Jeff Flake for the seat vacated by Congressman Matt Salmon, who did not seek a third term. This district was a heavily registered Republican district with few Latinos.

Proposition 203

With no other statewide office of significant importance to Latino voters, Latino interest in the election largely rested on the controversy surrounding the citizen initiative: Proposition 203. This proposition was backed by a group called English for the Children and was bankrolled by Ron Unz, the Palo Alto software millionaire who campaigned for California's Proposition 227, which dismantled bilingual education in California schools in 1998. This measure, if adopted, would establish English-only instruction in Arizona's classrooms, where about 5 percent of students participated in bilingual education programs, but far more spoke another language at school. The adoption of Proposition 203 would replace bilingual education programs with a one-year curriculum of "structured English immersion" regardless of the individual needs of children learning English, the advice of educators, or the desires of parents. Local school boards would also have no say in the matter. Under the law that existed before the November election, parents had the right to choose between bilingual education and other educational options (which included English immersion programs), but under Proposition 203 there would be virtually no choice.

Probilingual education groups mobilized during the 2000 elections campaign to oppose Proposition 203. These groups included the Arizona Language Education Council, the Arizona Association of Chicanos in Higher Education (AACHE), the Mexican American Legal Defense Fund, as well as organizations representing twenty-one Native American tribes in Arizona (Cart 2000; Doolen 2000). These groups shared a common fear of the detrimental impact 203 would have on educational outcomes for their children.[3]

Latino groups such as the AACHE attacked Proposition 203 using Arizona Department of Education data, which showed that children learning English in bilingual classrooms were outperforming their counterparts in English-only classrooms. These Latino groups argued that the real problem facing performance of all Arizona school children was not bilingual education but the low level of state educational spending. In 1999, Arizona ranked last in the nation in classroom spending per pupil. Native American groups argued that 203 would destroy American Indian–language revitalization programs on Arizona's Native American reservations that were central to maintaining their culture (Cart 2000).

Throughout the three months prior to the election, heated public debates between Proposition 203 supporters (English for the Children—the Ron Unz group, which included some Latino parents, but no visible or prominent Latino spokespersons) and the bilingual education community groups took place throughout the state. Despite the mobilization efforts on the part of Latino and Native American community groups, they were outspent by the English for the Children by a ten to one margin. While English for the Children was able to produce television and radio ad spots, the opposition groups had to rely on public forums and word of mouth to get their position across to the public. By the end of September, public opinion polls showed registered voter support for 203 at 71 percent (Merrill 2000). Whether Proposition 203 would be a rallying cry for Latinos to turnout in record numbers would determine the level of impact they would have on the presidential race in Arizona.

ELECTION RESULTS

As late as one week prior to election day, polls showed the Arizona presidential race to be dead even; the final outcome, however, provided Bush with a comfortable ten point margin, 53 to 43 percent. An analysis of the Latino vote indicates that neither the closeness of the presidential election nor interest in Proposition 203 was enough to substantially increase voter turnout among the Latino electorate. Nevertheless, block voting among the Latinos for Gore (75 percent) remained as high as it had been for Clinton in 1996 (see table 6.2).

The impact of this block voting was again muted by turnout, which has traditionally been substantially lower than the non-Latino vote. Turnout among registered voters in the most highly concentrated Latino precincts in the two most populated Arizona counties (Pima and Maricopa) was lower than elsewhere in the state. In Maricopa County, turnout in the most heavily concentrated Latino precincts was 27 percent below the statewide turnout. Turnout in the highest concentrated Latino precincts in Pima County was at 60

Table 6.2 Latino Democratic Bloc Voting and Turnout among Registered Voters in Arizona in 1992, 1996, and 2000 Presidential Elections (%)

	1992		1996		2000	
	Vote	*Turnout*	*Vote*	*Turnout*	*Vote*	*Turnout*
Maricopa County	58	53	77	42	75	45
Pima County	60	56	72	52	76	60
Statewide	37	78	47	64	45	72

Note: Maricopa County data based on thirty-two high-density Latino precincts; Pima County data based on thirty-nine high-concentration Latino precincts.

Source: Author's calculations based on county-turnout data.

percent, but this, too, was 20 percent below Pima County's overall rate of 80 percent.

As expected, Proposition 203 won easily, by a statewide margin of 63 to 37 percent. Despite the controversy, it did not spur mobilization in the Latino community. The majority of Latino voters in Arizona opposed the proposition, but they were far from universal in this opposition. In the thirty-two most heavily populated Latino precincts in Maricopa County, only 52 percent of the electorate voted against Proposition 203 and for bilingual education.

In other key statewide races involving Latino candidates, Pastor easily won reelection for his Second Congressional District seat by defeating Bill Barenholtz by a 69 to 27 percent margin. In the First Congressional District, Democratic David Mendoza made a surprisingly strong showing in a heavily Republican district, losing to Republican Jeff Flake by a 54 to 42 percent margin. Mendoza's strong showing may be attributed to his tireless campaign efforts and the fact that he did not use any racial cues or engage in discussion of race-based issues in his campaign. This, coupled with the fact that Flake was unknown to most of the Republicans in the district, created a situation in which voters probably paid more attention to issues than personality.

In the state legislature, a shift in power mirrored national election results in the U.S. Congress. Arizona voters, angry over an alternative-fuel vehicle legislation fiasco that cost Arizona taxpayers millions of dollars, shifted the balance of power in the state senate out of Republican hands for the first time in seven years. After the 2000 elections, the Arizona Senate had an equal number of Democrats and Republicans (at fifteen each); this reflected a loss of four seats for the Republicans. In the Arizona House of Representatives, Democrats picked up two seats over 1996, but Republicans remained in control as they had for the past twenty years, by a 36 to 24 percent margin.

The Latino legislative caucus after the 2000 elections stood at eleven members—seven in the Arizona House of Representatives and four in the Senate—an increase of two members in the house and one in the senate from 1996. The increase in the Latino legislative caucus came from victories in central Phoenix districts (one in the senate and one in the house), where increasing Latino populations have overtaken the few concentrations of African Americans.

The other increase in Latino representation came from the victory of the only Republican Latino in the legislature who resides in a Republican district in northern Arizona.

CONCLUSION

The impact of the Latino vote in Arizona in many ways mirrors the political realities of Latinos in other southwestern states. While Latino population growth continues across the United States and in Arizona, this alone does not ensure a significant increase in overall voting strength. The Latino population in Arizona is projected to grow from 25 percent to 34 percent in 2025, but the percentage of the population who are of noncitizen adults (32 percent) will continue to limit Latino voting strength in the years to come. The continuing low rates of registration (under 50 percent) among eligible adults must be addressed if Latinos in Arizona hope to become a significant influence on electoral outcomes.

If we look to Latino voting in Arizona over the last three presidential elections, several observations can be made with regards to their electoral impact. Several key contextual factors—outside Latino control—are necessary for the mobilization of the Latino vote, but are often absent in Arizona. These include competitive elections, mobilization, Latino candidates for statewide offices, and ballot issues of significant concern to Latino voters.

The dearth of competitive elections is particularly crucial in Arizona. Competitive elections make each voting block or group more appealing for the major parties as they seek to develop strategies to capture the votes of these groups (Guerra and Fraga 1996). Unfortunately, there has been little history of competitive party elections for most statewide offices over the past decade in Arizona. The lack of competitive elections means that Democratic and Republican presidential candidates have not targeted many resources toward the Latino vote in Arizona. Despite the fact that Latinos have increased their percentage of the electorate from 9 percent in 1990 to 15 percent in 2000, and voted as a block for Democratic candidates over the past decade, the impact of block voting has been offset by low voter turnout.

Arizona Latinos face a second barrier. Voter mobilization through voter registration and naturalization drives is largely absent. And Latino political elites are unable to place themselves in positions of influence within state and local and national parties. As long as naturalization, registration, and voter turnout rates among the Latino electorate remain low, they will have great difficulty in reaching their electoral potential commensurate with their increasing population.

If Latinos are to increase their electoral impact in Arizona, a number of changes must occur. Historically, the Latino community in Arizona has lacked a political tradition of effective participation within the state Democratic Party and therefore has had difficulty in effectively ensuring that resources will be dedicated to mobilization. However, given the changing demographics of the state and the increase in the Latino population in the next decade, Latino Democrats must begin to capture leadership positions within the party. The creation of eight Latino minority-majority state legislative districts in 2002 presents such an opportunity and challenge. Latinos have begun to size this opportunity. The number of Latino legislators increased from eleven in 2000 to fifteen in 2003.

Despite the large share of noncitizens (33 percent), Latinos have managed to increase their percentage of the electorate in the state from 9 percent in 1990 to 15 percent in 2000. In order to continue this upward trend of an increasing Latino electorate, much work will be needed to help noncitizens through the naturalization process, to develop effective voter registration drives, to get voters to the polls on election day, and to implement strong mobilization efforts. Attention to these strategies will increase the potential to organize a Latino block vote to increase Latino representation in elected offices at the state and federal levels in Arizona.

The constituency efforts mentioned earlier should be attended to by the Latino organizations and elected representatives, as they are in the best position to develop, organize, and advocate for the Latino community. Notably, there is the capacity for Latino elites to realize an impact within the Democratic Party and the state legislature. While Republicans continue to dominate state politics, Latinos within the Democratic Party have the potential to become a group with considerable impact. Seventeen of Arizona's thirty newly drawn legislative districts will be Republican majority while the other thirteen will be majority Democratic districts. Of the thirteen

Democratic districts, eight are Latino majority-minority districts, which have the potential of electing as many as sixteen Latinos to the house and eight members to the senate. As such, Latinos in the state legislature could potentially control the leadership of the Democratic Party in Arizona in the near future.

NOTES

1. If McCain had become the Republican nominee, he might have been able to capture more Arizona Latino votes than Bush, but only because Arizona Democrats, Latinos included, tend to be much more conservative than in other states. The likelihood that McCain would have brought more Arizona Latinos into the Republican fold is unlikely. Conservative Democrats in Arizona regularly vote Republican without changing party identification.

2. The post-2000 census reapportionment added two new congressional districts. Of the eight congressional districts created, two were majority Latino districts (58 percent Latino in the Fourth District and 51 percent in the Seventh District). A third majority Democratic district was also created (First District). Thirty-two percent of the voting-age population in the First District are racial minorities, with the largest group being American Indians (18 percent).

3. Most of the Latino groups that opposed Proposition 203 were existing educational organizations but not necessarily groups tied to bilingual education issues per se. 203 did bring together a number of Latino groups across the educational spectrum in a unified effort to defeat the antibilingual proposition. These groups continue to be active and have been working to create bilingual instruction options for parents in the public schools.

7

Still Waiting in the Wings

Latinos in the 2000 Texas Elections

LISA J. MONTOYA

In his second gubernatorial race, George W. Bush received an increased share of the Latino vote. Exactly how large a share is debated (de la Garza, Shaw, and Lu 1999), but estimates range from 33 to 49 percent. If he could transfer his appeal from Texas Latinos to Latinos in the other important electoral college states of Florida, New York, Illinois, California, and New Jersey, he would become the next president. Thus, Latino support for Bush as governor contributed both strategy and momentum to his presidential campaign. Unfortunately, once developed, Bush did not pursue the Latino strategy in Texas.

Aside from being the source of promise for this presidential hopeful, Texas Hispanics did not play an influential role in the election. Latino votes made no difference. If no Latino had voted, the results would have been the same. Three factors explain this lack of influence. First, the presidential and stateside campaigns were not competitive. Second, the Democratic Party failed to recruit Hispanic candidates. Finally, no campaign addressed issues salient to Latinos (Guerra and Fraga 1996).

This chapter is concerned with documenting the changing partisan landscape in Texas and how Latinos help shape it. I first discuss how the presidential campaigns targeted Latinos, calling attention to events and actors that may shape Latino influence in the future. Second, I present an overview of the major state races on which Latinos might have played a role. Finally, I evaluate how Latinos responded to the campaigns and what lies ahead.

THE 2000 ELECTIONS IN TEXAS

Because Al Gore was not going to be competitive in Texas, his campaign spent little time in the Lone Star State. Gore made three short visits to Texas between March and November, stopping once before a Hispanic audience. Bush's campaign paid lip service to the importance of Texas Latinos and made appearances before Hispanic audiences in El Paso and San Antonio. Beyond these appearances, the Bush campaign did little to court Texas Latinos. Neither candidate ran Spanish-language ads.

Primary

The Democratic and Republican primaries were nonevents in many respects. As the Texas primary approached, both candidates were already certain of their parties' nominations, and each was confident he would win his party primary in Texas. Instead, both candidates spent their time in battleground states. Vice President Gore scheduled an overnight stop in Dallas and Houston the weekend before the primary, where he met with his base. In Houston, Gore dined with Olympic champion Carl Lewis and spoke at a predominantly African American church with Representative Sheila Jackson Lee. Before departing, he lunched with local Hispanic officials and voters at a Mexican restaurant. State senator Mario Gallegos had organized the event and hoped he could bring Gore back to help candidates down the ticket. Gore did not return until November, just before the general election.

When the primary results were tallied, Vice President Gore won 80 percent of the Democratic vote and Governor Bush won 88 percent of the Republican vote ("Race Summary Report" 2000). Bush carried every age, income, and ideological group among Texas Republican primary voters, including 85 percent of Hispanic Republicans' votes. Ninety percent of GOP voters said they would vote for Bush in November. Gore's support was softer. He did well among minorities, receiving 90 percent of Hispanic Democrats' votes and 95 percent from African American Democrats. But only 75 percent of Democrats polled said they would vote for Gore in November (Koenig 2000). An El Paso exit poll revealed that 26 percent of Hispanics voted for Bush and 68 percent voted for Gore in the March primary (Koidin 2000).

General Election

As the campaign heated up across the country, Bush announced he would skip the Texas Republican convention. Traditionally, the governor is chair of the convention and delivers a keynote address, but Bush had never cultivated strong ties with the conservative leaders of the state party. In fact, party leaders had denied Governor Bush the traditional honor of chairing the convention in 1996. Attending the convention would highlight some fundamental differences between Bush and the party leaders that he probably did not want to see on the evening news. While Bush opposed abortion, he hadn't yet ruled out a running mate who favored abortion. The party also opposed bilingual education, even as the governor was trying to sway Latino voters in his favor. Finally, although Bush opposed gay marriages, he had been making overtures to gay and lesbian voters. His actions were sure to come under fire at the convention, where the Texas GOP would not allow, for the third time in a row, the Log Cabin Republicans, a gay rights group, to set up its information booth at the convention (Robison 2000a).

In June, Gore trailed the Texas governor by thirty-three percentage points overall, according to the Texas poll. At that time, Bush even led among Texas Latinos, 50 percent to 37 percent. The same was true for women, men, and all age categories. The only constituency group that favored Gore at this time were African Americans, 55 percent to 13 percent (Robison 2000b). The Texas numbers reflected the national polls and highlighted Gore's failure to get his message to the Democratic base. As Democratic political consultant George Christian put it, "Any Democrat should get as

much as 40 percent of the vote or better, just as a matter of course.
. . . And he's the Vice President of the United States" (2000b).

Bush was clearly enjoying a home court advantage. The June
Texas poll found his approval ratings as governor remained high at
71 percent, significantly higher than the 66 percent his predecessor,
Governor Ann Richards, attained at her peak. The campaign
claimed the high approval rating was a response to Bush's record of
reform in Texas. But Texans were not sure why they approved of
their governor. Fifty-two percent of Republican voters and 75 percent of Hispanics could not name a reform their governor had authored (Manfuso 2000).

At midsummer, Texas Democrats tried to make something of
Bush's failure to renounce the Texas state GOP platform, which included the "abolition of Social Security, the minimum wage and the
Education Department." State senator Gonzalo Barrientos challenged Bush's commitment to Hispanics in Texas. He said, "While
Bush has taken credit for legislation that helped Hispanics, the governor fought Latino legislators when they sought to pass health insurance for children and improved conditions at colonias" along the
border (Flores 2000). At the same time, the Rand Corporation had issued a report arguing that the education miracle in Texas was a
myth. It charged that the testing system imposed on the schools had
not resulted in the improved test scores and learning that Bush took
credit for. Each of these issues received media attention but they did
not change the momentum of the campaign.

Even as Democrats and nonpartisans denounced the governor,
the Bush campaign had made inroads with some conservative Democrats. By the end of the summer, Bush had sought and won the
support of several prominent Democratic Hispanics, including El
Paso mayor Carlos Ramirez and former Corpus Christi state representative Hugo Berlanga. Mayor Ramirez even campaigned with
Bush in California and New Hampshire. Calling himself a conservative Democrat, Ramirez said, "My support for him is because I have
gotten to know him as a person. I have gotten to know his values. I
know I can trust him" (Koidin 2000). Perhaps Bush's most influential but least surprising Democratic supporter was Tony Sanchez, a
wealthy businessman who was thinking about a run for governor
himself. Sanchez and Bush had supported each other in the past.
Bush had appointed Sanchez to the University of Texas Board of Re-

gents and Sanchez had contributed $106,000 to Bush's two guberna-
torial races. He also raised or contributed over $100,000 to the pres-
idential campaign (Herman 2000).

These Democratic defections may be attributed to the strong ties
that Bush built while he was governor and to the perception in Texas
that there would be substantial rewards to early supporters when
Bush won the presidency. Another factor was that Gore's campaign
was failing to grab the attention a vice president should attract.

By September, Bush's sizable lead over Gore had closed and he
was running on an underdog theme. Still, Bush remained ahead of
Gore by twenty-three percentage points in Texas (Ratcliffe 2000).
After the state and national conventions, both presidential campaigns stayed away from Texas until the election. Bush's support in
the polls remained in the middle fifties (see table 7.1).

Gore spent little time in Texas. He made an unscheduled stop
in San Antonio in July and did not return until late October when
he helped celebrate the opening of a megachurch in Dallas. Introduced by former secretary of state and Dallas mayor Ron Kirk, an
ambitious and talented African American Democrat, the vice president spoke about his support for family values and for hate crimes
legislation before a mostly African American audience. He did not
meet with Hispanic leaders or voters on this visit.

Shortly before election day, the presidential campaign began to
take a toll on the governor's approval ratings. Republicans believed
his numbers were a product of the Texas bashing coming from the
Gore campaign. Bush's approval numbers had fallen to 62 percent,
from a peak of 81 percent in 1999. The slide was most dramatic
among women. Still, his lowest rating was two points higher than
Governor Richard's highest ratings (Hughes 2000).

Table 7.1   Texas Poll Results, 2000 (%)

			May–June		
	February	*May–June*	*Latinos*	*August*	*October*
Bush	66	57	50	53	57
Gore	23	24	37	30	27
Nader	—	2	—	—	3
Buchanan	—	1	—	—	1

Sources: Freemantle (2000); Hughes (2000); Ratcliffe (2000); Robison (2000b).

ELECTION RESULTS

Bush took his home state with 59 percent of the vote, Gore won 38 percent, and Nader 2 percent. In Florida, Democrats were fuming that Nader had taken votes from Gore, a grab that arguably "cost" him the election. Nader's 2 percent of the votes in Texas would not have helped Gore.

How well Bush did among Hispanics is not too clear. According to the Willie C. Velásquez Voter Research Institute (WCVRI), Bush won 32 percent of the Latino vote and Gore 68 percent (2000c). The Voter News Service, which is less likely to conduct exit polls in high-concentration Latino areas, found that Bush did somewhat better, at 43 percent (and Gore at 54 percent). Thus, whichever total is used, Bush did very well for a Republican presidential candidate in Texas (Christenson 2000; Willie C. Velásquez Voter Research Institute 2000c).

The WCVRI estimated Hispanic turnout at 51 percent of registered voters immediately after the election (2000d). WCVRI estimates are generally drawn from high-concentration Latino areas that would include more low-propensity voters. The Census Bureau found a more respectable 68 percent Texas Hispanic turnout (U.S. Bureau of the Census 2002c). Actual turnout is probably much closer to 51 percent.

Senator Kay Bailey Hutchison, who won easily by a margin of 65 percent, helped Republicans in tight local races, but there were no Democrats to help local candidates down the ballot. Hutchinson may have included a Hispanic plurality in her victory margin. A WCVRI exit poll (2000b) found that she took 49.7 percent of the Hispanic vote against the 48.6 percent won by her Democratic opponent, Gene Kelly, who ran a limited and poorly funded campaign that included no Latino outreach.

Statewide, there were no close calls and Republicans were able to solidify their hold on state government by capturing *all* statewide offices and maintaining a slim majority in the state senate. The Democrats retained their majority in the congressional delegation and held on to their narrow margin in the state house.

All the Hispanic members of the Texas congressional delegation won reelection by comfortable margins. Henry Bonilla, the only Mexican American Republican in Congress, faced a more serious challenge than other Texas incumbents in 2000, but he was never in any real danger of losing. His challenger, Isidro Garza, received 39 percent of the vote, most of which probably came from the Hispanics in the district.

The most promising Latino challenger was Regina Montoya Coggins, a Wellesley-educated Dallas attorney and former Bill Clinton assistant who ran in the Fifth Congressional District in Dallas. She faced two-term incumbent Pete Sessions. Montoya Coggins raised approximately $560,000 in the primary, an amount ten times more than her Democratic opponent and later raised $1.5 million to run against Sessions. She lost but took 44 percent of the vote.

In all, six Hispanics challenged sitting house members, though only two of these mounted well-financed campaigns (Garza and Montoya Coggins). Four challenged other Latino members and three mounted those challenges in majority Hispanic districts. Ideologically, they were a diverse group. Two were Democrats, two were Libertarians, one was Republican, and one was Independent. The Democrats were the most competitive challengers. These candidates demonstrate that Latinos are willing to move beyond the Democratic Party, but they also represent a small demographic among Hispanics. They are the well-educated, activist, and politically savvy. Their presence shows diversity but not a splintering of the Democratic base among Texas Latinos.

The only Hispanic to win a statewide race was Alberto Gonzales, who was elected justice to the Texas Supreme Court. Gonzales had been appointed to the court by Governor Bush in 1999 and won his Republican primary easily. He faced no Democratic opposition in the general election (a Libertarian candidate won 19 percent of the statewide vote). Soon after the election, Gonzales was tapped for White House counsel and is considered a likely U.S. Supreme Court nominee.

The only other Hispanic holding statewide office was Tony Garza, a Republican Latino from Brownsville. Garza ran for Texas attorney general in 1994 and lost but was appointed secretary of state by Bush. In 1998, he was appointed to the Railroad Commission, an agency charged with overseeing oil and gas interests across the state. Garza held one of three commissioner positions and was the only Hispanic nominated to a statewide office in 1998.

In the state senate and house, all the Hispanic members up for

reelection won by comfortable margins. State Representative Leti-
cia Van de Putte, a Hispanic lawmaker from San Antonio, ran a successful campaign for the senate, doubling the number of Latinas in
the Texas Senate.

The Texas Supreme Court remained in Republican hands and
the GOP picked up four more seats on the state's appellate courts,
giving them forty-five justices out of seventy. Bush's strong coat-
tails are credited with the win. All five Hispanic Democratic incumbents returned to their positions as justices for district courts
of appeals and one Democratic challenger lost to a Republican incumbent in a very close race.

The election results show that Latino incumbents, whether Democrat or Republican, are retaining their seats as incumbents do.
But, while Republican Latinos are seeking higher offices, Democratic Latinos are mostly staying put. In an informal poll of five Latina
elected officials, each argued that Anglo party insiders are not supportive of Latinos seeking higher positions. There are many sea-
soned Latino state legislators who could be tapped to run statewide,
but they have not been recruited by party leaders or have been actively discouraged from running.

CONCLUSION

The 2000 elections provide insight on the electoral future of Texas
Latinos, on Bush's tenure as governor, and on the immediate
prospects for the Republican and Democratic Parties in Texas.

Texas Latinos were ignored by both presidential campaigns in
2000, but in different ways. The Gore campaign made the usual
promises to fight for an important electoral college state, but early
on, everyone knew his promises were insincere. Bush took Latino
votes for granted in a state he knew he would win even as he was
making overtures to Latinos across the country. Once again, Texas
was a noncompetitive presidential state, and Latino votes did not
count.

At the same time, Latino demographics will continue to drive political interest in Hispanics. Texas is the second largest state in the
nation with a population of 21 million people. Since 1990, Latinos
account for 60 percent (2.3 million) of its population growth, making

Latinos 32 percent of Texans up from 25 percent in 1990. Latinos will continue to become a more sizable portion of the electorate. In 2000, Latinos cast about 16 percent of the total votes.

Latinos have been geographically concentrated along the border and in west Texas, and they are the largest ethnic group in Texas's four largest cities: Houston, Dallas, Austin, and San Antonio. Yet, their future growth will not be restricted to these areas and cities only. The census reports that Latinos are more dispersed across the state than ever before. The implication here is that local parties across the state will have to consider how to woo Latino voters.

The 2000 elections also show that Governor Bush's strategy of engagement with Latinos was more successful in his gubernatorial race because of a weak Democratic challenger. Although Democrats had an able politician in Garry Mauro, the land commissioner, he proved a less able candidate and was hurt greatly by his ties to President Clinton. In the 2000 presidential election, Latino Democrats knew their presidential candidate and gave him their vote. Bush's performance with a strong Democratic candidate shows that Latinos, while open to other candidates, must have a good reason to vote for someone other than a Democrat (Montoya 1999; Martinez 1996).

Moreover, Bush's strategy to woo Hispanics did not change the Texas Republican Party. It is still a party led by social conservatives who have little sympathy or interest in Hispanic issues. They are more likely to continue to feature the few elected and appointed Hispanics as proof of their willingness to open their doors wide.

Democrats hit bottom after a long slide down as the 2000 elections came to a close. While the state house and the congressional delegation held onto its Democratic majority, the Democrats lost control of all statewide offices and of the state supreme court. The losses were a painful reminder of the 1998 elections, when Democratic candidates lost the three statewide races they entered.

Why is the Democratic Party so weak? State Representative Irma Rangel says the party is too divided. "Even the Chair of the State party used to be a Republican," she quips. "The division comes in part from liberals not wanting to cede control to minorities, especially to Hispanics" (2001). This viewpoint is widespread among Latino elected officials and candidates. One longtime labor insider gives three reasons for party weakness. One, the Democrats have never gotten over losing whites to the Republican Party. Two, the Democrats are running candidates who have money and have lost connection with their base. The rising cost of campaigns has everything to do with this. Three, the core Democratic constituencies are weaker than they used to be. Labor is divided and some of the most prominent African American and Hispanic leaders are busy building personal fiefdoms (Labor Leader 2000). The party is going through a lengthy reorganization. In both 1998 and 2000, Democrats tacitly agreed to focus on races that were winnable because the candidate pool was so slim. The outcome has been increasing the dominance of Republicans.

8

Unquestioned Influence

Latinos and the 2000 Elections in California

LUIS RICARDO FRAGA, RICARDO RAMÍREZ,
and GARY M. SEGURA

~~~~~~

IT MAKES LITTLE SENSE TO THINK OF CALIFORNIA AS ANYTHING BUT the most important state to all candidates in recent presidential elections. Its fifty-five electoral votes represent 20 percent of all the votes needed to win the presidency. In the post–Ronald Reagan era, it is difficult to think of any Democratic strategy to win the White House without victory in California. In the eighteen presidential elections since 1932, California has supported the winning candidate in all but three elections (1960, 1976, and 2000). This, of course, provides an incentive for Democrats to make sure that it stays in their camp. It provides an even stronger incentive to Republicans to limit Democratic support in the state.

One cannot begin to understand the continued population growth in this state, and its similarly growing Democratic partisanship, without a full understanding of Latinos as residents, citizens, and voters. By seeding the growth in Democratic registration, Latinos are the primary catalyst to this increased importance of the state in national politics. The partisan shifts that now characterize the California electorate are reflected even more starkly in the partisanship of its congressional delegation, its senate, and its assembly. California is now one of the three most Democratic states in the country after West Virginia and Hawaii. This could not have been predicted just ten years ago in the political birthplace of Richard Nixon, Reagan, and Pete Wilson. The primary reason for the Democratic advantage in California is its growing Latino population and the consistent propensity of Latinos to support Democratic candidates by a two-to-one margin. Stated differently, in national elections, as California goes, so go Democratic chances. And increasingly, as California Latinos go, so go Democratic victories.

We will argue that Latinos in California played an important role in the 2000 elections in at least three distinct ways. First, the rapid and substantial mobilization of the Latino electorate in California has placed the state out of reach to the GOP for statewide contests. While California was, until very recently, highly competitive in statewide contests, the mobilization of the Latino community has tipped the balance in the direction of the Democrats.

Second, California contributed substantially to the Democratic effort to retake the state house of representatives. Five seats in California switched party as a result of the 2000 elections, and Latinos played a substantial role in at least four of those contests.[1] An additional seat, considered threatened, was held by the Democrats. Had the Democrats simply broken even elsewhere, California's shift would have very nearly allowed them to retake a congressional majority.

Finally, the Democratic tilt to the election resulted in a lopsided advantage for the party in both chambers of the state legislature and a substantial growth in Latino legislators, giving Democrats, with the previously elected Democratic governor, and a Democrat lieutenant governor who is Latino, unprecedented opportunities to dominate state legislative decision making and especially to shape the redistricting process resulting from the 2000 census.

LATINO MOBILIZATION AND THE DEMOCRATIC ADVANTAGE IN STATEWIDE CONTESTS

In the early 1990s, there was much speculation as to whether the sizeable increases in the Latino population would ultimately result in Latinos determining the outcome of state elections. By 2000, this was definitely the case, at least in California. To best appreciate the significance of Latinos in the 2000 elections, it is necessary to place that election within the context of changes in California's population, voter participation, voter impact, and representation over the last ten years. It is this context that shows how 2000 was not an aberration in the capacity of Latinos to influence California politics. It was, rather, the culmination of a ten-year trend. This influence should only increase in the future.

The Latino population grew from 26.0 to 32.4 percent of the California population between 1990 and 2000. By comparison, the Asian population grew from 9.0 to 10.8 percent and the African American population decreased from 7.0 to 6.4 percent. Of special note, the white non-Hispanic population declined from 57 percent in 1990 to 46.7 percent in 2000. Among adults, 28.1 percent were Latino in 2000 and 51.1 percent were non-Hispanic white.

Latino voter registration has been steadily increasing as well. Using Current Population Survey data, the National Association of Latino Elected and Appointed Officials estimates that Latinos were 10.8 percent of all registered voters in California in 1992 and 14.7 percent in 2000 (National Association of Latino Elected and Appointed Officials Educational Fund 2002). A study by the Field Institute estimates that in May 2000 16 percent of all registered voters in California were Latino. This represented an increase of about 1 million Latino registered voters since 1990. This growth accounted for just over 90 percent of all newly registered voters in the last ten years (Field Institute 2000). During this same time period, there was a net decrease in white non-Hispanic registered voters of about 100,000. Whites were estimated to comprise 72 percent of the state's registered voters; down from 79 percent in 1990. This study by the Field Institute also estimates that African Americans experienced an absolute decline of about 50,000 voters and now comprise 6 percent of the registered voters in the state. Asian Americans and others, by contrast, have grown by 300,000 voters since 1990, and they now comprise 6 percent, up from 4 percent in 1990, of the registered voters in the state.

The Field Institute study also presents several additional findings regarding Latino voter registration. They estimate that there were 6,025,641 Latino adults in California. Of these, 75 percent were U.S. citizens. Latino registered voters in 2000 totaled 2,350,000, or 52 percent of all adult Latino citizens. If all Latino adult citizens registered to vote, they could comprise as much as 31 percent of all registered voters in the state. Notably, 46 percent of all Latino voters in the state have registered since 1994. Of these more recently registered voters, 50 percent are under the age of thirty, 44 percent were born outside of the United States, 42 percent reside in Los Angeles County, 38 percent have less than a high school education, and 34 percent have incomes of less than $20,000 per year (Field Institute 2000: 3–4). Perhaps most significantly, 59 percent of these recently registered voters have registered as Democrats and only 18 percent have registered as Republicans. This pattern is similar to that of Latinos who registered prior to 1994, of whom 61 percent are currently registered as Democrats and 24 percent are registered as Republicans. Despite the claims made by advocates and some pundits regarding Latino partisan loyalties, every survey conducted between the 1990 and 1998 primaries that asked this question has found that a clear majority of Latinos identify with the Democrats. In 1990, 64 percent of Latinos identified as Democratic partisans (Alvarez and Nagler 1999). By 2000, this share had declined to 60 percent, with 22 percent registered as Republicans. The California population as a whole saw 42 percent registered as Democrats and 39 percent registered as Republicans (Field Institute 2000: 4).

Using the estimates based on exit polls conducted by the *Los Angeles Times* and CNN, figure 8.1 provides estimates of the Latino share of the statewide electorate from 1992 through 2000 (it should be noted that these estimates have a sampling error of ±4 percent). Latino voters have doubled their size within the California electorate over this period of time. In 1992, they were 7 percent of the statewide electorate and in 2000 were 14 percent. It is apparent that this trend has been gradual and consistent. The trend for African American voters is distinct. They have remained relatively stable at 6 to 8 percent from 1992 to 2000. The rate of growth for Asian American voters is similar to that experienced by Latinos, although their numbers are smaller. They increased from 3 to 6 percent. These changes are mirrored by a sizeable decrease in the presence of the white electorate over the same period. Whites declined from 82 percent of the California electorate in 1992 to 71 percent in 2000.

Figure 8.1   Racial/Ethnic Shares of the California Electorate, 1992–2000

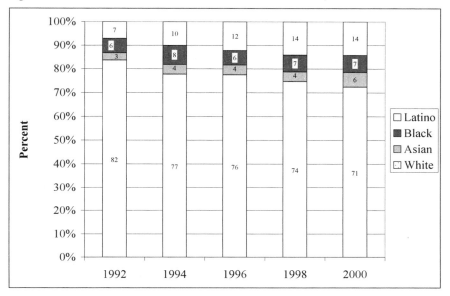

Source: *Los Angeles Times* Exit Polls 1992 and CNN Exit Polls 1994–2000

The growth in the Latino population and the Latino share of statewide voters is likely to continue. Democratic partisanship also appears to be a continuing characteristic of California Latino voters. Latino influence in the 2000 presidential election, however, was limited. The explanation for this can be found in several strategic conditions exogenous to California's Latino voters. Their influence was felt more firmly in congressional and state legislative races.

Conditions Allowing Latino Influence

Regarding the 1988 elections, Fernando Guerra (1992) argues that in the absence of six important strategic conditions the California vote and Latino voters within California were largely irrelevant. In addition to a unified Latino vote, he argues, the conditions that might have made the Latino vote significant were a close election, registration and mobilization, Latino presence in the convention and campaign, prominent Latino candidates in other races or ballot issues especially relevant to Latinos, and candidate-specific mobilization that does not alienate white voters (100).

Building on this work, Guerra and Luis Ricardo Fraga (1996) outline a more extensive set of "contextual" and "strategic" conditions necessary for the Latino vote to be a major factor in the 1992 presidential election. Contextual conditions refer to circumstances that were not in the direct control of Latino voters and leaders. Among these conditions were competitive elections, the minimization of white backlash, opportunities to elect Latino candidates, and the presence of ballot issues of particular concern to Latino voters (132–133). Strategic conditions were much more in the control of Latino voters and their leaders. These conditions were divided into those that were voter focused and those that were elite focused. The voter-focused conditions included voting as a block and effective voter mobilization strategies on election day. Elite-focused conditions included voter registration and naturalization drives, substantive advocacy for Latino interests during campaign strategy sessions, "unity and intensity of endorsement by Latino political elites, organizations, and media," and community-based "organizational development and coordination" (134–137). The limited relevance of the Latino vote in the 1992 elections prompted Guerra and Fraga to go so far as to state "if none of California's Latino voters had been allowed to participate, this would not have made any difference in the outcome of the presidential election" (131). This circumstance has changed dramatically since 1996 and perhaps was most apparent in 2000. Although Latino votes did not determine the outcome of California's vote, they gave the Democrats a strong advantage that prevented California from being competitive in the presidential race.

Latino Influence on California Elections in the 1990s

The data provided in figure 8.2 provide evidence for the varying role Latinos have had in affecting major elections for president, U.S. senator, and governor from 1990 to 2000. These data specify the percentage of the statewide vote represented by each racial and ethnic partisan voting block. This method combines the size of a group of voters in the statewide electorate with the extent to which that vote is cast as a block for each candidate.

Latinos were critical in determining the outcome of one senato-

Figure 8.2   Racial/Ethnic Electoral Influence in California Races, 1990–2000

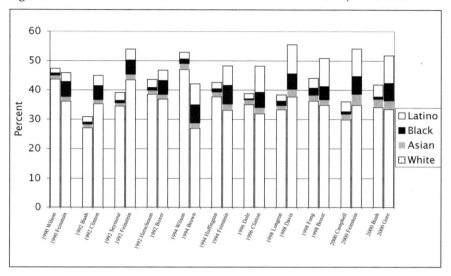

Source: *Los Angeles Times* Exit Polls 1998–1998 and CNN Exit Polls 1994–2000

rial election in 1992. They were not significant, however, in affecting the outcome of the presidential race that year, nor were they critical in the other senatorial race. Barbara Boxer, the Democratic candidate, lost the white vote to her opponent. She would not have been elected senator in 1992 if it had not been for the vote provided by Latino, African American, and Asian American voters. In the cases of both Bill Clinton and Diane Feinstein, each received such an overwhelming share of the white vote that the votes of communities of color were insignificant in determining the outcome of their elections. This same situation appeared in the gubernatorial election in 1994. In his reelection campaign, Governor Pete Wilson received a clear majority of the statewide vote. White voters comprised the vast majority of his total support.

The situation was very different for Senator Feinstein in her 1994 reelection campaign. In this race, the white vote clearly split in favor of her opponent. Voters of color, however, represented 31.4 percent of her statewide total and provided critical support to her victory. This election was the first time that Latinos represented the largest segment of the minority vote received by a winning Democratic candi-

date. Feinstein would not have won her reelection without the support of Latino and other minority voters.

   This pattern of Latino voters who are the largest block of voters
of color for successful Democratic candidates appears in the presidential election of 1996 and in both the gubernatorial and senatorial elections of 1998. Because of the split in the white vote, Clinton would not have won California in 1996 without the support of
communities of color, including Latinos. Latino voters provided
President Clinton with 18.7 percent of his statewide vote, as compared to African Americans who provided him with 10.8 percent
and Asian Americans who provided 4.4 percent. By comparison,
white voters provided him with 66.2 percent of his vote. Similarly,
in 1998 voters of color also provided gubernatorial candidate Gray
Davis and incumbent Senator Boxer with important components of
their victory margins. Davis won a majority of the votes of all racial
and ethnic segments of the California electorate, but would have
lost the election without the support from communities of color.
Latinos provided him with a full 17.8 percent of his statewide vote.
Senator Boxer did not receive a majority of the white vote in her
election.

   Latinos comprising the largest portion of the votes from communities of color for successful Democratic candidates statewide
was especially evident in 2000. Senator Feinstein won reelection in
2000 and again it was the votes she received from communities of
color that allowed her to defeat her Republican opponent. The votes
of communities of color were even more critical to Al Gore's margin
of victory in the presidential race. Gore split the white vote in California. According to Voter News Service exit polls, Bush received 48
percent of the white vote and Gore received 47 percent. They also
split the Asian vote (with Gore at 48 percent and Bush at 47 percent). Gore, however, won an overwhelming majority of the votes
cast by African Americans and Latinos. He won the African American vote 86 percent to Bush's 11 percent and he won the Latino vote
68 percent to Bush's 29 percent. Of these two groups, Latinos comprised the largest percentage of his statewide votes from communities of color: a full 18.3 percent, compared to the African American
contribution of 11.6 percent.

   From 1990 to 2000, California held eleven statewide elections
for governor, U.S. senator, and president. Democrats have won nine

of these races. In seven of these nine (78 percent), Latino voters were significant contributors to the winning Democratic candidates. Three of these nine (33 percent) successful Democratic candidates would not have won without Latino votes (making the unlikely assumption that Latino Democratic voters stopped voting while Latino Republican voters voted at levels seen in the actual election). Over the decade, Latino voters increasingly used their share of the California electorate and their Democratic block voting to provide ever-larger shares of the state Democratic vote. This was unequivocally demonstrated in the 2000 elections for president and for U.S. senator. Whenever the Democratic candidate loses the white vote, it is the Latino vote that represents the critical and ever-growing margin of victory in California.

THE 2000 PRESIDENTIAL ELECTION

At the start of the campaign season, California Latinos looked to be the targets of both parties' attentions. The Democratic Party chose Los Angeles—the city with the largest Latino population in the United States—to be the site of its national convention, in part out of an acknowledgment of the importance of Latino voters to Gore's presidential campaign. Given the anticipated Republican emphasis on appealing to Latino voters in the Bush campaign, choosing Los Angeles would make sense to the Gore campaign.

The Bush campaign's efforts to appeal to Latino voters nationally are well documented. The *Atlanta Constitution* noted that this effort would surely include California, "where there are 2.3 million Latino voters." Lionel Sosa, the media director of Bush's 1998 campaign, stated that "the campaign is buying 'all available Spanish media everywhere we go'" (Heath 1999). Michael Madrid, a California GOP consultant, stated, "The party genuinely believes that Hispanics will be a conspicuous part of the New Majority" (Marinucci 2000). In January 2000, the Republican National Committee (RNC) announced that it would mount a "multimillion-dollar bilingual ad campaign aimed at Latino voters" and that front-runner Bush was pursuing an "unprecedented Latino-aimed television and print advertising campaign in California before the March 7 primary." Sosa stated that "whoever wins the Hispanic vote in California will win the presidency. And make no mistake about it—we will win the Hispanic vote here." Jim Nicholson, the RNC chair, stated that the Republican Party would "spend up to $10 million to run the spots in California and nine other key states" (2000).

In the end, though, neither campaign made much of an effort to sway California or California Latino votes. Because California is such a safe Democratic state and also because its media markets are among the most expensive in the nation, the Gore campaign did little to win California votes. Until the last weeks of the campaign, Bush and the Republicans did even less. Although California Latinos often served as a backdrop to one campaign or the other's aspirations for Latino votes nationally, the bulk of the Bush and Gore Latino campaigns took place in other states.

Despite moving its primary forward, the primary campaign was largely over before the state held its primary in early March. California held a nonpartisan primary (in which all candidates appeared on the same ballot). In this primary, Gore received 34 percent of the vote, Bush 29 percent of the vote, John McCain 23 percent, and Bill Bradley 9 percent. Gore earned 81 percent of registered Democrats' votes and Bush 61 percent of registered Republicans' votes. Both candidates did visit the state repeatedly in the primary season, but this was to raise money, not to win votes.

In the period between the primaries and the party conventions, California Latinos saw more of the candidates than at any point in the campaign. Gore held rallies and campaign visits in Latino areas in April and May as part of a strategy to reinvigorate his campaign after a decline in the polls. Bush also spoke to Latino audiences in this period as part of his national strategy to show interest in and win support from Latinos. Media coverage of these events indicated that the audience was national, not state. Both campaigns had unofficially conceded the state to Gore.

The Republican demonstration of its sensitivity to Latino voters, and especially their language and culture, was especially apparent at the Republican national convention in Philadelphia. California Republican assemblyman Abel Maldonado gave the first-ever convention speech entirely in Spanish (Calvo 2000). California Latinos were even better represented at the Los Angeles Democratic convention. Unlike the 1996 Democratic convention, which had been held in Chicago, however, the 2000 convention did not extensively use Latino institutions as venues for convention-related events.

The general election saw little of either major-party candidate. Each campaign did send surrogates to the state. More importantly, the Democratic, mostly in an effort to win several close congressional races, invested in a field mobilization effort or "coordinated campaign" to turn out likely Democratic voters. The Gore campaign itself did little to target Latino voters. There were campaign ads run on Spanish-language television and radio, but they were as a response to the efforts of the Bush campaign. In fact, it was reported that the Gore campaign decided to only buy time on Latino and African American radio. It had "no plans to counter Bush's TV buy" (Novak 2000). In the last weeks of the campaign, the Bush campaign made the decision to spend $8 million in California, with a sizeable portion going to Latino media. This was reported as not an easy decision for the campaign to make, but one that Republican leaders in California argued for very strongly (2000).

Despite its limited scope, the Gore strategy worked. He won the California vote by almost 12 percent and the Latino vote by a very comfortable 68 percent to Bush's 29 percent. Reports of the very limited success of the Republican efforts to win voters in California, especially Latino voters, has in part been attributed to "'mishandled' expenditures and management 'blunders.'" It has also been attributed to the claim that the California Republican Party is dominated at the grassroots level by conservatives (Jeffe 2001). As stated earlier, the Latino vote was a very important contributor to Gore's margin of victory in California, but it must be acknowledged that he received this support without any well-developed targeted efforts to secure their votes.

RACES FOR THE HOUSE OF REPRESENTATIVES

Nowhere in the context of the 2000 campaign did California have a greater opportunity to affect national outcomes, nor Latinos the chance to affect those California events, as in the races for the U.S. House of Representatives. The effects of demographic change in the electorate are manifest in California's U.S. House races.

Democratic hopes of recapturing the House of Representatives were premised on a good showing in California. Going into the fall election, Republicans held a 223-210-2 advantage in the House. Since the Independents split in alignment with the major parties, the Democrats needed a net gain of seven seats nationally to take control, one of which they were sure to get in the Thirty-first District of California (Representative Matthew Martinez's district).

All of the action in the California U.S. House races focused on these seven seats. The ultimate outcome in the Thirty-first District was ensured, given the absence of a Republican candidate in the general election. The important contest was in the Democratic primary, where state senator Hilda Solis defeated long-time incumbent Matthew Martinez. The seat was solidly Democratic, where the party held an astounding 31 percent registration advantage over the GOP, so no Republican candidates chose to enter the primary. Out of pique, Martinez changed his party and, in some instances, his floor-voting behavior.[2]

Of more interest were the six competitive seats. One of these was an open seat—vacated by Tom Campbell for his U.S. Senate run—in the South Bay/Silicon Valley area. Though Democrats hold a registration advantage in the Fifteenth District, Campbell—a moderate Republican—had won the seat in the past and many felt that the GOP could hold the seat with a good effort. It was not to be. Democrat Mike Honda defeated a well-funded Republican, Jim Cunneen, by 28,679 votes, or about 12.1 percent. This victory in a district held by Republicans was, at least in part, accomplished on the strength of Latino and Asian American voters, who are about 26 percent of the district. While overall district registration favored Democrats by about ten percentage points, among Latinos, the registration advantage was 45.6 percent. Though their numbers were not sufficient to have determined the outcome, Latinos undoubtedly contributed to Honda's victory margin.

In only one of the six closely contested seats was a Democrat the incumbent. Cal Dooley, a non-Hispanic white, represented the Twentieth District even though the district, in the primarily agricultural southern San Joaquin Valley, was drawn in the 1990 redistricting as a majority-minority district. The district is approximately 67 percent minority and 55 percent Latino. Not surprisingly, Democrats enjoy a substantial registration advantage. This race was interesting for two reasons. First, the Republican challenger was Rich Rodriguez, a well-known Latino television news anchor with considerable support from the party. His ethnicity put to test the question of whether race or partisanship predominates in minority vote choice. Second, both of the California Assembly members whose districts are nested within the Twentieth Congressional District, Sarah Reyes and Dean Florez, were to be "termed out" in 2002 or 2004 and would be looking for new opportunities. Latino political leaders, then, had to choose between supporting a Latino from the other party or an Anglo from their own party, while simultaneously figuring which would be easier to defeat in two or four years. In the end, the Latino political establishment closed ranks behind their copartisan and that, combined with a series of political gaffes by Rodriguez, secured Dooley's reelection (by less than 7 percent of the vote; for a fuller discussion of the race, see Michelson 2001). Especially given the presence of a Latino GOP nominee, the choices of Latino voters were clearly what drove the outcome.

In the remaining four contests, Republican incumbents faced substantial challenges from well-funded and/or experienced Democrats and, in the end, the GOP lost three of these four seats. The only seat that the GOP held was Steve Horn's, in the Thirty-eighth District, in the Long Beach area of south Los Angeles County. Democrats hold a sizable registration advantage, and the district has large Latino and gay populations. Despite these apparent advantages, Horn and the GOP managed to hold his seat by the narrowest of margins. Horn's opponent, Gerrie Schipske, a lesbian nurse-practitioner with little political experience, came within 1,800 votes of defeating this four-term incumbent with a huge funding advantage. Latino voting in the district has grown substantially (increasing by over 11,000 Latino registrants from 1998 to 2000).

Democrats did manage to take three seats away from GOP incumbents. In all three instances, the raw number of Latino registered voters increased significantly in the 1990s. In what was probably the closest watched race nationally, state senator Adam Schiff defeated incumbent Jim Rogan, in the Twenty-seventh District, which is located in the Glendale and Pasadena area of Los Angeles County. Rogan gained national visibility as a U.S. House "manager" in the impeachment trial of President Clinton. Latinos increased their share of the electorate from about 9.2 percent in 1994 to about 13.7 percent in 2000. That shift, and the loss of moderate support over the impeachment issue, combined to defeat the incumbent.

In the Thirty-sixth District, in the coastal areas of Los Angeles County south of Venice, former representative Jane Harman, who had vacated the seat two years earlier to run for governor, defeated incumbent Steve Kuykendall. Harman edged out Kuykendall in a very close race, with only about 1.7 percent of the votes separating them. Latinos represent about 10.4 percent of the voters in the district, but almost a third of them have registered in the last four years, dramatically improving Democratic chances in a district where, until recently, Republicans actually enjoyed a small registration advantage.

Finally, in the Forty-ninth District in coastal San Diego County, Democratic councilwoman Susan Davis defeated incumbent Brian Bilbray by a margin of about three percentage points. This is a moderately Republican district that the *California Journal* once described as having a minority population with little impact on election results. In recent years, however, the Latino share of the electorate climbed to 8.2 percent, more than one-quarter of which have registered since the 1996 elections.

The effect of California Latinos on Republican incumbents for the House of Representatives is summarized in table 8.1. The Democratic Party picked up five seats—admittedly Martinez's seat was no surprise—in California alone, nearly got one more in Long Beach, and beat back a significant challenge in the Central Valley. After the 1994 elections, in which the GOP took control of both the U.S. House of Representatives and the California Assembly, the California delegation to the U.S. House was twenty-six Democrats and twenty-six Republicans. In the intervening years, Democratic fortunes improved to the point that, as a result of the 2000 elections, the California delegation had thirty-three Democrats and nineteen Republicans. Growth in the Latino electorate and the strong Democratic preference of these new voters played a role in this strong performance.

After the election, the Republicans controlled the House of Representatives 221-212-2, a net Republican loss of two seats. Had the Democrats broken even elsewhere, California's results would have brought the Democrats within two seats of controlling the House.

Table 8.1   Registration and Results in U.S. House Races of Interest with GOP Incumbents, California 2000 General Election

Congressional District	Latino Share in 1994 (%)	Latino Share in 2000 (%)	2000 District Party Reg. D/R (%)	2000 Latino Party Reg. D/R (%)	Republican Share of the Vote, 1998 (%)	Republican Share of the Vote, 2000 (%)	Total Votes Cast, 2000	Democratic Margin of Victory (Defeat) 2000
15th	7.3	8.0	44.1 / 34.1	61.6 / 18.5	60.5	42.2	236,904	28,679
27th	9.2	13.7	43.9 / 37.4	59.8 / 23.5	50.7	43.9	215,774	19,190
36th	7.6	10.4	40.9 / 39.1	55.3 / 24.9	48.9	46.6	239,131	4,452
38th	12.3	20.6	51.8 / 30.7	63.2 / 18.7	52.9	48.5	180,122	(1,768)
49th	6.4	8.2	39.1 / 36.1	52.1 / 24.0	48.8	46.2	228,489	7,885

Sources: Authors' compilations based on minority registration data from the Statewide Database, Institute for Governmental Studies, University of California, Berkeley, and registration and election data from the official Statements of the Vote, Office of the Secretary of State, California.

The relatively poor performance of the party in the rest of the country, where the Democrats suffered a net loss of three seats, thwarted the achievement of their ultimate goal of retaking the House.

The State Legislature: The Institutionalization of Democratic Hegemony

While it is easy to look at changing Democratic fortunes in the California U.S. House elections and be impressed, those improvements pale in comparison with improved Democratic fortunes in the California legislature.

Some context here is appropriate. In 1994, California Republicans took control of the state assembly, by a slim and troublesome margin,[3] which they lost in 1996. The senate, too, was extremely close. Since 1994, the GOP has lost seats in both chambers of the state legislature in every election, including and especially 2000. Entering the 2000 electoral cycle, the partisan division was forty-six Democrats, thirty-two Republicans, one Green, and one vacant in the assembly, while in the senate it was twenty-five Democrats and fifteen Republicans. As a result of the 2000 elections, the Democrats enjoyed huge majorities in the legislature, controlling the assembly by a fifty to twenty-nine margin (with one Green Party member) and the senate twenty-six to fourteen margin.

As Democratic fortunes in the legislature have improved, so too have Latino fortunes. As a result of the 2000 elections, Latinos held twenty seats in the assembly (sixteen Democrat and four Republican) and seven more in the senate (all Democrat). By contrast, those numbers a decade ago were strikingly smaller. In 1990, only seven seats total were occupied by Latinos, three in the senate and four in the assembly, all Democrat.

These gains in Latino representation in the state legislature are in part driven by increased population concentration in specific districts. However, as the data in figure 8.3 demonstrate for the assembly, gains have been made in Latino representation from areas with overwhelming Latino concentration and in districts where Latinos are clearly not the largest ethnic grouping of voters. For example, of the twenty Latinos currently serving in the assembly, nine of them were elected from districts where Latinos were 40 percent or more of the registered voters. However, eight were elected from districts where Latinos were 20 to 39 percent of the registered voters in the district and another three were elected from areas where Latino voter registration was under 20 percent. Interestingly, of the four Republicans elected to the assembly, two were elected from districts where Latino voter registration was below 20 percent and two were elected from districts where it was between 20 to 39 percent. Stated differently, Latino increases in legislative representation have occurred in a range of districts. The largest and perhaps most stable base of Latino legislative representation is from districts where they are the plurality of the registered voters. However, they have also made considerable gains in districts where they are not the dominant group of registered voters. This pattern developed gradually throughout the 1990s and was displayed in full force in the 2000 elections.

It is important to note that the sixteen Democratic Latinos in the assembly and the seven in the senate make influential blocks of votes for party leadership positions. The sixteen Latino Democrats comprise 32 percent of the Democratic voter power in the assembly.

Figure 8.3   Latino Registration and Representation in Assembly Districts, 1992–2000

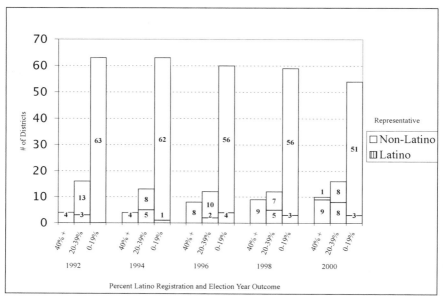

They, of course, could be outvoted by fellow Democrats. It is clear, however, that they, to the extent that they vote as a block, are major players in any party vote. Similarly, the seven Latinos in the state senate comprise 28 percent of the Democrat voting power in this body.

The gains to both Democratic and Latino fortunes in both houses of the state legislature served both groups in the redistricting that occurred in 2001. For the first time since 1981, redistricting was in the hands of the Democratic Party. By contrast, the redrawing of district lines in 1991 was left to judicially appointed special masters, whose work was necessitated by the inability of the Democratic legislature and then-governor Pete Wilson (R) to come to agreement.

Redistricting was not necessarily without adverse implications for Latinos. The potential for conflict between the Latino Caucus and the Democratic leadership existed on three issues. First, safeguarding existing Democratic incumbents could thwart the desire to increase the number of Latino seats. In one instance, a white Democrat representing an area with a large and fast-growing Latino electorate was appointed to a leadership position in the redistricting effort, all but guaranteeing that this area will not be redrawn to elect a Latino. Second, the growth of Latino populations in what had been African American areas raised the stakes in redistricting and created the potential for interethnic competition and ill feelings. Third, maximizing Democratic seat share is not the same as maximizing Latino seat share. That is, high concentrations of Latino voters can be used to bolster existing Democratic districts or make others more competitive without necessarily enhancing the chance that a Latino candidate wins the seat.

Interestingly, the redistricting process that occurred was one of the most noncontroversial in California history. The legislature developed a plan after extensive public hearings that served to protect incumbents. Both Democrats and Republicans voted in favor of districting changes, perhaps out of incumbent self-interest. Twenty-three of the twenty-six Latino state legislators voted for the measure including all Latinos in the senate. The number of Latino seats might increase marginally, but this was not a major concern of the Latino Caucus. Governor Davis signed the plan on September 27, 2001.

The Mexican American Legal Defense and Education Fund (MALDEF) filed suit on behalf of Latino voters residing in two proposed congressional districts and one senate district alleging a violation of the equal protection clause of the Fourteenth Amendment and a violation of section 2 of the Voting Rights Act (*Cano v. Davis* 2002). It is interesting that MALDEF would pursue this case given the overwhelming support the Latino Caucus gave to the redistricting plan. MALDEF argued that it understood its goals as simply maximizing the representation of Latino voters and that the current plan did not serve Latino voters in the districts in question. MALDEF also questioned that among the primary advisors in the redistricting process was Michael Berman, a long-time participant in California redistricting and brother to Representative Howard Berman (D-Los Angeles), whose district was itself in question. MALDEF claimed that Latino voters were removed from Berman's district to make it unlikely that he could be seriously challenged by a Latino in a Democratic primary. After an extensive oral hearing, the court decided on June 12, 2002, to grant in full defendants' and defendants-intervenors' motions for summary judgment.

In the end, the redistricting process in California maintained its noncontroversial status. With the defeat of MALDEF's suit, Latino voters still maintain considerable representation in the U.S. Congress and in the state senate and assembly. Whether this representation influence will lead to policy gains at the state level is beyond the scope of this chapter. It is certainly reasonable to expect that this representational clout can be used to benefit Latinos all across the state.

LATINOS AND THE FUTURE OF CALIFORNIA POLITICS

Our analysis of the role of Latinos in the 2000 elections allows us to reach several conclusions. First, it is clear that California is key to any Democratic presidential victory. It is hard to fashion a viable national Democratic plan that is not built on a foundation of the fifty-five California electoral votes. Relatedly, the likelihood that the Democratic Party can be the majority in the House of Representatives is very dependent on Democratic legislators coming from California. The Democratic Party, therefore, has every incentive to maintain its support in this state. Most importantly, the Republican

Party has an equal incentive to try to limit this Democratic support. Since more Latinos live in California than any other state, Latino interests should be served by the bipartisan focus on the national strategic importance of the state. Second, our analysis demonstrates that the Latino vote is an increasingly important contributor to Democratic margins of victory in close elections. This Latino statewide influence, however, is still entirely dependent on a potentially competing white block vote in opposition to Latino preferences. Herein lies the lesson in our first two conclusions. It is reasonable to expect that California will be an increasingly Democratic state. To the extent that this occurs, however, if the Republican Party does not actively compete for the Latino vote, Democratic Latino voters are at the risk of being increasingly taken for granted by the Democratic Party and its candidates. Latino influence in affecting statewide elections in California is unquestioned. Whether Latinos will benefit from this influence is much less clear.

A third conclusion we draw from our analysis is that Latino influence in the state legislature is clear, growing, and demonstrating a level of political sophistication that was unimaginable just ten years ago. The numbers of Latinos, both Democrats and Republicans, have risen to unprecedented levels in the assembly. In the senate, Latino influence is impressive. Is this influence likely to lead to considerable policy gain? One scenario suggests that it will do so, although perhaps not immediately. Despite term limits, as Latino representatives become more and more sophisticated in the policy process, and especially as institutional memory grows in legislative staff including those staff of the Latino Caucus, the chances of state policy reflecting Latino interests and needs should be greater. An alternative scenario interprets the likelihood of Latino policy benefit similar to the caveat noted earlier. Although the assembly and senate may be dominated by the Democratic Party, it is possible that a Democratic governor, as exemplified by former governor Gray Davis, would be overwhelmingly concerned with not pursuing policies that are perceived as "too" beneficial to Latinos and thus risk alienating a sufficient number of white voters to make a statewide official vulnerable; a Republican governor, such as Arnold Schwarzenegger, would be even less concerned since Latinos make up such a small share of the Republican electorate. Democratic domination of the legislative process, in other words, is not inevitably one that will consistently serve Latino interests. Clearly, how distinctly Latino interests are articulated from those of California generally, and how Latino leaders choose to package Latino interests, will affect how supportive any Democratic governor will be.

Finally, at no time in the history of the state have Latinos been better positioned to institutionalize their electoral, representational, and policy influence. Institutionalizing such influence does not, however, provide guidance as to how to address the complex realities facing many Latinos in California today. Issues such as school reform, immigration, the resource deficiencies caused by the legacy of Proposition 13, and the boom-bust cycles of the California economy require conceptualization and analysis that go far beyond traditional identity politics. At least we know that Latino interests are very likely to be articulated in the halls of governance in California. Much less clear is what the substance of those interests is and how they can be addressed by public policy. Perhaps this is the greatest lesson that Latinos' unquestioned influence in affecting California elections in 2000 provides.

NOTES

1. One seat—held by Representative Matthew Martinez—became a GOP seat because Martinez had been defeated for Democratic renomination; in a fit of pique, he switched parties. Given the absence of a Republican nominee in the general election, the outcome of that seat—a switch back to the Democrats—was not in doubt.

2. David Lublin (2001) demonstrates that Martinez's voting record also changed, specifically with regard to his support for gay and lesbian rights, which dropped precipitously after the party switch.

3. The close division of the lower house in early 1995 led to a variety of highly visible political shenanigans, including one Republican moderate refusing to vote for his own party's leader, and two Republican members—one of which was later defeated in a recall election and the other in the next general election—serving as speaker by virtue of Democratic votes. Though they achieved majority status in November 1994, the GOP never fully gained operational control of the assembly.

9

"Pues, At Least We Had Hillary"

Latino New York City, the 2000 Elections, and the Limits of Party Loyalty

ANGELO FALCÓN

DURING THE 2000 PRESIDENTIAL ELECTION, LATINO VOTERS RECEIVED unprecedented attention from the major candidates. This attention, however, was not distributed equally throughout the country. Instead, the candidates followed what could be called a "Latino southern strategy" that focused on Mexican Americans and Cuban Americans in the Southwest and Southeast, respectively. For Puerto Ricans, Dominicans, and other Latinos in the Northeast and Midwest, it was business as usual as far as the national political parties were concerned. In New York, in particular, Latinos are largely outsiders to the Democratic Party, despite their consistent loyalty to it; in 2000, they were once again ignored by the Democrats. Republicans also followed their historic pattern of writing them off. Focusing on New York City, where Latinos outnumber all racial and ethnic groups except non-Hispanic whites, this chapter will explore this inattentiveness (see table 9.1). Specifically, I ask how the 2000 campaign played itself out in New York and what roles did the Latinos play in the election's outcome.

The study of presidential elections largely occurs at an abstract

Table 9.1   Racial and Ethnic Composition of New York City, 2000

	Population	%
Latinos	2,160,554	27.0
Blacks	1,962,154	24.5
Asians	783,058	9.7
American Indian	17,321	0.2
White	2,801,267	36.0
Other Race	58,775	0.7
Multiracial	225,149	2.8
Total	8,008,278	

Source: Author's compilation.

level of analysis. How these elections, which elevate the level of political participation in the country significantly every four years, are linked to local politics is largely overlooked, however. Presidential elections, in other words, represent a rare moment when national political elites and parties are forced to develop strategies for dealing (or not dealing) with local political elites and parties. These elections present a rare opportunity to look at the nature of the local Latino politics largely missed by mainstream political science. While the bottom line of whether or not the Latino vote influenced the outcome of the presidential election is important, it is also important to use these unique elections to see how national politics is shaped by city and neighborhood Latino politics (de la Garza, Menchaca, and DeSipio 1994). This is a major focus of this chapter.

LATINO POLITICS IN NEW YORK CITY

Over the last decade, Latino politics in New York City went from what could be described as an "access" to a "postaccess" stage. Until the 1990s' round of redistricting, the main concern of Latinos in the political arena was the issue of underrepresentation. In the last ten years, Latino representation in elected public office has reached parity with its share of the electorate. Not only did Latinos elect officials at the local, state, and federal levels, but some achieved seniority in these positions. In the Bronx, which has the largest number of Latino elected officials among the city's five boroughs, Puerto Ricans occupied the positions of borough president (Fernando Ferrer) and chairman of the Bronx Democratic County Committee (Roberto Ramirez), positions Puerto Ricans continued to hold after these particular individuals moved on. Brooklyn and Manhattan also had Latino elected officials at these levels (except borough president); Queens and Staten Island did not (although the congressional seat held by Nydia Velazquez was mostly in Brooklyn, it also includes parts of Manhattan and Queens).

Two of the twenty-three Latino elected officials in office at the beginning of 2000 were Dominican Americans and the other twenty-one were Puerto Rican. Dominican inroads in electoral politics, despite their relatively recent arrival in large numbers in New York, were dramatic, but tied largely to their residential segregation in the Washington Heights area of Northern Manhattan. This representational pattern reflects the continuing dominance of Puerto Rican and Dominican voters that followed the city's Latino politics in the new century (Mollenkopf and Miranda 2002).

Because Puerto Ricans are the only group of Latinos to arrive in the United States already as U.S. citizens, they do not have to overcome the hurdles imposed by the lack of U.S. citizenship other Latino groups have to confront to become eligible to vote in New York. On the other hand, the high population concentration of Dominicans in Washington Heights compared to the residential pattern of other Latinos (including Puerto Ricans and Dominicans) in the rest of the city appears to be what accounts for the surprising rapidity of their ability to successfully elect their own to elected office in the city council and the state assembly, despite their high proportion of noncitizens.

There are several major demographic developments that were relevant to the role Latinos played in the 2000 elections. One was the census finding that, for the first time, the number of Puerto Ricans in the city had declined. In a phenomenon shared by four other cities in the Northeast and Midwest (Jersey City, Newark, and Patterson, New Jersey; and Chicago, Illinois), New York City's Puerto Rican population dropped dramatically in the 1990s by close to 110,000 (a 12.2 percent decline), with Puerto Ricans going from being 49 to 36 percent of the Latino population between 1990 and 2000 (Navarro 2000; Falcón 2001). Despite this, Puerto Ricans remained the largest Latino group in the city, and their political status is enhanced relative to the other groups because they are all citizens. The increased numbers of other Latino immigrants, however, combined with continuing increases in naturalization will no doubt accelerate the erosion of Puerto Rican preeminence. Indeed, because of continued immigration, low naturalization rates are perhaps for the first time an important obstacle to New York Latino political mobilization (Mollenkopf, Olson, and Ross 2001; Minnite, Holdaway, and Hayduk 1999; Minnite, Shapiro, and Fuchs 1997).

A second demographic factor is how transnational factors have also had an important role in redefining the city's politics in this period. The citizenship status of Puerto Ricans compared to other Latinos falls away here, as the "simultaneity" (to borrow from Graham 2001) of the New York and homeland politics becomes increasingly salient for non–Puerto Rican Latinos as well as for Puerto Ricans. The trend toward Latin American countries increasingly trying to develop closer ties with the diasporas has influenced how Latinos deal with elections in New York and in the homelands. Puerto Rican events, like the aftermath of President Bill Clinton's granting of clemency to eleven Puerto Rican "political prisoners" in 1998, the movement to remove the U.S. Navy from the island of Vieques, the short-lived campaign to grant the residents of Puerto Rico the right to vote for U.S. president, and the gubernatorial election in Puerto Rico all became issues during the 2000 elections in varying degrees. At the same time, major elections in the Dominican Republic, Colombia, and Mexico had homeland politicians reaching out to their compatriots in New York City and elsewhere in the United States, adding further political stimulus to these communities during the 2000 elections.

The third development is that since the mid-1980s New York City's population has become "majority minority" (Falcón 1988). The 2000 census revealed a city that was 65 percent Latino, black, and Asian. This demographic growth has not, however, translated automatically into more political power for these communities of color, despite the election of the first African American to the mayoralty in 1989 (David Dinkins) for one term. Instead, because of a number of factors such as age, citizenship status, and high poverty levels, this 65 percent of the population translated to perhaps only 40 percent of the electorate (Mollenkopf, Olson, and Ross 2001). Thus, despite having attained parity between the number of Latinos elected with the community's share of the total electorate, the consistent retention of major political positions (mayor, city council speaker, public advocate, and so on) by whites is indicative of a racial and ethnic disparity in political power that continues to contribute to the city's racial and ethnic political tensions.

Similar demographic changes in all of the largest U.S. cities have stimulated a potentially paradigmatic shift in urban political analysis. Historically, calls for going beyond a black and white perspective were often little more than rhetoric. With the new immigration, multiethnic coalitions in which minorities are the majority are now a fact of urban political life. This means that the notion of a minority-liberal white coalition, which until recently was viewed as the most effective minority urban political strategy (Browning, Marshall, and Tabb 1984), should be reassessed. Is such an approach superior to a pure minority coalition in cities where minorities constitute majorities? The need for this reassessment is especially relevant in the face of the increasing hostile critique by the Left (such as it exists) and the Right of "identity politics" in which Latinos, African Americans, and Asian Americans still engage. In short, the New Democrat formulation of a more centrist liberal politics or what some would call a "postliberal" politics that downplays ethnicity on the assumption that racial and ethnic minorities have no place else to go beyond the Democrats has made the minority-liberal white coalition strategy increasingly suspect within African American, Latino, and Asian American communities.

Moreover, issues such as police brutality in black and Latino communities illustrate the extent to which local politics remain racialized. The police killings of Patrick Dourismand and Amadou Diallo in New York City, among others, became issues that spoke directly to the terms by which New York's racial and ethnic changes were being played out in political and policy realms. Other issues, like the reform of bilingual education and educational access and the police response to the Central Park rampage against women following the National Puerto Rican Parade also conditioned Latino participation in 2000.

This is the context in which the 2000 elections played themselves out in New York City. The city is dominated by the Democratic Party with an electorate overwhelmingly registered as Democrats and most elected officials are of this party. Since 1992, however, the mayor has been Republican, indicating that Democratic dominance is not absolute and that political outcomes can be determined by more than party affiliation, especially in this age of the candidate-centered campaign. With so many of the city's political institutions being controlled by one party, however, the result is all too often in a type of, to borrow pundit William Stern's term, "commercial politics" devoid of serious issues beyond patronage and lacking in political vision.

THE 2000 CAMPAIGN

The March 7 Super Tuesday primaries included both the electoral vote-rich states of California and New York and twelve states with Republican primaries and sixteen with Democratic contests. In New York, Al Gore beat challenger Bill Bradley by a two-to-one margin. With Gore having the support of every major Latino elected official in the city, Bradley had little support among Latino voters. When he spoke to issues of interest to Latinos, he chose to do so largely in African American venues (highlighted in the media by a February 7 visit to a black church in Queens and the February 22 debate with Gore in Harlem's Apollo Theater). Bradley dropped out of the presidential race altogether only two days after Super Tuesday.

In the Republican primary, George W. Bush easily beat John McCain in New York City, getting sixty-nine to McCain's twenty-four delegates. For McCain, New York was an uphill battle from the start since he had to take the state's GOP to court to allow him to appear on the ballot in all the state's counties. Both candidates, however, focused their efforts on the California primary because of the greater number of electoral votes it represented and because, compared to Democratic-dominated New York, it was a state that was seen as being more in play politically for Republicans. Since Bush basically ceded New York to Gore, the focus of efforts to mobilize voters in the city was the more hotly contested U.S. Senate race.

In November 2000, Gore won the popular vote in New York City over Bush by the margin of 78 percent to 18 percent, with Ralph Nader trailing with only 3 percent and Pat Buchanan with less than 1 percent. Among Latino voters in New York City, Gore received 89.8 percent of the vote, compared to 95.1 percent of blacks,

Table 9.2   Presidential Vote in New York City, by Race and Ethnicity, 2000 (%)

	Latino	Black	Asian American	White
Gore	89.8	95.1	72.9	66.0
Bush	8.1	3.4	22.6	20.9
Nader	1.6	1.1	4.1	4.6
Buchanan	0.1	0.1	0.2	0.2

Note: Column totals do not add up to 100 percent because of the estimating technique.
Source: Author's calculations (see note 1).

72.9 percent of Asian Americans, and 66.0 percent of whites (see table 9.2). Latinos in New York City, therefore, continued to follow the pattern of giving most of their vote to the Democratic candidate for president: 78 percent for Michael Dukakis in 1988; 77 percent for Bill Clinton in 1992 and 90 percent in 1996 (Falcón 1992, 1996, 1999) (see table 9.3).

Latinos turned out at a rate considerably lower than all other groups, except for Asian Americans (see table 9.4). Approximately 28 percent of Latino registered voters turned out to vote compared to a citywide average of 38 percent. Blacks in New York saw the highest turnout rates, at 40 percent.

The Latino and black votes at the citywide level were distinctive from the white and Asian American votes. Disaggregating the vote at the neighborhood level reveals that the Latino vote was consistently high with some variation. Gore received less than 85 percent of the vote in only six of thirty Latino neighborhoods, and 90 percent or higher in fourteen.[1] Puerto Rican and Dominican neighborhoods were the most supportive of Gore, and the Latino neighborhoods of Queens, which are predominantly Central and South American, were the least supportive (but still significantly more

Table 9.3   Latino Vote for Presidential Candidates in New York City, 1988–2000 (%)

	Democrat	Republican	Other
1988	78	20	2
1992	77	20	3
1996	90	7	3
2000	90	8	2

Sources: Falcón (1992, 1996, 1999); author's calculations.

Table 9.4   Turnout and Roll-off Rates in New York City, by Race and Ethnic Group, 2000 (%)

	Voter Turnout	Presidential Blank Votes	Senatorial Blank Votes	Difference (Sen. — Pres.)
Latino	28.3	6.1	5.5	−0.6
Asian	18.7	3.6	5.4	1.8
Black	40.4	3.9	3.6	−0.3
White	32.3	3.2	3.9	0.7
Total	37.6	3.9	4.2	0.3

Source: Author's calculations based on Voter Registrar data.

supportive than the citywide white vote). In western Brooklyn, the predominately Puerto Rican neighborhoods of Sunset Park and Lower Park Slope also exhibited lower levels of support for the Democratic candidate, probably influenced by a more conservative home owner population and, in the case of Lower Park Slope, a significant white progressive population that gave Nader support.

Each of these neighborhoods is organized differently in terms of political party influences and machineries, some determined by the county-level organization, others by distinctive local power structures. Nonetheless, when looking at voting by political party, these same patterns hold up, except for the significant vote that the Working Families Party received in Manhattan's largely Puerto Rican section of the Chelsea neighborhood. Unfortunately, we know very little about the reason for these distinct electoral outcomes despite the fact that this is probably the most useful unit of analysis to use in developing concrete strategies for Latino voter mobilization.

The U.S. Senate Campaign

The First Lady, Hillary Rodham Clinton, won the historic race for U.S. Senate with a surprisingly large lead in New York City where she beat Long Island Republican Rick Lazio by a margin of 73.6 to 25.3 percent. Among Latinos in the city, Clinton attracted 91.4 percent of the vote, compared to 96.0 percent of blacks, 72.9 percent of Asian Americans, and 55.9 percent of whites. Clinton did slightly better than Vice President Gore among blacks and Latinos and the same among Asian Americans and worse among whites.

The U.S. Senate race to replace the retiring Daniel Patrick Moynihan occurred in a number of phases. First was the New York state Democratic Party's leadership decision to seek out the First Lady as a candidate and her accepting the challenge. Second was the short-lived campaign between the First Lady and then–New York mayor Rudy Giuliani. Third was Guiliani's dropping out of the campaign and being replaced as the Republican standard-bearer by Long Island congressman Rick Lazio. Fourth was the Clinton-Lazio campaign resulting in Clinton's victory.

While Clinton and Lazio had distinct positions on many issues, the driving force behind much of the campaign was the First Lady's celebrity status and connection to the Clinton White House, with all the political perks and baggage that brought with it (Harpaz 2001; Noonan 2000; Olson 1999). For Latinos, Clinton's political credentials made the choice easy, especially given Lazio's poor efforts to reach out to Latino voters, which consisted mainly of photo-op visits to Latino neighborhoods like El Barrio and marching in parades; his 1996 congressional vote to make English the official language was not very helpful (Archibold 2000).

The U.S. Senate race was interesting from a Latino (and black) perspective because the First Lady benefited from her connection to President Clinton's policies. For white voters and Asian Americans, on the other hand, this connection was problematic. In late 1999, President Clinton granted clemency to eleven Puerto Rican *independentistas*, who had spent disproportionately long terms in federal prisons on charges of sedition against the United States. This was a highly controversial decision that some speculated was rooted in efforts to help Hillary Rodham Clinton with Puerto Rican voters. To allay this charge, she criticized her husband's decision to grant them clemency, which she had initially supported, angering local Puerto Rican elected officials who had supported her campaign. South Bronx congressman José Serrano publicly denounced the First Lady and threatened to withdraw his support of her, while all major Puerto Rican elected officials held a news conference to criticize her. Eventually, however, they all wound up supporting her candidacy.

Another important issue to Puerto Rican voters was the campaign to remove the U.S. Navy from the island of Vieques (Waldman 2000; Pérez Viera 2002). While President Clinton had negotiated a

deal that would have the navy leave by 2003 depending on the results of a referendum to be held among its residents, Puerto Rican
leaders demanded the immediate removal of the navy. Hillary Rodham Clinton, critical of her husband's position on this issue,
charged that the navy should leave immediately. This, along with
efforts to hire Latinos on her staff, allowed her to mend fences with
Puerto Rican politicians angry at her for her opposition to her husband's granting of clemency for the Puerto Rican independentistas.
Lazio, on the other hand, initially supported President Clinton's position and, as the campaign closed, supported Hillary Rodham Clinton's position.

Vieques attained national significance. Only a few days before
the election, a group of twelve activists were arrested for protesting
at the Statue of Liberty against the navy's presence in Vieques. New
York governor George Pataki also took on the Vieques issue as part
of a strategy to reach out to Latino voters locally while, ironically,
national Republican leaders were critical of Puerto Rican demands
for the naval withdrawal. In view of how uninterested non-Cuban
Latinos across the country were in the Elián Gonzalez issue, it was
uncertain how this purely Puerto Rican issue would play politically
with other Latino groups. Politicians like Pataki and Clinton correctly concluded that it would be important to them.

The nature of New York City's electorate, and the city's increasing political clout in the state, forced the candidates to try to
distance themselves from their respective national tickets, which
was especially the case with the Lazio campaign that at one point
tried to go as far as, to quote his staff, "forge a Gore-Lazio alliance"
in the minds of voters (Hardt and Birnbaum 2000).

At the Latino neighborhood level, the senatorial vote followed
the pattern of the presidential vote. Lazio did best (though still not
very well) in the Central and South American sections of the
Queens neighborhood of Elmhurst and the Puerto Rican sections of
Ridgewood. In Brooklyn, Lazio did best in the Lower Park Slope and
Sunset Park areas, while in the Bronx he did best in the largely
Puerto Rican sections of Belmont, Parkchester, and Soundview-
Castle Hill. In East Harlem, which he visited most frequently, he
only received 4.9 percent of the vote. In terms of party voting, the
Working Families Party, which endorsed Hillary Rodham Clinton,
received its greatest support in the Latino sections of the Brooklyn

neighborhoods of Bedford-Stuyvesant and Lower Park Slope and the Manhattan neighborhood of Chelsea.

The U.S. Senate race received as much, if not more, attention from the media and public for reasons already discussed. One indication of this was the very little roll-off in the vote between president and the U.S. Senate. "Roll-off," also known as the "drop-off" in the vote, occurs between higher and lower offices in an election in which voters leave their ballots blank for a particular office, with the usual pattern being that people vote more for higher rather than lower offices. In New York state, the roll-off can be measured by looking at the category of blank, mutilated, or voided votes. The percentage of blank votes increased only slightly from 3.9 to 4.2 percent between the presidential and U.S. Senate votes in New York City (see table 9.4). This was the same pattern among white voters (from 3.2 to 3.9 percent) and Asian American voters (3.6 to 5.4 percent). Among Latino and black voters, however, the pattern was surprisingly reversed: for Latinos it went from 6.1 to 5.5 percent, and for blacks from 3.9 to 3.6 percent. In other words, more Latinos and African Americans voted in the U.S. Senate race than in the presidential race. This could be a good indicator of the more intense mobilization of black and Latino voters that occurred in the U.S. Senate race, especially by labor. It is also interesting that the percentage of blank votes among Latino and Asian American voters was significantly higher than that among whites and blacks, perhaps indicating less mobilization of these voters and/or less interest in or information about the election.

THE ROLE OF LOCAL LATINO POLITICS

As a largely Democratic Party city, the local primaries determine, for the most part, the results of local general elections. They also, of course, indicate the strengths of different sectors within the political parties. This provides, in turn, important information about the nature of Latino politics.

The Latino population in New York City is spread throughout its five boroughs (counties) and within each borough among over twenty-one neighborhoods and another thirty-three subneighborhood areas (Hanson-Sánchez 1996: 7–8). In contrast to most other major cities where the Latino population is concentrated in a relatively small number of areas, in New York it is much more dispersed and politically complex.

The center of Latino politics in New York City is the south Bronx. The Bronx is a borough where the Puerto Rican community has been able to achieve a major influence with the election of Fernando Ferrer to the borough presidency in 1987 and of Roberto Ramirez as chair of the Bronx Democratic Committee in 1994. It is the only borough where Latinos are close to half the population (48.4 percent in 2000) and it is the only borough to have had a Puerto Rican as its president (Ferrer was elected in 1987 and Herman Badillo in 1965). It is also one of the two boroughs with a Puerto Rican sitting as a U.S. representative, with José Serrano currently occupying this post that was once also held by Badillo and Robert Garcia.

Queens, the borough with the second largest number of Latinos, is the most ethnically diverse with Puerto Ricans in the minority and Colombians, Dominicans, and Ecuadorians being the largest Latino communities. Although making up 25 percent of the population, Latinos up to 2000 had not elected one of their own to any major political post in this borough.

Brooklyn has the third largest number of Latinos, who make up 19.3 percent of its population. In 2000, this borough had elected Latinos, all Puerto Ricans, to all three levels of government. The second Puerto Rican congressperson in the city is from Brooklyn, Nydia Velazquez, who was the first Puerto Rican women elected to Congress (her district also includes Manhattan's Lower East Side and a small part of Queens). Because of the dispersed pattern of Latino settlement in Brooklyn, however, Latinos in this borough have not been able to achieve the degree of influence in its Democratic Party organization that is the case in the Bronx.

The fourth largest Latino borough, Manhattan, is 27.2 percent Latino. Like Brooklyn, Manhattan has elected Latinos to all levels of government. However, unlike the other boroughs, the Latino population is not concentrated in contiguous neighborhoods. Instead, they cluster in three major areas in different parts of the borough. The largest is Northern Manhattan/Washington Heights, which is overwhelmingly Dominican. Next is East Harlem, also known as El Barrio, which is on the other side of black Harlem of Washington Heights. El Barrio has been going through major demographic changes with a rapidly growing Mexican population, although in 2000 the census still found that Puerto Ricans made up 55 percent of its population. The third cluster is the Lower East Side, also known as Loisaida, which has undergone major gentrification over the last decade and has lost much of its original Latino population.

The smallest Latino population is found on the borough of Staten Island, also known as Richmond. Along with Queens, this has been one of the boroughs with the largest Latino population growth in the 1990s, with Latinos now making up 12.1 percent of the population clustered on its northern coast. This is the borough with the strongest Republican Party presence, and it is also the most isolated of the five boroughs. The Latino population of Staten Island is the newest and smallest and has yet to elect one of its own to any political office.

During the 2000 election season, much local political discussion focused on the 2001 mayoral race, since Mayor Giuliani had been term limited. Despite the racial and ethnic makeup of the city, there were no potential black candidates emerging, save for the controversial Reverend Al Sharpton. In the Latino community, Bronx borough president Ferrer, who is Puerto Rican, had been preparing for this race for some time. In the 1997 elections, he threw his hat in the ring but dropped out unexpectedly. Ferrer himself was "termed out" of office in 2001, so he was definitely interested in running for mayor in 2001. With the control that his lieutenant, state assemblyman Roberto Ramirez, had as chair of the Bronx Democratic Committee, Ferrer had the political machinery to launch a credible campaign for mayor. Television personality Geraldo Rivera, who is also Puerto Rican, flirted as well with the idea of running for mayor, but dropped the idea once he realized it would compromise his journalistic career.

In 2000, the big question for Ferrer was whether the Bronx Democratic machine could deliver electorally. Ramirez, in preparation for 2001, had been aggressively reaching out to black politicians in anticipation of the development of a black-Latino coalition effort in a future mayoral campaign. His most controversial move in this regard was his withdrawal of support for a party incumbent, twelve-year Bronx congressman Elliot Engel, a white, to support state senator Larry Seabrook, a black, against Engel in the Democratic primary.

Even *salsero* Willie Colon, who had in the past run against Engel, supported him this time around against his bigger political opponents: the Ferrer-Ramirez machine.

As 2000 came to a close, the Ferrer-Ramirez political machine was weakened at the local level by losing four important local primary races, but maintained its legitimacy with state and national Democratic Party players, such as the nearly deposed Sheldon Silver, state assembly speaker, and the newly elected Senator Clinton, both of whom received Ramirez's support. Locally, the reelections of Congressman Engel and former state senator Pedro Espada (who was under indictment when he ran) stood, along with the other two losers in the state senate races that he backed, as reminders of the Bronx machine's vulnerability. Engels won with a relatively close 49 to 42 percent lead. But, despite all this it was not clear what this would mean politically for the resilient "Bronx Boys."

In the rest of the Latino community, 2000 largely represented the status quo politically. Manhattan and Brooklyn largely retained its cadre of elected officials, while Queens and Staten Island continued to have no Latino elected officials. In Manhattan's El Barrio, former city Councilmember Adam Clayton Powell unseated incumbent state assemblyman Nelson Denis, thus returning a legendary political name back into the mix of both black and Latino politics. In Brooklyn, Congresswoman Velazquez was convincingly reelected despite her congressional district having been reconfigured in 1998 as a result of a successful lawsuit (*Diaz v. Silver*) challenging its constitutionality.

In 2000, the nonpartisan New York Immigration Coalition and others began to systematically mobilize immigrants as a voting block. In Brooklyn, there was a high-profile race in which Congressman Major Owens was challenged by a protégé, term-limited city councilmember Una Clarke, a native of Jamaica. This was a brutal campaign among former friends whose significance laid in the growing immigrant consciousness in the black community as Clarke claimed that Owens was out of touch with his largely black immigrant constituency. Owens was reelected in a close election but, for both blacks and Latinos, this race pointed to the potential new salience of the immigrant factor in the city's politics, as well as the new pressures on term-limited officials to seek alternative elective opportunities.

CONCLUSION

The electoral behemoth known as the presidential election blows across the country every four years and, in its wake, leaves both devastation and innovation. While the bulk of mainstream political science views these elections from largely national or state-based perspectives, a real challenge remains in exploring how they interact with more local politics (a good example is Maisel 2002).

New York was largely bypassed by both major parties in their presidential campaigns because they saw the outcome as fixed. The Republicans under Bush finally targeted Latinos via a Latino southern strategy that put their resources largely behind mobilizing Mexican American and Cuban American voters, while ceding Puerto Ricans and other Latinos in the Northeast and Midwest to the Democrats. As the campaign developed, some of this changed, with some states in the Midwest becoming more important in the Republican campaign. The Democrats continued to take the Latino vote for granted in New York, convinced it had nowhere else to go.

This created an electoral vacuum in New York City that was filled by the U.S. Senate race. This hotly contested and nationally high-profile campaign went beyond being a mere extension of the presidential election at the local level. Both the First Lady and her Republican opponent had to distance themselves at various points from their national counterparts and develop locally responsive campaigns. The Clinton campaign took positions in its early stages that aroused the public anger of Latino politicians but which eventually got her campaign more linked with the network of Latino elected officials. Clinton, in essence, backed her way into the Latino community. The Lazio campaign followed the Bush lead in talking about the importance of the Latino vote, but found that his party had done little to work in this community and that his campaign's positions on issues (which were not very numerous) did not resonate well among Latinos. The campaign centered on the character of Clinton and her carpetbagger status, neither of which was important to Latinos.

The New York state Democratic and Republican Parties were out of touch with the Latino voter. The Democratic Party's main connection to Latinos was through its secretary, Dennis Rivera, the head of the powerful Local 1199 union, and through Roberto

Ramirez, the chair of the Bronx Democratic Committee. Besides the fact that both of these actors have interests that compete with a purely Latino agenda, at various points their role was largely marginal to other party interests. The Republican Party, on the other hand, is barely present in New York City (outside of Staten Island) and exists exclusively as a label for candidate-centered campaigns. Institutionally, it had no interest in reaching out to Latinos, doing so only when its candidates decided it was a priority, as this began to be the case with Governor Pataki in 2000 as he prepared for his 2002 reelection bid. Third parties, like the Liberal Party, the Conservative Party, the Right to Life Party, the Working Family Party, the Green Party, the Independence Party, and others have not been able to connect in significant ways to Latino voters.

The political center of the Latino community in New York City, the Ferrer-Ramirez machine of the Bronx Democratic Committee, was strengthened by its broker role with the state and national Democratic Party organizations in relation to the city's Latino voters. In anticipation of the need for a strong black-Latino coalition in the 2001 mayoral election in support of Ferrer, the Ferrer-Ramirez machine made a number of endorsements that backfired. It also was not able to defeat political rivals for power within the Latino community. Despite these losses, the Bronx Boys delivered for both Gore and Hillary Rodham Clinton, although it is doubtful that their contributions were all that important in this regard given the long-term Latino voter loyalty to the Democrats. However, they were able to capitalize on the newfound recognition of the importance of the Latino vote among the major parties and their local political weaknesses were offset as a result. Being the token Latino players in the state and national Democratic structures was sufficient to overcome their apparent inability to adequately mobilize Latino voters on their own behalf in 2000. Thus, a weak Latino political infrastructure was buttressed by a state and national Democratic Party apparatus that was largely inattentive to Latinos.

This created a situation in which the larger Democratic Party structures propped up a local Latino political machine. This was the case for a number of reasons, including the larger party structures' need to display some connection to the Latino electorate. The role that the Ferrer-Ramirez machine played because it represented the largest number of Latino elected officials made it the center of Latino party politics in the city, giving it a greater representational role than it deserved from the standpoint of the number of Latino voters it represented. The large Brooklyn, Queens, and Manhattan Latino communities had their political agendas filtered through the Bronx Boys apparatus, at times creating tensions and disproportionately concentrating patronage and other political dividends in one borough at the expense of the rest of the city's Latino community. This concentration would prove critical to an eventual run for mayor in 2001 by Ferrer, but would reinforce the uneven political development of the Latino community in the city.

By propping up this group of largely marginal Puerto Rican politicians, who were experiencing internal challenges and displayed continual problems of fragmentation, the state and national Democratic Party organizations maintained the Latino vote in a marginal position within its ranks. With Rivera's Local 1199 as the other major mechanism to reach Latino voters, the Democratic Party could play one against the other. However, whether this strategy would continue to work in the future as the Latino population continued to grow is not at all ensured with the possibility that the Democrats could be legitimating a potentially aggrieved group of Latino politicians if they continued to treat them as very junior partners, while largely ignoring Latino politicians outside of the Bronx.

At the same time, this arrangement advantages Puerto Ricans over other Latino groups in Democratic Party politics in New York City. Over 90 percent of the twenty-three Latino elected officials in the city at the boroughwide, city, state, and federal levels are Puerto Rican. However, as the composition of the city's Latino population changes, making Puerto Ricans a smaller portion of the total despite remaining the largest Latino subgroup, the Puerto Rican leadership will be under increasing pressure to incorporate the other groups.

The Dominican political ascendancy of the past decade did not have to confront the Puerto Rican political block because it was so centered in one geographic area: the Washington Heights area of Manhattan. The concentration of Central and South Americans in Queens, which, because of their citizenship status and relative recency of arrival, have been unable to elect one of their own or make inroads into the Queens Democratic organization. This has also kept these groups from having to confront the Puerto Rican leadership in a serious way. As the Dominican population continues to grow and disperse throughout the city, and the Central and South American population begins to mount more serious challenges in Queens, however, their relationship to the Puerto Rican leadership will change. The dramatically growing Mexican American population is another factor in this equation of inter-Latino group relations, especially in Manhattan, that will add to the pressure on the Puerto Rican leadership to incorporate them. There may be other paths of political development for these groups that may not directly involve Puerto Ricans, but these have not emerged as yet.

Despite the open nature of these Latino intergroup relations and the fact that they have been relatively conflict-free, scholarly commentary on the subject has been rather superficial, ahistorical, and exaggerated. John Mollenkopf, David Olson, and Timothy Ross, in their otherwise useful comparison of immigrant political participation in Los Angeles and New York, conclude, for example, that "established native minority politicians are quite unlikely to promote political mobilization of immigrant groups. Nor are they likely to support bids for elective office by emerging leaders from those groups, even from those from racially or ethnically related immigrant groups" (2001: 44). In an analysis of Central and South American politics in Queens that is misleadingly cast as a book on Latino politics in New York City, Michael Jones-Correa (1998) takes a decidedly uninformed, hostile, and cynical tone toward Puerto Rican relations with other Latinos. He refers to "considerable tensions among the various Latino groups" in New York City and to the relationship between Puerto Ricans and Dominicans as "particularly edgy" (114–116). These types of comments certainly are not based on any examination of the evolving Latino intergroup history of New York, nor do they acknowledge the fluidity of these relations (Flores 2000; Laó-Montes and Dávila 2001). Rather, they appear to be based on the behavior of a relatively small number of Latino political elites whose politics are, despite some low-level ethnic posturing, much more malleable in practice.

The presidential candidates' strategies of, for all intents and purposes, bypassing New York can only reinforce the alienation among the state's Latinos. The local high-profile U.S. Senate race reinforced the notion that the state parties viewed Latinos in the same way. These circumstances resulted in a state of continued uneven Latino political development in New York City tenuously centered in the

Ferrer-Ramirez Democratic machine in the south Bronx. As the Latino population continues to grow and become increasingly diverse, it is not at all clear what this all portends for the future of New York City politics. In the end, however, we could say about the 2000 elections in New York that, *pues*, at least we had Hillary.

NOTE

1. The voting preferences and levels of the various racial and ethnic groups reported in this chapter were calculated by analyzing those election districts that were 60 percent or greater of a particular group. This ecological approach has yielded results over time that have been consistent with polls, although its does have its limitations. Where it appears to accurately reflect a group's vote, reference is made to the group; where it may not because the sample is small, reference is made to the geographic area dominated by the group. For a discussion about the limitations of this approach, see King (1997).

1 0

Battleground Florida

KEVIN A. HILL and DARIO MORENO

〜〜〜〜〜〜〜〜〜〜〜〜〜〜〜〜〜〜〜〜〜〜〜〜〜〜〜〜〜〜〜〜〜〜

THE 2000 PRESIDENTIAL ELECTION IN FLORIDA WAS THE CLOSEST AND most controversial in the state's history. Governor George W. Bush of Texas barely won the state with an "official" margin of 537 votes of over 6 million cast, making his margin of victory an incredible 1/100th of 1 percent. Bush's razor-thin victory brought the national spotlight to all the irregularities and mistakes that plagued the election in the Sunshine State. Chads, dangling and pregnant, entered the national dialogue and became material for late-night television comedians. But despite all the jokes at Florida's expense, the 2000 presidential election reaffirmed Florida's role as a pivotal swing state in U.S. presidential politics. Florida's newly found importance in national politics also served to enhance the importance of the state's Hispanic voters, especially Miami-Dade County's Cuban Americans.

The 2000 presidential election in Florida restored the political influence of the Cuban American community. Many journalists and political analysts had predicted that in the aftermath of the Cuban American leadership's disastrous public performance during the Elián Gonzalez saga, the community would lose its political clout.

213

The conventional wisdom was that current U.S.-Cuban policy would change after the presidential election because the Cuban American leadership had squandered so much political capital and public good-will during the Elián affair. This perception was reinforced when some congressional Republicans began advocating the end of the U.S. economic embargo against Cuba. The decisive support that Miami Cuban Americans gave the Bush campaign during and after the presidential election, however, has created a new political reality in Florida. The GOP now understands that the political health of the Bush brothers (Jeb and George) depends on maintaining the solid support of Miami's Cuban community. Any change in Cuban policy would likely have disastrous political implications for George W. Bush in 2004. The Bush dependency on Miami's Cuban vote is partially a result of their unpopularity with the state's other important minority constituencies, specifically African Americans and Jews.

FLORIDA AS A BATTLEGROUND STATE

Florida was not supposed to be a battleground state. Florida is traditionally one of the most Republican states in the South. The GOP controls both houses of the state legislature by large majorities and since 1952 Florida has voted for the Republican candidate for president in all but three elections (1964, 1976, and 1996). George W. Bush's father carried the state in both the 1988 and 1992 presidential elections, and his brother is a popular governor. According to an April 1999 Mason-Dixon poll, 57 percent of those surveyed approved of Jeb Bush's performance as governor and only 27 percent disapproved (Silva 2000). Moreover, Jeb and George W. Bush's brand of "compassionate" conservatism seem to be a good match with the state's moderate Republican and Independent voters. In this political climate, the Cuban American vote was regarded by most political commentators as relatively unimportant. Cuban Americans comprised only about 8 percent of the state's electorate and were viewed as already heavily committed to the GOP ticket. Some political commentators even speculated that there could be a backlash against the Cuban American community because of the Elián affair. According to this argument, both candidates would avoid campaigning in Cuban Miami because it could lose them votes in other parts of the state. But overall the expectation was that there would be little campaigning in the state as it was already "safely" in the Republican win column. The conventional wisdom was that the Democrats would concede Florida to George W. Bush and concentrate their efforts in the industrial Midwest. However, Florida's political landscape changed radically in the Democrats' favor in 2000.

First, while the state has been electing more and more Republicans, it still has a powerful Democratic Party. In fact, Democrats still enjoy an edge of 373,572 in overall registration in the state, with 3,862,933 Democrats compared to 3,489,391 Republicans (41 to 39 percent) (Florida Secretary of State, Division of Elections 2000). Although the Democrats lost control of the governor's mansion and both houses of the state legislature in the 1990s, they are still very competitive in statewide elections. President Bill Clinton solidly defeated Senator Bob Dole in the 1996 presidential election by over 302,000 votes in Florida, while President George H. W. Bush barely won the state with a margin of 100,000 votes in the 1992 presidential election. Arguably the state's most popular politician, former Democratic governor and current U.S. Senator Bob Graham, retains his Senate seat with a landslide victory every election cycle; in 1998 he won reelection with a decisive 972,652 vote margin (2,436,407 to 1,463,755). Floridians' recent political behavior in statewide elections indicated that the Democrats could be competitive if they could energize their traditional voters and put forward quality candidates.

Second, Jeb Bush offended the state's large African American population with his "One Florida Initiative." The governor's initiative was a response to Ward Connerly's effort to place on the Florida ballot an antiaffirmative action referendum. Connerly's referendum would have amended the Florida constitutional to make affirmative action programs illegal. Jeb Bush hoped to avoid a divisive debate on race relations by proposing a compromise. The One Florida Initiative ended all state-sponsored affirmative action programs and instead guaranteed admission to the top 20 percent of all Florida high school students to the state university system. The initiative also replaced state minority set-asides with a new office for encouraging state contracts to minority-owned businesses. The initiative backfired. African American leaders, even those who supported Bush in the 1998 gubernatorial election, reacted angrily to the One Florida Initiative. Florida's black leadership especially resented the fact that Bush did not consult with them before ending the state's affirmative action program. They responded with a campaign of civil disobedience, protest, and voter mobilization, including a mass rally at the state capitol in Tallahassee. After the One Florida Initiative, Jeb Bush's job disapproval rating jumped 15 percentage points to 42 percent (Silva 2000).

The One Florida Initiative served to mobilize an important Democratic Party constituency on the eve of the presidential campaign. African Americans turned out in large numbers during the 2000 presidential election. During the 1998 gubernatorial election, African Americans made up 10 percent of the state's voters at the polls; in the 2000 presidential election, African Americans consisted of 16 percent of the voters casting ballots.

The selection of Joe Lieberman as Al Gore's vice presidential running mate was another important factor making Florida competitive. Lieberman mobilized Florida's important Jewish community. Jewish voters make up 6 percent of the state's total. Lieberman spent more time in Florida than in any other state. The Gore-Lieberman ticket was rewarded with huge margins in the two heavily Jewish counties of Broward and Palm Beach (209,801 and 116,781 votes, respectively). In fact, the Gore-Lieberman ticket won these counties by larger margins than did Clinton-Gore in 1996 (177,902 and 96,859 votes, respectively).

Finally, the Democrats expended significant resources in the state. Gore refused to concede the state to Bush. He spent lots of time and money in the state. The last stop in Gore's campaign was a massive rally on South Beach on election eve. In defiance of the political pundits and conventional wisdom, the Democrats made Florida a key battleground state, and they were helped in their efforts by Florida's increasing diversity.

Florida's demographic mix of liberal Jewish retirees, conservative midwestern transplants, African Americans, Hispanics, seniors, and traditional southerners made the state competitive for both parties. The rapid growth of the state's population has made the state and its twenty-five electoral votes critical in a close election. The 2000 presidential election in Florida was characterized by heavy voter participation. Everybody seemed to have had a reason to vote for or against someone. Many of the state's Jewish voters were excited by the selection of Lieberman as the Democratic vice presidential candidate. African Americans upset over Jeb Bush's One Florida Initiative voted in record numbers to reject Jeb's brother. Cuban Americans, outraged by the Clinton administration's decision to send Elián Gonzalez back to Cuba, showed up in large numbers to vote against the Democratic ticket.

THE ELIÁN SAGA AND THE CAMPAIGN

The Elián Gonzalez case led to a meltdown of support for the Gore-Lieberman ticket among Miami's Cubans. Cuban Americans make up 8 percent of the state voters and about 42 percent of the voters in Florida's largest county—Miami-Dade. While Cuban Americans have traditionally supported Republican presidential candidates with large margins, there were important signs of growing support for the Democrats (see table 10.1). Clinton in 1992 was the first Democratic presidential candidate to campaign in Miami's Cuban community. Although he received only 25 percent of the Cuban vote in 1992, by 1996 Clinton's support in Miami's Cuban community had climbed to nearly 40 percent (Moreno and Warren 1999).

The expectations going into the 2000 presidential campaign cycle were that the Democrats were going to make a serious effort to retain their growing support among Florida's Cuban Americans. After all, the Clinton administration had strengthened the U.S. eco-

Table 10.1   Hispanic Support for Democratic Presidential Candidates in Miami-Dade County

	% Democratic Vote Hispanic Precincts	% Democratic Vote Countywide
1980 Jimmy Carter	20	44
1984 Walter Mondale	12	41
1988 Michael Dukakis	15	45
1992 Bill Clinton	22	46
1996 Bill Clinton	38	57
2000 Al Gore	25	53

Sources: Authors' calculations based on Official Election Results, Metro-Dade Elections Department (1980, 1984, 1988, 1992, 1996, 2000).

nomic embargo against the Castro regime (Helms-Burton Bill in 1996), maintained Radio and TV Marti, and made many presidential trips and fund-raisers to Miami. Gore also had the support of Miami-Dade's young Cuban American mayor Alex Penelas. The popular Penelas was the highest ranking Cuban American Democrat and had been an important supporter of Clinton in 1996 and was expected to play a pivotal role in Gore's campaign in Florida. It was widely speculated that Penelas would receive a cabinet appointment in the Gore administration; at one point, he was even mentioned as a possible vice presidential nominee.

Democratic prospects in the Cuban American community ended with the Elián saga. The decision of the Immigration and Naturalization Service to deny the six-year-old boy an asylum hearing sparked an emotional backlash against the Clinton administration. This backlash was captured in a January 2000 public opinion poll conducted among Miami-Dade County's Cuban voters by Campaign Data, Inc. The poll showed that over 83 percent of the respondents believed that the Republican Party better represented the interests of the Cuban American community, while only 8 percent felt the Democratic Party did so (Campaign Data 2000). Even more disturbing for Democrats was the fact that even among Cuban Democrats, there was strong support for the GOP. Forty-eight percent of the Cuban Democrats responded that the Republican Party better represented the interests of the Cuban community, while only 40 percent held that their own party did. This rising feeling against the Democratic Party was not only bad news for Vice President Gore's campaign, but for Mayor Penelas as well.

Penelas, who faced reelection in 2000, began to worry openly that his close association with the Clinton-Gore administration would jeopardize his standing with his Cuban American constituents. In an infamous March 2000 news conference, Penelas condemned the Clinton administration's handling of the affair and promised his constituents that local law enforcement agencies would not cooperate with federal officials to seize Elián Gonzalez from his Miami relatives. The mayor also warned that any violence resulting from the seizure of the boy would be the fault of the Clinton administration. The mayor's statement of defiance of federal authority, reminiscent of George Wallace and Orvil Faubus, energized the Cuban community and caused a major anti-Cuban backlash

among Miami's non-Cubans, complicating the Florida political landscape a few months before the presidential election.

The Elián affair deeply affected the Florida Hispanic campaign
of both parties. Vice President Gore was forced to abandon his campaign among Miami's Cubans. In fact, Gore could not venture into
Cuban parts of Miami for fear of massive protests over the Clinton
administration's handling of the Elián affair. Few prominent Cuban
Americans except Raul Martinez, the mayor of Hialeah, campaigned for the Democratic ticket. Mayor Penelas, still angry over
the Elián affair, concentrated instead on his own reelection. After
his first-round victory in the mayoral race in September 2000,
Penelas pointedly took an extended vacation in Spain. Dispirited
Cuban Democrats were left leaderless and without resources as
Cuban Republicans were energized by the prospects of punishing
the Clinton administration.

The Gore campaign instead concentrated their Florida Hispanic
campaign in central Florida. Their campaign strategy was to concede the Cuban vote and instead try to attract non-Cuban Hispanics in central Florida. Almost all of Gore's Spanish-language media
was bought in the Tampa and Orlando markets. The Gore campaign minimized the importance of the Cuban American vote by
rationalizing that it constituted only 8 percent of the Florida vote
and that it was a traditional Republican vote anyway. Ironically, the
Bush campaign also avoided, at least during the early stages of the
presidential race, any overt campaigning in the Cuban community.
Fearing a backlash from Anglo voters because of the Elián affair,
Bush kept his appearances in Miami to low-key affairs. The campaign's only pre–Labor Day event in Miami was an invitation-only
speech on U.S.-Latin American relations at Florida International
University in Miami.

The Bush campaign, however, quickly abandoned its quiet campaign among Miami Cubans when statewide polls began showing a
tightening race in Florida. A close election, with Democrats mobilizing their traditional base of Jewish and black voters, made it critical for Republicans to energize their Cuban American supporters.
The Bush campaign kicked off a more aggressive campaign with a
major campaign rally at the Coconut Grove Convention Center in
Miami. The Republicans also poured resources into Miami's Spanish-
language media, running an extensive campaign both on radio and

television to mobilize Cuban Americans. By the weekend before the election, Florida was one of the last remaining battleground states. Both candidates spent the campaign's last weekend criss-crossing Florida and ending their tours of Florida with major rallies in Miami. Governor Bush ended his Florida campaign the Sunday before the election at Tamiami Park with a rally geared toward Miami's Cuban community, while Vice President Gore ended his campaign on election eve with a rally on South Beach geared toward his young Anglo and Jewish constituents.

THE RESULTS

Bush's victory in Florida was partly due to the overwhelming support he received in Miami's Cuban community. While there were many factors that contributed to the outcome of the election, it is clear that Bush would not have won if he had not done exceptionally well among Miami's Cuban Americans. In the 1996 presidential election, Clinton won Florida with a margin of 302,644 votes. Clinton's victory was due to his ability to obtain huge majorities in the three heavily Democratic southeast counties: Broward, Miami-Dade, and Palm Beach. Clinton's margin of victory in those three counties totaled 382,455 votes. Although he lost the state, Gore actually had larger margins of victory in Broward and Palm Beach Counties than Clinton. Gore was helped in those counties by Jewish and black voters, the so-called "Lieberman effect." However, in Miami-Dade County Gore did much worse than Clinton. While Clinton won Miami-Dade by 107,694 votes, Gore's margin was only 39,272.

Why did Gore do so poorly in the traditional Democratic stronghold of Miami-Dade County? The answer lies in his poor showing among the county's Hispanic voters. In 1996, Clinton received nearly 40 percent of the Hispanic vote in Miami-Dade County (Moreno and Warren 1999). In the 2000 presidential election, Bush won 67 percent of the Hispanic vote in Miami-Dade. However, among Cuban Americans, Bush received 75 percent. Hispanics in Miami-Dade gave Bush a total of 230,178 votes, which is 429 times his total margin of 537 votes statewide. Bush's margin of victory in Miami-Dade's Hispanic community was uniform throughout the county. Bush won by similar margins in the working-class precincts of Hialeah and Little Havana and the more affluent areas of Kendall, Village Green, and Westchester.

Bush's strong support in the Hispanic areas of Miami-Dade County helped offset Gore's almost universal support in the African American community. Gore received a staggering 97.5 percent of the votes in the African American precincts. In contrast, an analysis of the homogenous precincts showed that Bush received only 3,189 votes out of 127,548 African American votes cast.[1] Gore also did very well among non-Latin white voters; he received 61 percent of their votes. Gore's support grows dramatically among Jewish voters in the northeast condos of Aventura and Miami Beach, where the vice president received over 84 percent of the vote. Bush was able to offset Gore's strong showing in Miami-Dade's non-Hispanic community by winning three-fourths (75 percent) of the Cuban American vote.

Vice President Gore's poor showing among Hispanic voters in Miami-Dade County was somewhat offset by his performance among non-Cuban Hispanics elsewhere in the state. Gore was the first major presidential candidate to target Florida's diverse non-Cuban Latino population. The non-Cuban Hispanic population constitutes about 6 percent of Florida's voting-age population and about 3 percent of the electorate.[2] They are concentrated in the center of the state along the Interstate 4 corridor (the highway between Orlando and Tampa) in Orange, Osceola, and Seminole Counties. In large part, because of Gore's strong showing among non-Cuban Hispanic, the vice president became the first Democratic presidential candidate since 1944 to carry Orange and Osceola Counties. There are also significant Hispanic populations in Hillsborough County, which is made up of the remnants of the nineteenth-century Cuban colony in Ybor City and new immigrants from Colombia, Venezuela, and Puerto Rico and in Broward County (mostly Cubans, Puerto Ricans, and South Americans). However, it is difficult to find homogenous precincts of non-Cuban Hispanics, as there are significant Cuban populations in all these counties. In fact, Mel Martinez, the Cuban-born secretary of housing and urban development, was chair of the County Commission in Orange County.

Exit polls show that Gore edged out Bush among non-Cuban Latinos 53 to 43 percent. This was according to CNN and the Voter

News Service (VNS). However, it should be noted that the VNS severely undercounted the number of Cubans in its survey. Cubans comprised 2 percent of the statewide total in the VNS survey instead of 8 percent of the total, which all other pollsters use. This is one of the reasons that the networks misprojected the Florida result. Although the VNS overcounted non-Cuban Hispanics (8 percent of the total instead of 3 percent), the percentage should be a valid indication of the preference of non-Cuban Hispanic in Florida. The differences between the presidential preferences of Cubans and non-Cuban Hispanics was also confirmed in an April 2001 survey by the Florida Institute of Government, which showed that while 75 percent of Cubans believed that Bush won the Florida presidential contest, only 35 percent of the non-Cubans Hispanic believed Bush won Florida (MacManus et al. 2001).

THE RECOUNT

Cuban Americans only played a relatively minor role in the long postelection controversy over the Florida vote. The butterfly ballot was in Palm Beach and the alleged intimidation of African American voters occurred in the panhandle. Miami-Dade only entered the national spotlight when the Gore campaign asked for a manual recount of the county's ballots. The Gore campaign targeted the three largest Democratic counties in Florida (Palm Beach, Broward, and Miami-Dade) in an attempt to overcome Bush's narrow lead.

In Miami-Dade, the Gore campaign requested a manual recount of, at first, 1 percent of the vote in three precincts as provided for in Florida law. Of the three precincts that were picked for a sample recount, two were overwhelmingly black and one was a predominantly Jewish retiree precinct in North Miami Beach. After hand recounting 8,000 ballots, the three-member Canvassing Board only found six new votes (all for Gore) and decided two to one against a full manual recount. Inexplicably, two days later a member of the Canvassing Board, Cuban American county judge Miriam Lehr, reversed her decision and voted for a full manual recount of almost 700,000 ballots in Miami-Dade County. Lehr had just been reelected to a four-year term. She is a Democrat, though her husband is a high-profile, successful Republican fund-raiser.

During the hand recount, the Florida Supreme Court issued a decision calling on all counties to have their manual recounts completed and certified by Sunday, November 26. On the day before Thanksgiving, with the Miami-Dade count about 15 percent complete, the Canvassing Board in the county decided that there was not enough time left to complete the full recount by the court-appointed deadline. By this point, the board had discovered many hundreds of new votes that had not been noticed by the machines, with Gore picking up a net of 167 votes here, a substantial percentage of what he needed statewide to reverse Bush's lead. Then the Canvassing Board faced a very important decision. If it stopped the recount at this point, would it "throw out" all the newly discovered votes or would it submit a partial recount to Tallahassee including this net swing of 167 votes to Gore? This question became injected with a Cuban American angle because of the way in which the count was being conducted. The Canvassing Board was manually recounting the county's votes in numerical precinct order. It turns out that the lower-numbered precincts in the county are the overwhelmingly Democratic areas of Miami Beach, Aventura, and heavily black areas of northeast Miami-Dade. It was after recounting these ballots that the Canvassing Board decided to suspend the recount. The board was at the point in the count where the next regions to be counted would have been Hialeah, Westchester, West Miami, Little Havana, and Flagami, neighborhoods with overwhelmingly Republican and Cuban American voters. The Bush campaign lawyers, led by prominent Cuban American lawyers, Bob Martinez, a former U.S. attorney, and Miguel De-Grandy, a former state legislator, argued that stopping the count at this point and including only partial results from heavily non-Hispanic areas would have been a dilution of the votes of Cuban Americans and thus a violation of the Voting Rights Act and the Fourteenth Amendment's equal protection clause. This argument, though it must have seemed bitterly ironic to Democrats and especially African Americans, apparently worked to at least influence the Canvassing Board not to submit partial results and instead fall back to the machine recount of November 8. This was a devastating blow to Gore's recount effort. According to press reports, Gore called on Mayor Penelas to intervene with the Canvassing Board, but the mayor demurred.

HISPANIC POWER IN FLORIDA

The 2000 elections saw few major gains for Hispanic politicians in Florida. Cuban Americans retained their eleven seats in the state house of representatives, three seats in the state senate, and two congressional seats. Moreover, Penelas easily won reelection as county mayor of Miami-Dade despite offending many non-Latino whites and African Americans with his strong stance on behalf of Elián Gonzalez's Miami relatives. Cubans continued to consolidate their hold over Miami-Dade politics, electing more and more municipal officials in such traditional Anglos enclaves as Miami Beach, Coral Gables, and Miami Lakes. Cuban Americans also made major gains in neighboring Broward County as Diana Wasserman-Rubin became the first Hispanic elected to the Broward County Commission, and Barbara Herrera-Hill became the first Hispanic city commissioner in the county when she was elected to the city commission in upscale Weston. Both are Cuban American and are the only Hispanic elected officials in Broward County. Interestingly, both represent constituencies that are not majority or even plurality Hispanic. Both are also Democrats. In a June 30, 2002, feature story on the thirty most powerful people in Broward County, both of these Cuban American politicians were named by the *Sun-Sentinel* as among the most influential people in the county, partly because they represent an extremely rapid demographic shift. All the Hispanics cited in that article were Cuban Americans. Time will tell whether or not this demographic shift translates into a political shift and whether or not that shift will be as ugly as the one that occurred in Miami-Dade County in the 1980s and 1990s (Nevins 2002; Moreno and Warren 1992, 1996).

Elsewhere in the state, Hispanic politicians fared poorly. An Anglo Republican recaptured the seat won by Anthony Suarez in Orlando, the first non-Cuban Hispanic elected to the state legislature. Central Florida Hispanics lost the highest elected official in Orange County when Mel Martinez resigned in March 2001 to become secretary of housing and urban development, and they also lost a non-Cuban Hispanic Commission seat in Osceola County. The only Hispanic elected official in Florida outside Miami-Dade and Broward Counties above the rank of city commissioner or school board member is state representative Bob Henriquez, a fourth-generation Cuban American, representing the traditional Cuban enclave around Ybor City in Hillsborough County. Thus, despite impressive population gains for Hispanics around the Interstate 4 corridor, Hispanics in central Florida have made relatively little progress in capturing political power. Moreover, almost all the Hispanic elected officials outside of Miami-Dade are Cuban Americans. Despite the rising media and academic attention paid to other Hispanic groups in Florida, these groups have simply not been able to translate their numbers into political power like Cuban Americans have. Although the *New York Times* and other out-of-state media continually write about the rise of non-Cuban Hispanics in politics, this is simply not borne out by political realities on the ground in Florida. The political power of the non-Cuban Hispanic voter in Florida for several years has been like the eponymous Godot from the play—people are waiting, but it has yet to show up in reality.

The 2002 redistricting cycle resulted in some gains for Cuban Americans. Florida created a third Hispanic majority congressional district in Miami-Dade and Collier Counties, and one additional state representative seat with a Hispanic majority in Miami-Dade and western Broward. For some reason, the state senate gave up on a plan to create a fourth Hispanic majority senate district, even though one could have easily been drawn. Non-Cuban Hispanics lobbied hard for a Hispanic seat in central Florida, though demographic and political realities conspired against its creation. The possibility of vote dilution lawsuits to create additional Hispanic majority legislative seats remains a possibility. Then again, demographic shifts may take care of this situation since, in addition to the three Hispanic majority state senate seats created in Miami-Dade County, three other counties contain over a 33 percent Hispanic population and are seeing rapid growth in their Latino populations.

CONCLUSION

The 2000 elections underscored the importance of Miami's Cuban American community in presidential politics. Although tiny in size—less than 5 percent of the nation's total Latino population—Cuban Americans have been able to exercise inordinate influence because of the competitive nature of statewide elections in Florida. Representing 8 percent of the state's electorate and practicing bloc voting, Cuban Americans are a critical part of any Republican effort to forge a wining electoral coalition in Florida. It can be argued that Cuban American voters swung Florida to the Republican column in three recent statewide elections: the 2000 presidential election, 1992 presidential election, and Connie Mack's 1988 election to the U.S. Senate. Cubans have also been an important part in the GOP's successful effort to capture both houses of the state legislature.

The Republicans, especially the Bush brothers, have been quick to recognize the importance of Cuban voters in keeping Florida Republican. President George W. Bush named the first Cuban American to a presidential cabinet when he appointed Mel Martinez to the Department of Housing and Urban Development. Just as important was his nomination of Cuban-born Otto Reich to be assistant secretary of state for inter-American relations, signaling Bush's willingness to give Cuban Americans greater influence over Cuba policy. Similarly, Jeb Bush has rewarded his Cuban supporters by backing Al Cardenas's efforts to become chair of Florida's Republican Party and naming Cuban Americans to prominent positions in his administration. President Bush made a well-publicized trip to Miami for the May 20, 2002, Cuban independence day celebration. There have also been no changes in the embargo, despite some pressure from midwestern Republicans.

Cuban American success in Florida has come as an anomaly in national Latino politics. Other Latinos, even in Florida, do not share in Cubans' enthusiasm for the Republican Party. Conversely, Cubans complain about the lack of sensitivity of other Latinos (especially Mexican Americans and Puerto Ricans) to the issues of human rights and democratization in Cuba. The lack of support for the Cuban community among Latinos outside Miami during the Elián affair (and outright hostility from a few Hispanic members of Congress) reinforces this chasm in national Latino politics. However, as long as Florida is the largest battleground state in presidential elections, Cuban Americans as a key swing vote will continue to wield a political influence far out of proportion to their small numbers and will remain as one of the few Latino groups who influence presidential election outcomes.

NOTES

1. This analysis is based on the thirty-nine precincts where African Americans make up at least 90 percent or more of the voters and the twenty-seven precincts where non-Latino whites make up 85 percent or more of the voters.

2. This estimate is based on statewide polling figures from the Florida Voter and Schroth and Associates.

11

Electoral College Dropouts

Illinois Latinos in the 2000 Presidential Election

LOUIS DESIPIO

~~~~~~

THE PRESIDENTIAL ELECTION AGAIN PASSED ILLINOIS LATINOS BY. IN neither the primaries nor the general election did presidential candidates or political parties seek their votes. Latinos themselves did little to organize to increase their influence. They were not relevant to the outcome and, had no Latino voted, the outcome would have been no different.

Previous studies have identified several factors—particularly the relatively even balance between Democrats and Republicans among non-Latino voters and Latino concentration in the city of Chicago—that potentially raise the salience of the Illinois Latino vote (Fraga 1992). In addition, Chicago's Latinos have experienced mobilization in a close election: Harold Washington's mayoral victory in 1983. Arguably, this mobilization, and the strong support that Latinos gave to Washington, won him the race (Torres 1991; DeSipio 2002).

Despite these potential advantages, studies of Latinos and state election cycles have found a recurring pattern: their votes are not the subject of candidate or party competition and there is little effort among Latino leaders to overcome this absence of external mobilization. As a result, Illinois Latinos participate at relatively low rates and their votes prove irrelevant to the outcome of the election (Valadez 1994; Rey 1996; DeSipio 1999). Although this pattern also appears in other states with large Latino populations, Illinois in the period since 1988 has seen among the lowest levels of Latino mobilization. In addition, Illinois Latino politics is shaped by a demographic characteristic that has only recently appeared in other states with large Latino populations. Specifically, Illinois Latinos (and particularly Illinois Latino voters) are divided between two national-origin groups: Mexican Americans and Puerto Ricans. With occasional notable exceptions (Padilla 1986; Torres 1991), these two populations have not been able to build a sustained pan-Latino coalition that mobilizes Latino votes in national elections. As this pattern of multiple Latino national-origin groups residing around each other and sharing a political space is becoming more common in other states, the experiences of Illinois Latino politics may presage poorly for national Latino political mobilization and influence.

THE CAMPAIGN

Despite polls that showed the presidential race to be close until the last week of the campaign, Illinois was not central to either candidate's strategy. It was neglected by both parties in the primaries and by both candidates until the last two weeks of the general election. Races within the state did not add significantly to the level of competition for voters, whether for Latinos or for the state's population as a whole. There were no statewide races and local races with Latino candidates were largely noncompetitive.

Primaries

Illinois's presidential primary in late March was largely a nonevent. By the time of the primary, both George W. Bush and Al Gore had eliminated their opponents and were well on the way to capturing their parties' nominations. The period after the primary, but before the commencement of the general election, was similarly quiet for the state as a whole as well as for its Latino voters. The seeming

quiet did mask some efforts by Latino leaders to position themselves for the redistricting that would follow the 2000 elections.

This quiescence through the 2000 primary season was something
of a contrast to 1999, when the campaigns began in earnest. In 1999,
it seemed as if Latinos might have a more significant role than they
had in past races. Competition for Latino votes, or at least Latino
elite support, was high. Vice President Gore sought and earned endorsements from prominent (and not-so-prominent) Latinos
throughout the state. In this, he followed the same strategy as in
other states, seemingly seeking to corral every Latino with electoral
office or community prominence. Senator Bill Bradley, however, was
able to snag two key Latino endorsements, one from the state's only
Latino member of Congress, Luis Gutierrez, and the other from the
state's longest serving Latino state senator, Miguel del Valle (Neal
1999a, 1999b). These early endorsements for the challenger made it
appear that Illinois's Democratic Latino votes would be contested in
ways that they had not been in recent memory (or, perhaps, ever). In
making his endorsement, del Valle commended Senator Bradley's
commitment to handgun registration and licensing and, more generally, to spurring a debate within the Democratic Party about its pri-
orities. His endorsement also criticized President Bill Clinton, and
by extension Vice President Gore, for supporting the 1996 Welfare
Reform Bill. Gutierrez linked his support to Bradley's endorsement
of universal health care and campaign-finance reform.

Underlying the Gutierrez and del Valle endorsements of Bradley
were the twisted arms of Chicago's political machine. Gutierrez (and
his ally, del Valle) were positioning themselves to undermine challenges from the machine and Mayor Richard Daley, an active supporter of Vice President Gore (Mendieta, Sadovi, and Carpenter
2000). Gutierrez's congressional seat was to be redrawn prior to 2002
and the resulting "Latino" district could be much more concentrated
in the city's Mexican American neighborhoods, putting Gutierrez, a
Puerto Rican, in electoral jeopardy (DeSipio 1999). State senators and
legislators who are not supported by the machine face continuing
challenges, so del Valle had reason to establish (ultimately unsuccessfully) a separate power base. Thus, these efforts to ally with the
nascent Bradley campaign should be seen both in terms of criticism
from the left of the Clinton-Gore administration and of creating a
power base that supplants the machine in Chicago politics.

Ultimately, the Bradley challenge failed. In the March 21 primary, Gore handily won the state and carried Cook County with nearly 87 percent of the Democratic vote. Senator del Valle was not elected as a convention delegate. Neither Democratic candidate actively campaigned for Latino votes. While both visited the state prior to the primaries for fund-raising events, these events did not target Latinos. On the Republican side, Governor Bush did visit the state in March, but again, he did not reach out to Latinos.

The period after the primary saw no change in the candidates' competition for the state's votes. Governor Bush, for example, did not visit the state from March to mid-July. Although this neglect, in large part, reflected a recognition that the state was likely to support Vice President Gore in the general election, some in the press also argued that Bush was distancing himself from Illinois's governor, George Ryan, who was facing ethics charges relating to the sale of drivers' licenses while he served as secretary of state. The governor had also alienated many in the Republican Party by imposing a moratorium on executions in the state in response to evidence that several innocent people had been on death row for long periods. Some in the Bush campaign thought that the concern for prisoners' rights that guided this moratorium reflected poorly on Bush and Texas, which leads the nation in executions.

Bush's failure to compete may have reflected confidence that he could win the national race with other state's electoral college votes, but seems surprising in retrospect. Polls conducted both before and during the primaries showed Bush ahead more often than not. As late as mid-July, an American Research Group poll showed Bush ahead by 7 percent. This early Bush support probably included few Latino voters.

The party's conventions did not add any particular excitement to the presidential race. In 1996, the Democratic convention had been in Chicago, creating electoral excitement for Democrats and Democratic Latinos in the state after what had been a very dull primary season. In 2000, the dull primary season was repeated but without the energy of a convention.

Four of the state's seventy-four delegates to the Republican convention were Latino, making up 5.4 percent of the delegation (Orosco 2000). The Democrats had a higher share, though the count varies by source. Between 15 and 19 percent of the 152 Illinois Democratic delegates and alternates were Latino. These Democratic delegates included Congressman Gutierrez, who earned a seat as a "super" (non-elected) delegate. Illinois Latinos did not have a prominent place as speakers at either party's convention. The Democrats did hear from Grace Delgado, who spoke about her experiences with community-oriented policing and praised the Clinton administration initiative that provided funds to hire up to 100,000 new police officers.

In sum, the primary season did little to mobilize Illinois Latinos (or Illinois residents in general). Although early in the campaign season, it appeared that Illinois Latino votes might be contested in the Democratic primary, an opportunity that soon disappeared. Through the primaries and the conventions, none of the candidates and neither of the parties expended much effort to mobilize the state's votes, regardless of ethnicity.

General Election

The general election proved to be an unfortunate carbon of the primaries. Neither candidate dedicated much time to the state and little money was spent on advertising. Illinois only entered the candidates' and parties' strategies twice—first at the start of the campaign around Labor Day and then in the last two weeks of the campaign. In the end, this lack of competition for the state's votes proved justified. Vice President Gore handily won Illinois's popular vote by a 55 percent to 43 percent margin, though polling evidence indicates that the Gore lead grew steadily through the fall and particularly in the campaign's final week.

With the exceptions of visits to the state to appear on *Oprah*, Bush and Gore only visited Illinois to attend fund-raising events between Labor Day and the last week in October. The Bush campaign's Labor Day visit is not a pleasant memory. At a rally in suburban Chicago, Bush called *New York Times* reporter Adam Clymer "a major league asshole" in what he thought was an off-microphone comment to running mate Dick Cheney.

The Bush campaign did run some ads in selected Illinois media markets around Labor Day, but these ended in early September. Both campaigns removed their campaign staffs (transferring them, for the most part, to neighboring Wisconsin) in early September. Although the state parties' conducted absentee voting drives and get-out-the-vote efforts, the formal infrastructure of the presidential campaigns largely disappeared in September never to return.

The candidates' absences, as they related to Illinois's Latinos, became particularly apparent in late September. The annual meeting of the U.S. Hispanic Leadership Conference attracted 8,000 Latinos to Chicago, but neither of the presidential nor vice presidential candidates appeared despite repeated invitations (Puente 2000). Henry Cisneros represented the Gore campaign through a meal-time address to the conference, though the Democrats did not host a booth. The Bush campaign representative was Carlos Ramírez, the Democrat mayor from El Paso. Mayor Ramírez was not on the program and addressed the conferees though a press conference.

The Bush campaign appointed a steering committee for Latino outreach in the state that included thirteen business owners and educators. None had a statewide prominence and it is not clear that this steering committee did much to promote Bush. The Gore campaign also had a *Ganamos con Gore!* committee in place from the primaries. As was the case with the paid staff, the *Ganamos* volunteers largely directed their energies toward other states.

The bipartisan neglect of Illinois voters became cautious interest beginning in the final two weeks of the campaign (Belluck 2000). As part of what appeared to be a national trend at the end of the campaign, Governor Bush began to campaign and advertise in states that he had previously conceded to Gore. Although the goals of this strategy were not so clear (see chapter 1 in this volume), there was a bit more reason for it in Illinois than in other states. Polls, including a highly publicized *Chicago Sun-Times* poll released on October 22, showed the race narrowing to a statistically insignificant Gore lead of just 2 percent.

During that final two weeks, the state became a more common stop for both candidates and the Bush campaign resumed limited advertising. These candidate visits, of which there were more from Bush, were creatively strategic. Both candidates visited media markets that reached more competitive states, for example, Moline, which also reached eastern Iowa, and Chicago, which also reached southern Wisconsin. November 2 was the high point for the Illinois campaign, when Bush, Cheney, and Gore all appeared in the state. Gore's failure to respond to the Bush campaign's advertising expenditures and appearances in the state in weeks before the campaign's end reflected a confidence in the state Democratic Party's get-out-the-vote efforts. The party committed to calling 3 million Democratic households in the week before the election. The Chicago Democratic Party also contributed; it invested extensively in a very successful get-out-the-vote effort among the city's African Americans. The Chicago machine's successes in this strategy was noted by the state's Republican governor who enviously praised Mayor Daley for bringing out such a high share of the city's African American voters. No comparable effort was made to reach the city's Latino Democrats.

Ultimately, the Bush campaign's outreach in the final weeks of the campaign had little effect. As the election neared, tracking polls indicated a steady increase in Gore support. One week before the election, several polls had Gore in the lead, but at a level just above the polls' margins of error. By election day, his lead had grown to 12 percent.

Despite the low competition for Illinois Latino votes in the 2000 elections, the race offers an important insight into the broader question of Latino politics in presidential elections. In any list of the "major" Latino states, Illinois appears. The 1.28 million Latinos in Illinois make it the state with the fifth highest Latino population. Of these, more than 262,000 were registered to vote (U.S. Bureau of the Census 2000a, 2002c). Yet, when Illinois became noncompetitive, the Gore campaign was strategic in moving its Latino campaign staff to Wisconsin—a state that would never appear on a list of the "major" Latino states. Wisconsin had many fewer Latinos than did Illinois (no more than 150,000) and few registered Latino voters (34,000 in 2000). Wisconsin Latinos could only add 1,000 to 2,000 *new* Gore votes. By *new*, I mean votes that Gore would not get if his campaign did nothing to mobilize Wisconsin Latinos. Yet, in a race as close as the 2000 race was nationally, and particularly in the electoral college, 2,000 new Latino votes in Wisconsin were more important than the tens of thousands of new Latino votes that could be earned in Illinois with a comparable mobilization effort. So, a lesson of the 2000 presidential race is that in close races, the states with large Latino populations will not necessarily be the targets of the campaigns' Latino mobilization efforts. Instead, cohesive Latino partisanship in highly contested states makes Latinos a target for mobilization even if the total number of votes that can be won are few.

Illinois Latinos and Nonpresidential Elections

Other than the presidential race, Illinois had no statewide races in 2000. At the local level, no races with viable Latino candidates were competitive. Several congressional seats were actively contested, though only one of these—the Tenth District—had a Latino population exceeding 5 percent. Illinois's one Latino member of Congress (Luis Gutierrez) did not face significant opposition. Neither Latino state senator faced reelection. Two Latino members of the state legislature faced primary challenges, but the winners of these two races (both machine-supported challengers who beat the incumbents) and two other Latino incumbents who did not face primary challenges had no opposition in the general election. This absence of statewide races and of local competitive races with Latino candidates added to the turnout-dampening impact of the low salience presidential race.

In the Fourth Congressional District, Representative Gutierrez did not face a Republican opponent. Instead, Libertarian Stephanie Sailor ran what can only be seen as a symbolic campaign against the incumbent. Although it probably does not suggest any troubling weakness in Gutierrez's hold over the district, Sailor's 11 percent of the vote nearly doubled the 6 percent earned by Gutierrez's Libertarian (and only) opponent in 1996.

Although neither Gutierrez nor Sailor actively campaigned, Gutierrez actively raised funds for his campaign. In 1999 and 2000, Gutierrez raised approximately $454,558 for his campaign fund. After expenses, he had $314,224 on hand. Sailor did not file finance reports with the Federal Election Commission as are required if she raised funds for her campaign.

One of the two competitive congressional races in the state included a small number of Latino voters (7 percent in 1990, and perhaps as many as 10 percent in 2000). Despite their small number, the potential importance of Latino votes was amplified by the closeness of the race and the fact that one of the candidates—Republican Mark Kirk—reached out to Latinos (as well as African Americans) throughout the campaign (Fornek 2000; Giroux 2000; Mellen 2000). Kirk's outreach was primarily symbolic. He spoke Spanish, distributed Spanish-language lawn signs, and attended Latino community events. The issues he addressed in his campaign—reducing government regulation, promoting small business, and assisting small business owners to obtain health insurance for their workers—did not resonate with those identified by Latinos as being important. Nevertheless, Kirk's outreach to Latinos and African Americans was of sufficient concern to his Democratic opponent, Lauren Beth Gash, that she brought Luis Gutierrez and Jesse Jackson Jr. to the district to campaign on her behalf. Kirk's narrow margin of victory, 51.2 percent to 48.8 percent (or 5,649 votes), led some to wonder whether his Latino outreach, which was nontraditional for a Republican, sealed his victory in a toss-up district (Fornek 2000). Considering the size and partisanship of the district's Latino vote, it is impossible that Latinos were responsible for Kirk's margin. Nevertheless, outreach by a Republican in a close race shows new ways in which Latinos will likely be mobilized in the future. Kirk also represents a new generation of Republicans who are able to and interested in reaching out to Latinos and do not see a risk in this strategy to their core constituencies. Finally, it represents the first evidence of large-scale Illinois Latino politics taking place in Chicago's suburbs.

In sum, conditions exogenous to the Latino community limited their impact on the outcome of all levels of the election. The presidential and other races were noncompetitive. With Kirk's exception, candidates did not seek their votes and parties did not actively seek to mobilize their participation. The relative unimportance of the Latino community, it should be noted, did not distinguish them significantly from non-Latinos in Illinois. The election season did allow political elites to position themselves for upcoming events. Chicago's political machine strengthened its hold by unseating two of its opponents in the state legislative primary.

ILLINOIS LATINO ATTITUDES AND VALUES IN THE 2000 ELECTIONS

Illinois Latinos were frequently polled in the 2000 elections. Four issue and candidate-preference polls were conducted at different points in the campaign season. In addition, one statewide poll of candidate preference conducted just before the election reported data on its Latino respondents, though it provided no data on the number or characteristics of its Latino respondents. Table 11.1 presents data from these polls on Illinois Latino candidate prefer-

Table 11.1   Polls of Illinois Latinos, 2000 (%)

	WCVRI 1	PBS	PBS Registered	WCVRI 2	TRPI	McCulloch
Partisanship Voters						
Democrat	—	37.1	—	78.0	69.9	—
Republican	—	14.0	—	12.3	16.4	—
Independent/Other	—	48.9	—	9.7	13.7	—
Candidate Support						
Gore	37.8	43.6	50.0	58.6	56.1	72.7
Bush	34.7	34.5	34.4	19.1	23.1	18.2
Undecided/Other	27.5	21.9	15.6	22.0	20.8	9.1
Intended Party of Congressional Vote						
Democrat	—	46.1[a]	—	74.5	64.1	—
Republican	—	18.5[a]	—	12.9	14.2	—
Other/Not Sure	—	35.4[a]	—	12.6	21.7	—
Nativity						
U.S.-born	—	18.5	—	49.1	71.0	—
Puerto Rican-born	—	1.0	—	14.2	8.0	—
Overseas	—	80.5	—	36.7	21.0	—
National Origin						
Mexican	—	87.9	—	72.7	57.8	—
Puerto Rican	—	4.5	—	19.9	26.0	—
Other	—	7.6	—	7.4	16.2	—
n	238	200	84	529	394	?

Notes:

WCVRI 1—William C. Velásquez Research Institute telephone poll of 238 registered Latino voters, conducted November 1999.

PBS—Public Broadcasting Service poll of 200 Latino adults, conducted June and July 2000. I report data separately for registered voters from this survey in the third column.

WCVRI 2—William C. Velásquez Research Institute telephone poll of 529 registered voters, conducted September 13–21, 2000.

TRPI—Tomás Rivera Policy Institute telephone poll of 400 Latino registered voters, conducted October 2000. The data are weighted to reflect statewide distributions of native born, Puerto Rican born, and foreign-born Latino registered voters.

McCulloch—McCulloch Research and Polling Illinois Tracking Poll of 800 likely voters statewide (it does not provide data on the number of Latino respondents). The poll was conducted November 1, 2, 3, and 5, 2000. The respondents all resided in households that had voted in two of the last three elections.

[a] In the PBS survey, data on intended party of congressional vote is the answer to the question "Which party in Congress will best handle problems facing Latinos?"

Sources: Public Broadcasting Service (2000); Tomás Rivera Policy Institute (2000a); William C. Velásquez Research Institute (2000f).

ences, partisanship, and intended party of congressional vote. For the three surveys that ask Illinois Latinos a range of questions about their attitudes toward the candidates and the issues, I also report some key demographic characteristics: nativity and national origin/ancestry.[1]

Two patterns emerge. First, Gore was the choice of Illinois Latinos. Second, his Latino margin of support grew as the election neared and as polls narrowed their focus to registered voters or likely voters. In the initial William C. Velásquez Research Institute (WCVRI) poll, conducted a year before the election, Latinos were evenly divided with just a slight preference for Gore. Nearly one-third were undecided. By election day, Latino support for Gore had grown, support for Bush had diminished, and the number of undecided voters had declined. Although the utility of the McCulloch poll is diminished by its failure to provide sample demographics or even a sample size, it indicates that by the time of the election, Gore had increased his margin over Bush to nearly four to one. There are no exit polls of Illinois Latinos against which to test this poll result, so this is the best estimate of how Illinois Latinos voted in 2000.

The polls also confirm what is widely known. Specifically, Latinos are strong Democratic partisans in Illinois. Democrats have an advantage among Illinois-registered Latino voters of between four to one and six to one. Latinos intended to tap this partisanship when voting in congressional races. Although the margins shown here for the Democrats in terms of likely congressional vote are quite dramatic, their actual votes were even more likely to be for the Democrats. Many Latinos only had Democrats on the ballot for Congress.

These polls also measured Illinois Latino issue preferences. The results show broadly that Illinois Latinos are concerned with the same issues that Latinos nationwide are, although there are some state-specific differences. In the Tomás Rivera Policy Institute pre-election poll, for example, Illinois Latinos were most likely to identify education and crime as the most important issues facing the nation (Tomás Rivera Policy Institute 2000a). Fourteen percent of respondents identified each of these issues. The third most-mentioned issue was the economy, with approximately 9 percent of respondents identifying it as the most important.

The WCVRI poll asked a somewhat different question, but came

up with similar results (2000). It asked Illinois respondents to identify the issue that would most determine their vote in the November election. Education was again ranked first, identified in this poll
by 24 percent of respondents. Rounding out the top three issues
were lack of health care access (15 percent) and strengthening jobs
and wages (10 percent). Amnesty for undocumented workers and
raising the minimum wage proved to be relatively less important issues for Illinois Latinos (8 percent and 5 percent, respectively).

The Public Broadcasting Service poll (which oversampled Latino
immigrants) broadly found the same issues at the top of the list,
though it did find at least one ethnic-specific issue among the top
three issues. In response to the question of the most important issue
facing the nation, the top three issues identified by Illinois Latinos
were economic conditions (15 percent), racism/discrimination (14
percent), and crime (14 percent). Illinois Latinos were more likely
than Latinos in California, Texas, New York, or Florida to identify
racism/discrimination as the most important issue facing the nation.

With campaigning for Latino votes in Illinois so rare, these
candidate-preference and opinion polls offer an invaluable tool to
measure their preferences and opinions. Although few surprises appear in these results, they offer important confirmations of what we
know about Illinois Latinos. They are Democrats and these Democrats were not swayed by Governor Bush's efforts to win Latino votes
nationally. The issues that shape their candidate preferences and partisanship are domestic social and economic issues, such as education, crime, health care, and the economy. These are not issues that
are unique to Latinos. Ethnic-specific issues do appear when Latinos
are asked about issues, but they are the exception rather than the rule.

ILLINOIS LATINOS AND THE OUTCOME OF THE ELECTION

Like Latinos in other states, Illinois Latinos turn out at rates lower
than other ethnic or racial groups. Arguably, the traditional barriers
Latinos face (see chapter 1 in this volume) are exacerbated in Illinois because so many of the recent election cycles have been noncompetitive in presidential as well as in nonpresidential races and
because of the divide between Illinois's Mexican Americans and
Puerto Ricans (Fraga 1992; Valadez 1994; Rey 1996; DeSipio 1999).

The cumulative impact of these noncompetitive elections on Latino turnout appeared in an analysis of Latino turnout conducted by the *Chicago Sun-Times* in early 1999 (Rodríguez 1999). In addition to measuring turnout in a specific election (the March 1998 primary), they measured the share of Latino and non-Latino populations that were eligible to vote in all elections between March 1994 and March 1998, but had voted in none. Slightly more than 36 percent of Chicago's Latinos did not vote in any election in this four-year period. Approximately 27 percent of non-Latinos were similarly situated. The gap between Latinos and non-Latinos widened outside of the city of Chicago. In suburban Cook County, 43 percent of registered Latinos did not vote between 1994 and 1998. In Kane County, more than half (56 percent) of registered Latinos had not voted once. The comparable rates of nonparticipation for registered non-Latino voters were 29 percent in both cases.

In the 2000 general election, Latino turnout increased. Statewide, 218,000 Latinos voted, an increase of 71 percent from 1996 (U.S. Bureau of the Census 2002c). This dramatic increase is probably somewhat overstated. The source is the Current Population Survey, which is based on self-reported voting as part of a survey of adults conducted in the weeks after the election. Smaller populations, such as Latinos, are subject to large sampling errors that could account either for too high an estimate in 2000 or too low an estimate in 1996. Even if accurate, this Latino vote was well below Gore's state victory margin of more than 500,000.

A second estimate also finds an increase, though not as dramatic. Turnout in Chicago increased relative to 1996 (see table 11.2). In high Latino concentration precincts, turnout increased by 18 percent over 1996 levels. This significance of this surge in turnout is not so clear, however. The increase in turnout between 1996 and 2000 is smaller than the decrease in these same precincts between 1992 and 1996. Thus, even with the 18 percent growth in turnout since 1996, turnout has declined by 3 percent between 1992 and 2000. In this same period, voter registration increased by 16 percent in these precincts. Thus, the 2000 race brought more Chicago Latinos to the polls, but the 1990s have seen an overall decline in Latino participation, both in raw numbers and as a percent of registered Latino voters.

No exit poll data are available for Illinois Latinos. As was the case in 1996, the Voter News Service consortium did not interview enough Latinos to report statistically reliable estimates of their candidate preferences. Based on the pre-election polls, it seems very likely that Gore did well among Illinois Latinos. Without exit polls, however, it is impossible to say exactly how well. The high-concentration precincts indicate that he might have done quite well (see table 11.2). In each of these seven precincts, Gore took at least 76 percent of the vote. In the precinct with the highest concentration of Latinos (the twenty-second, which is 77 percent Latino), Gore was the choice of nine of ten voters.

Table 11.2   Voter Registration and Turnout in High-Density Chicago Latino Wards, 1992, 1996, and 2000

Registration

Ward	% Latino	1992	1996	2000	Change (%) 1992–2000
22	77	14,985	15,191	18,490	+ 23.4
25	75	14,356	14,689	17,810	+ 24.1
12	73	12,035	12,183	14,677	+ 22.0
1	69	21,302	20,799	24,723	+ 16.1
26	68	22,783	23,250	25,558	+ 12.2
31	68	20,145	19,605	22,394	+ 11.2
35	65	19,719	20,614	22,009	+ 11.6
Total		125,325	126,331	145,661	+ 16.2

Voting

Ward	% Latino	1992	1996	2000	Change (%) 1992–2000	2000 Vote (%) Gore	Bush	Other
22	77	9,432	8,368	9,323	− 1.2	90.2	8.9	1.1
25	75	9,179	8,221	9,964	+ 8.6	80.9	15.3	3.4
12	73	7,574	5,968	6,230	− 17.7	79.2	18.7	2.2
1	69	13,370	10,956	14,391	+ 7.6	76.3	16.0	7.7
26	68	14,784	11,268	13,791	− 6.7	80.5	14.9	4.6
31	68	13,264	10,643	11,657	− 12.1	81.6	16.5	1.9
35	65	13,265	10,809	12,850	− 3.1	76.1	17.0	6.9
Total		80,868	66,233	78,206	− 3.3			

Note: The percentage of Latinos in these seven wards is based on 1990 census data. Each is likely to have become *more* Latino as the decade progressed, but Latinos are likely to make up a lower share of the voter population than they do of the population as a whole.

Sources: City of Chicago, Department of Planning and Development (1993); Chicago Board of Election Commissioners, 2001.

CONCLUSION

For the fourth presidential election cycle in a row, Illinois Latinos proved irrelevant to the statewide outcome in either the primary or the general election. Candidates and parties neglected them and they did little to counteract this neglect through community-based mobilization. This ongoing pattern of neglect and weak internal organization raises two questions. First, does it matter to the long-term empowerment of Illinois Latinos that they have repeatedly been neglected by the parties and candidates in election after election? Second, will the post-2000 redistricting give Illinois Latinos more opportunities to shape state and local electoral politics? If so, will parties and candidates have greater need to seek their votes?

The substantial increase in Illinois Latino voting in 2000, even in an election with so little mobilization, offers a note of optimism for future growth in Latino influence in Illinois. That said, the rapid increase between 1996 and 2000 is diminished if the period under investigation changes to 1992 to 2000. The 1996–2000 increase in Latino voting likely represents the steady increase in the voting-eligible population—that is, Latino adult U.S. citizens. As this population grows, more Latinos turn out to vote, even if the share of eligible Latinos voting stays the same. Without targeted efforts to mobilize new Latinos (or more competitive elections), it is unlikely that the high share of chronic nonparticipants identified by *Chicago Sun-Times* will diminish.

Redistricting, on the other hand, provided a jolt to state politics, but ultimately left the incentives for Latino mobilization much as they had been in the 1990s. Illinois saw its congressional delegation decline by one, necessitating the cannibalization of one district. A Latino district was secure, in part because a Latino district was guaranteed by the provisions of the Voting Rights Act, but also because one incumbent (Rod Blagojevich) gave up his seat to run for governor. Somewhat surprisingly, the Latino district that emerged looked very much like the Latino district of the 1990s, a "C" shape that connected Chicago's Mexican American and Puerto Rican neighborhoods while not touching the largely African American neighborhood in between. That the Illinois legislature chose to re-create this district was quite surprising. The oddly shaped district built explicitly around racial considerations would seem to be at constitutional risk in the wake of *Shaw v. Reno* (1993) and its progeny.[2] A district concentrated around Chicago's Mexican American population could have been drawn that would be compact and would not need to explicitly take ethnicity into account, but would nevertheless elect a Latino.

In the period before the Illinois legislature redistricted congressional seats, Chicago political actors—Latino and non-Latino alike—organized in a way unseen in the presidential election cycle. Representative Gutierrez's early endorsement of Senator Bradley and fund-raising can be seen as part of a strategy to prepare for 2002. He also raised his profile in national Latino politics and led the call for an expanded amnesty program for undocumented immigrants that was pressed by Latino leaders as the national Latino issue in the 2000 race (Mendez 2000; Zuckman and Stricherz 2000). Gutierrez's opponents in Chicago's machine also prepared. Alderman Danny Solis was seen as a likely Gutierrez challenger before the shape of the new district appeared (Mendieta, Sadovi, and Carpenter 2000). Mayor Daley also increased his criticism of Gutierrez. As soon as it became evident that the new district would look like the existing district, this contestation declined and the opportunity for a heavily contested race seeking Latino votes diminished considerably. To the extent that statewide politics continues to offer lopsided advantages for one party or the other, this would have been a rare opportunity for Latino mobilization. In its absence, however, conditions exogenous to Illinois's Latinos will continue to limit their voices and influence in statewide and national politics.

NOTES

1. The demographics offer a considerable note of caution of the accuracy of statewide polls of Latino communities. These polls—each purporting to accurately (within a margin of error, at least) represent the same population—shows a considerably difference. The Public Broadcasting Service poll, for example, is over 80 percent foreign born, while the William C. Velásquez poll is just 37 percent foreign born. The Tomás Rivera Policy Institute data are weighted to reflect the nativity composition of the state's Latino registered voters in 1998, with just 21 percent foreign born. Similarly, national origin varies among the three polls. The point of this methodological discussion is to suggest that it is wise to look

for common patterns as they are more likely to accurately represent the attitudes of Illinois Latinos than isolated findings not repeated in other surveys.

2. It should be noted that this district did survive two constitutional challenges before the U.S. Supreme Court that raised *Shaw* standards (*King v. Illinois Board of Elections*, No. 96-146; Elsasser 1998).

References

ABC News. 2000. "Exit Polls, State by State Voter Surveys." Http://abcnews.go.com/sections/politics/2000vote/general/exitpoll—hub.html (accessed June 15, 2003).

Abramowitz, Alan. 2004. *Voice of the People: Elections and Voting in the United States.* New York: McGraw-Hill.

Abramson, Paul R., John H. Aldrich, and David W. Rohde. 2003. *Change and Continuity in the 2000 and 2002 Elections.* Washington, DC: CQ Press.

Aguilar, Louis. 2001. "State's Latino Numbers Booming: Growth May Have 'Profound Impact.'" *Denver Post,* 8 March.

Alvarez, Michael, and Jonathan Nagler. 1999. "Is the Sleeping Giant Awakening? Latinos and California Politics in the 1990's." Paper presented at the annual meeting of the Midwest Political Science Association, Chicago, April.

Ames, Michele. 2000. "Negative Campaign Ads Can Do the Job." *Rocky Mountain News,* 12 November.

Andrew, Joseph. 2000. "Debating the GOP Record on Hispanics." *Washington Post,* 29 January.

Archibold, Randal C. 2000. "Between Cheek-Pinching and Pasta, Lazio Makes Appeals to Immigrants." *New York Times,* 23 October.

Arvizu, John R., and F. Chris Garcia. 1996. "Latino Voting Participation: Explaining and Differentiating Latino Voting Turnout." *Hispanic Journal of Behavioral Sciences* 18:104–128.

Avalos, Manuel. 1996. "Promise and Missed Opportunity: The 1992 Latino Vote in Arizona." In *Ethnic Ironies: Latino Politics in the 1992 Elections,* ed. Rodolfo O. de la Garza and Louis DeSipio, 95–110. Boulder, CO: Westview.

———. 1999. "Less Is More: Latinos in the 1996 Election in Arizona." In *Awash in the Mainstream: Latino Politics in the 1996 Election,* ed. Rodolfo O. de la Garza and Louis DeSipio, 117–136. Boulder, CO: Westview.

———. 2000. *Testimony in U.S. District Court: The Voting Integrity Project v. Mark Fleischer and Arizona Democratic Party.* U.S. District Court for the District of Arizona. March 1.

Barreto, Matt A., Gary M. Segura, and Nathan D. Woods. 2002. "Rest Assured? Estimating the Potential Mobilizing or Demobilizing Effects of Overlapping Majority-Minority Districts." Paper presented at the annual meeting of the Midwest Political Science Association, Chicago, April.

Barreto, Matt A., and Nathan D. Woods. 2000. "Voting Patterns and the Dramatic Growth of the Latino Electorate in Los Angeles County, 1994–1998." Claremont, CA: The Tomás Rivera Policy Institute.

———. 2001. "The Anti-Latino Political Context and Its Impact on GOP Detachment and Increasing Latino Voter Turnout in Los Angeles County." Paper presented at the Minority Representation Conference, Claremont, CA, January.

Belluck, Pam. 2000. "The Illinois Campaign: Where Gore Seemed Safe, There's a Race after All." New York Times, 3 November.

Block, A. G., and Richard Zeiger. 1990. "Constitutional Offices and Ballot Propositions—Election 1990—Term Limits." California Journal (December).

Booth, William. 2000. "A Key Constituency Defies Easy Labeling." Washington Post, 14 February.

Bragg, Rick. 1999. "Trump and His Portfolio Tour Miami." New York Times, 16 November.

Brooke, James. 1997. "Hispanic Leaders Feel Sands Shift beneath Them." New York Times, 15 July.

Brown, Fred. 2000a. "Why Play Favorites? Coloradans Prefer Bush, But Favor McCain vs. Gore." Denver Post, 5 March.

———. 2000b. "Only a Handful Show Hands." Denver Post, 10 August.

Brown, Fred, and Terri Cotten. 2000. "Lively Gore Promises to Fight for All." Denver Post, 29 February.

Browning, Rufus P., Dale Rogers Marshall, and David H. Tabb. 1984. Protest Is Not Enough: The Struggle of Blacks and Hispanics for Equality in Urban Politics. Berkeley: University of California Press.

Brownstein, Ronald. 2000. "Bradley's Drive for Minority Vote Is Raid on Gore's Home Territory." Los Angeles Times, 9 February.

Bruni, Frank. 1999. "Creating a Portrait of Bush, as an Upbeat Leader Promising a Fresh Start." New York Times, 26 October.

Bunis, Dena. 2000. "Democrat's Efforts with Latinos Pay Off." Orange County Register, 15 November.

Burns, Nancy, Kay Lehman Schlozman, and Sidney Verba. 2001. The Private Roots of Public Action: Gender, Equality, and Political Participation. Cambridge, MA: Harvard University Press.

"Bush Campaign Begins to Air Spanish-Language Ad." 2000. Santa Rosa Press Democrat, 7 February.

Bustillo, Miguel. 1999. "In Iowa, Latinos Bask in New Political Glow." Los Angeles Times, 8 November.

Calvo, Dana. 2000. "The Republican Convention: A New Accent; The Party That Spoke against Bilingualism in '96 Now Welcomes a Flood of U.S. Spanish-Language Media." Los Angeles Times, 3 August.

Calvo, Maria Antonia, and Steven J. Rosenstone. 1989. Hispanic Political Participation. San Antonio: Southwest Voter Research Institute, Inc.

Campaign Data. 2000. "Cuba Policy Poll." January 13–16. Miami: Campaign Data, Inc.

Caress, Stanley M. 1998. "Assessing Recent Research on Legislative Term Limits: The Case of California." American Review of Politics 19:253–266.

Carmines, Edward G., and James A. Stimson. 1989. *Issue Evolution: Race and the Transformation of American Politics.* Princeton, NJ: Princeton University Press.

Cart, Julie. 2000. "Tribal Languages Unintended Target in English-Only Drive." *Los Angeles Times,* 15 October.

————. 2000. "Missteps, Blunders Plaguing Tally in New Mexico's Biggest County." *Los Angeles Times,* 12 November.

Chicago Board of Election Commissioners. 2001. "Precinct Vote Totals." Unpublished data. Chicago: Chicago Board of Election Commissioners.

Chiu, L. 2000a. "Record Primary Turnout Dems' Vote Attracted across Racial Lines." *Arizona Republic,* 25 March, B1.

————. 2000b. "Net Vote Divided by Racial Lines." *Arizona Republic,* 12 April, B1.

Christenson, Sig. 2000. "Gore Big Hit with Hispanics, But Bush Sets GOP Record." *San Antonio Express-News,* 8 November.

City of Chicago, Department of Planning and Development. 1993. "Precinct Vote Totals." Unpublished data. Chicago: City of Chicago, Department of Planning and Development.

CNN. 2000a. "Exit Polls for Colorado." www.cnn.com/election/2000/epolls/co/p000.html (accessed December 10, 2000).

————. 2000b. "Exit Polls for Colorado." www.cnn.com/election/2000/epolls/co/i2000.html (accessed December 10, 2000).

————. 2000c. "Exit Polls for Colorado." www.cnn.com/election/2000/epolls/co/iten00.html (accessed December 10, 2000).

Coleman, Michael. 1999. "Domenici PAC Boosts Hispanics." *Albuquerque Journal,* 26 August.

————. 2000a. "Gore Aims to Attract Undecided." *Albuquerque Journal,* 27 April.

————. 2000b. "Buchanan Figures Bush Unprepared." *Albuquerque Journal,* 2 May.

————. 2000c. "Bush Addresses N. M. Topics." *Albuquerque Journal,* 1 June.

————. 2000d. "Hispanic Republicans Displeased." *Albuquerque Journal,* 16 June.

————. 2000e. "Bush's Nephew Visits Belen." *Albuquerque Journal,* 12 July.

————. 2000f. "N.M. Delegates Say Differences with GOP Must Be Pushed." *Albuquerque Journal,* 13 August.

————. 2000g. "Senator's PAC Gives $26,000 to N.M., Hispanics in GOP." *Albuquerque Journal,* 21 September.

————. 2000h. "Campaign to Bring Clinton to New Mexico." *Albuquerque Journal,* 21 September.

————. 2000i. "Gore Visits Hispanic Center." *Alburquerque Journal,* 23 October.

Colin, Sandra. 2001. Interview by Rodolfo O. de la Garza. Austin. January.

Colorado Reapportionment Commission. 2001. "Senate District Summary: Ethnic Breakdown of Districts Plus Voting Age Population." Colorado Reapportionment Commission, 30 July.

Colorado Secretary of State. 1980. *Abstract of Votes Cast 1980.* Denver: Secretary of State.

————. 1984. *Abstract of Votes Cast, 1984.* Denver: Secretary of State.

————. 1988. *Abstract of Votes Cast, 1988.* Denver: Secretary of State.

————. 1992. *Abstract of Votes Cast, 1992.* Denver: Secretary of State.

————. 1996. *Abstract of Votes Cast, 1996.* Denver: Secretary of State.

————. 2000a. *Abstract of Votes Cast, 2000.* Denver: Secretary of State.

————. 2000b. *Party Affiliation of Registered Voters as of November 6.* Denver: Secretary of State.

————. 2000c. "2000 Presidential Primary Election Results." www.sos.state.co.us/pubs/elections/2000PresPrimDem.htm (accessed November 2000).

Cottle, Michelle. 2000. "Campaign Journal: Mad Props." *The New Republic,* 24 July.

Cross, Beth. 1999. "Bush Launches Advertising Campaign in Iowa, New Hampshire." *CyberCaucus 2000 News Service,* 4 November.

Curry, Matt. 2000. "Bush's Election Still Uncertain; GOP Sweeps Other Texas Offices." *Associated Press State and Local Wire,* 8 November.

David, Yepsen. 1999. "New Bush Ads Include One in Spanish." *Des Moines Register,* 26 October.

de la Garza, Rodolfo O. 1992. "From Rhetoric to Reality: Latinos and the 1988 Election in Review." In *From Rhetoric to Reality: Latino Politics in the 1988 Elections,* ed. Rodolfo O. de la Garza and Louis DeSipio, 171–180. Boulder, CO: Westview.

————. 1995. "The Effects of Ethnicity on Political Culture." In *Classifying by Race,* ed. Paul E. Peterson, 333–353. Princeton, NJ: Princeton University.

————. 2004. "Latino Politics." In *Annual Review of Political Science,* ed. Nelson W. Polsby, 5. Palo Alto, CA: Annual Reviews.

de la Garza, Rodolfo O., and Louis DeSipio, eds. 1992. *From Rhetoric to Reality: Latino Politics in the 1988 Elections.* Boulder, CO: Westview.

————. 1993. "Save the Baby, Change the Bathwater, and Scrub the Tub: Latino Electoral Participation after Seventeen Years of Voting Rights Act Coverage." *Texas Law Review* 71 (June): 1479–1539.

————, eds. 1996. *Ethnic Ironies: Latino Politics in the 1992 Elections.* Boulder, CO: Westview.

————, eds. 1999. *Awash in the Mainstream: Latino Politics in the 1996 Elections.* Boulder, CO: Westview.

de la Garza, Rodolfo O., Louis DeSipio, F. Chris Garcia, John A. Garcia, and Angelo Falcón. 1992. *Latino Voices: Mexican, Puerto Rican and Cuban Perspectives on American Politics.* Boulder, CO: Westview.

de la Garza, Rodolfo O., Angelo Falcón, and F. Chris Garcia. 1996. "Will the Real Americans Please Stand Up: Anglo and Mexican-American Support of Core American Values." *American Journal of Political Science* 40:335–351.

de la Garza, Rodolfo O., Charles Haynes, and Jaesung Ryu. 2001. "Voting Frequency: An Analysis of Latino Voting Patterns in the 1992–1998 General Elections in Harris County, Texas." Working paper. Austin: University of Texas, Tomás Rivera Policy Institute.

de la Garza, Rodolfo O., Martha Menchaca, and Louis DeSipio, eds. 1994. *Barrio Ballots: Latino Politics in the 1990 Election.* Boulder, CO: Westview.

de la Garza, Rodolfo O., Daron Shaw, and Fujia Lu. 1999. "Where Have All the Democrats Gone? Latino Turnout and Partisanship in Texas." Paper presented at the annual meeting of the American Political Science Association, Atlanta, September.

DeSipio, Louis. 1996a. *Counting on the Latino Vote: Latinos as a New Electorate.* Charlottesville: University Press of Virginia.

———. 1996b. "Making Citizens or Good Citizens? Naturalization as a Predictor of Organizational and Electoral Behavior among Latino Immigrants." *Hispanic Journal of Behavioral Sciences* 18, no. 2 (May): 194–213.

———. 1996c. "After Proposition 187, the Deluge: Reforming Naturalization Administration While Making Good Citizens." *Harvard Journal of Hispanic Policy* 9:7–24.

———. 1999. "Election? What Election? Illinois Latinos and the 1996 Elections." In *Awash in the Mainstream: Latino Politics in the 1996 Elections,* ed. Rodolfo O. de la Garza and Louis DeSipio, 193–210. Boulder, CO: Westview.

———. 2000. "The Dynamo of Urban Growth: Immigration, Naturalization, and the Restructuring of Urban Politics." In *Minority Politics at the Millennium,* ed. Richard A. Keiser and Katherine Underwood, 77–108. New York: Garland.

———. 2002. "More than Passing Acquaintances: Latinos and Jews in Chicago." In *Latinos and Jews: Old Luggage, New Interests,* 102–112. New York: American Jewish Committee.

DeSipio, Louis, Rodolfo O. de la Garza, and Mark Setzler. 1999. "Awash in the Mainstream: Latinos and the 1996 Elections." In *Awash in the Mainstream: Latino Politics in the 1996 Elections,* ed. Rodolfo O. de la Garza and Louis DeSipio, 3–46. Boulder, CO: Westview.

Doolen, D. L. 2000. "Bilingual Ed Backers Flood TUSD Meeting." *Tucson Citizen,* 15 November, 1.

Downey, Tom. 2001. Interview by Rodney Hero and Patricia Jaramillo. Denver. January.

"Election Flip-Flops Put Gore in Front." 2000. *USA Today,* 14 November.

Election.com. 1999. "Arizona Democratic Party Selects Votation.com to Hold World's First Legally-Binding Public Election over the Internet." www.votation.com/us/pressroom/pr99/1216.htm (accessed June 2, 2003).

———. 2000. "Arizonans Embrace Online Voting." www.votation.com/us/pressroom/pr2000/0309.htm (accessed June 2, 2003).

Elsasser, Glen. 1998. "Hispanic District Gets High Court OK." *Chicago Tribune,* 27 January.

Ewegen, Bob. 2000. "Campaign 'Reform' Makes Things Worse." *Denver Post,* 23 August.

Fagan, Terrence. 2001. Interview by Rodney Hero and Patricia Jaramillo. Denver. January.

Falcón, Angelo. 1988. "Black and Latino Politics in New York City: Race and Ethnicity in a Changing Urban Context." In *Latinos and the Political System,* ed. F. Chris Garcia. Notre Dame, IN: University of Notre Dame Press.

———. 1992. "Puerto Ricans and the 1988 Election in New York City." In *From Rhetoric to Reality: Latino Politics in the 1988 Elections,* ed. Rodolfo O. de la Garza and Louis DeSipio, 147–170. Boulder, CO: Westview.

———. 1996. "Puerto Ricans in Postliberal New York: The 1992 Presidential Election." In *Ethnic Ironies: Latino Politics in the 1992 Elections,* ed. Rodolfo O. de la Garza and Louis DeSipio, 185–210. Boulder, CO: Westview.

———. 1999. "Beyond La Macarena? New York Puerto Rican, Dominican, and South American Voters in the 1996 Election." In *Awash in the Mainstream: Latino*

Politics in the 1996 Election, ed. Rodolfo O. de la Garza and Louis DeSipio, 249–268. Boulder, CO: Westview.

———. 2001. *"De'trás Pa'lante:* The Future of Puerto Rican History in New York City." New York: PRLDEF Institute for Puerto Rican Policy, January.

Farney, Dennis, and Eduardo Porter. 2000. "In Presidential Politics, Hispanics Are Taking on a New Significance." *Wall Street Journal,* 23 October.

Fecteau, Loie. 2000a. "Session Didn't Affect Party Loyalty." *Albuquerque Journal,* 22 March.

———. 2000b. "Lawmakers 'Not That Popular.'" *Albuquerque Journal,* 22 March.

———. 2000c. "Bush, Gore Each Score 41 Percent with State Voters." *Albuquerque Journal,* 20 March.

———. 2000d. "Bilingual Gore Woos UNM Crowd." *Albuquerque Journal,* 29 August.

———. 2000e. "GOP Tour Touts Bush in Northern Counties. *Albuquerque Journal,* 23 October.

Field Institute. 2000. "The Expanding Latino Electorate." Http://field.com/fieldpollon line/subscribers/Release1960.pdf (accessed July 17, 2003).

Fleisher, Mark. 2000. Deposition. *The Voting Integrity Project vs. Mark Fleisher.* United States District Court for Arizona, 18 February.

Flores, Juan. 2000. *From Bomba to Hip Hop: Puerto Rican Culture and Latino Identity.* New York: Columbia University Press.

Flores, Matt. 2000. "Demo Boss Sees a Texas Surprise." *San Antonio Express-News,* 1 July.

Florida Secretary of State, Division of Elections. 2000. "Registration for 2000 Presidential Election." www.dos.state.fl.us/elections (accessed October 10, 2000).

Fornek, Scott. 2000. "Kirk Gives Credit to Minority Voters." *Chicago Sun-Times,* 9 November, 18.

Fraga, Luis. 1992. "Prototype from the Midwest: Latinos in Illinois." In *From Rhetoric to Reality: Latino Politics in the 1988 Elections,* ed. Rodolfo O. de la Garza and Louis DeSipio, 111–126. Boulder, CO: Westview.

Freemantle, Tony. 2000. "Texas Is Bush Country, Latest Survey Suggests." *Houston Chronicle,* 4 March.

Fuchs, Ester R., Robert Y. Shapiro, and Lorraine C. Minnite. 2001. "Social Capital, Political Participation, and the Urban Community." In *Social Capital and Poor Communities,* ed. Susan Saegert, J. Phillip Thompson, and Mark R. Warren. New York: Russell Sage Foundation.

Gallegos, Gilbert. 2000a. "Gore Visit Highlights Wide Circle of Swing Votes." *Albuquerque Tribune,* 28 April.

———. 2000b. "New Mexico's Vote More Important than People Think, Experts Say." *Albuquerque Tribune,* 29 April.

———. 2000c. "Hispanics Hope GOP Gives Them More Than Just Lip Service." *Albuquerque Tribune,* 31 May.

———. 2000d. "Bush Advisers Wooing Hispanic Vote in N.M." *Albuquerque Tribune,* 2 August.

———. 2000e. "Gore Asked to Consider Universal Health Care." *Albuquerque Tribune,* 30 August.

Garcia, F. Chris. 1996. "Conventional Politics under Unusual Circumstances: Latinos and the 1992 Election in New Mexico." In *Ethnic Ironies: Latino Politics in the 1992 Elections,* ed. Rodolfo de la Garza and Louis DeSipio, 53–74. Boulder, CO: Westview.

Garcia, F. Chris, and Rodolfo O. de la Garza. 1977. *The Chicano Political Experience: Three Perspectives.* North Scituate, MA: Duxbury.

Garcia, F. Chris, and Bianca Sapien. 1999. "Recognizing Reliability: Hispanos in the 1996 Elections in New Mexico." In *Awash in the Mainstream: Latino Politics in the 1996 Election,* ed. Rodolfo de la Garza and Louis DeSipio, 75–100. Boulder, CO: Westview.

García, Ignacio M. 2000. *Viva Kennedy: Mexican Americans in Search of Camelot.* College Station: Texas A&M University Press.

García, James. 2000. "Bush Led Inroads among Latinos." *Politico,* 9 November.

Garcia, Michael. 2002. Interview by Rodney Hero and Patricia Jaramillo. Denver. June.

Giroux, Gregory L. 2000. "Illinois 10th Rivals Reach out to Hispanic Voters." *Congressional Quarterly,* 30 October.

Glover, Cindy. 1998. "Surname Not Big Factor in NM." *Albuquerque Journal,* 7 September.

Gonzalez, D. 2000. "Latinos May Hold the Key to Arizona's Electoral Votes." *Arizona Republic,* 2 October, B1.

"GOP 'Big Tent' Still Short on Hispanics." 2000. *Albuquerque Journal,* 18 June, B2.

"Gore Finally Claims New Mexico." 2000. Associated Press, 18 November.

Graham, Pamela M. 2001. "Political Incorporation and Re-incorporation: Simultaneity in the Dominican Migrant Experience." In *Migration, Transnationalization and Race in a Changing New York,* ed. Hector R. Cordero-Guzmán, Robert C. Smith, and Ramón Grosfoguel, 87–108. Philadelphia: Temple University Press.

Green, Donald P., Alan S. Gerber, and David W. Nickerson. 2003. "Getting out the Vote in Local Elections: Results from Six Door-to-Door Canvassing Experiments." *Journal of Politics* 65 (November): 1083–1096.

Green, Eric. 2000. "Hispanics Vote 2–1 for Gore over Bush in U.S. Presidential Election." *Washington File,* 14 November.

Guerra, Fernando. 1992. "Conditions Not Met: California Elections and the Latino Community." In *From Rhetoric to Reality: Latino Politics in the 1988 Elections,* ed. Rodolfo O. de la Garza and Louis DeSipio, 99–107. Boulder, CO: Westview.

Guerra, Fernando, and Luis Ricardo Fraga. 1996. "Theory, Reality, and Perpetual Potential: Latinos in the 1992 California Elections." In *Ethnic Ironies: Latino Politics in the 1992 Elections,* ed. Rodolfo O. de la Garza and Louis DeSipio, 131–145. Boulder, CO: Westview.

Guerra, Frank. 2001. Interviews by Robert Marbut Jr. Austin, TX. 1999–2001.

Hanson-Sánchez, Christopher. 1996. *New York City Latino Neighborhoods Databook.* New York: Institute for Puerto Rican Policy.

Hardt, Robert, Jr., and Gregg Birnbaum. 2000. "Team Lazio Will 'Call' on Gore Voters." *New York Post,* 26 September.

Harpaz, Beth J. 2001. *The Girls in the Van: Covering Hillary.* New York: Dunne.

Hawkins, Brett W., and Robert A. Lorinskas. 1970. *The Ethnic Factor in American Politics.* Columbus, OH: Merrill.

Heath, Jena. 1999. "Campaign 2000: Bush's Plan to Win Every Latino Vote Goes into High Gear." *Atlanta Journal and Constitution,* 19 December.

Herman, Ken. 2000. "The Texas Delegation: Democrats' Rising Star Is a No-Show." *Austin American-Statesman,* 14 August.

Hero, Rodney. 1992. "Latinos and the 1988 Elections: Arizona." In *From Rhetoric to Reality: Latino Politics in the 1988 Election,* ed. Rodolfo O. de la Garza and Louis DeSipio, 77–83. Boulder, CO: Westview.

———. 1996. "An Essential Vote: Latinos and the 1992 Elections in Colorado." In *Ethnic Ironies: Latino Politics in the 1992 Elections,* ed. Rodolfo O. de la Garza and Louis DeSipio, 75–94. Boulder, CO: Westview.

Hero, Rodney, E., Chris Garcia, John Garcia, and Harry Pachon. 2000. "Latino Participation, Partisanship and Office Holding." *PS: Political Science and Politics* 33, no. 3: 529–534.

Hero, Rodney E., Patricia A. Jaramillo, and John C. Halpin. 1999. "Similar Behavior, Different Results: Latinos and the 1996 Elections in Colorado." In *Awash in the Mainstream: Latino Politics in the 1996 Elections,* ed. Rodolfo O. de la Garza and Louis DeSipio, 101–116. Boulder, CO: Westview.

Heslop, Alan. 1990. "Prop. 140 Clips the Gerrymander's Claws." *San Diego Union-Tribune,* 2 December, C1.

Hibbing, John R., and Elizabeth Theiss-Morse. 2002. *Stealth Democracy: Americans' Beliefs about How Government Should Work.* New York: Cambridge University Press.

Hubbard, Burt. 2000. "Smear Mailing Targets Candidate." *Rocky Mountain News,* 9 October.

Hughes, Polly Ross. 2000. "Texas' Image Bruised by Campaign, Poll Shows." *Houston Chronicle,* 4 November.

Jackson, Robert A. 2003. "Differential Influences on Latino Electoral Participation." *Political Behavior* 25 (December): 339–366.

Jacobs, Lawrence R., and Robert Y. Shapiro. 2000. *Politicians Don't Pander: Political Manipulation and the Loss of Democratic Responsiveness.* Chicago: University of Chicago Press.

Jeffe, Sherry Bebitch. 2001. "California; GOP Mulls a New Face." *Los Angeles Times,* 9 September.

Johnson, James, Walter Farrell, and Chandra Guinn. 1997. "Immigration Reform and the Browning of America: Tensions, Conflicts and Community Instability in Metropolitan Los Angeles." *International Migration Review* 31, no. 4: 1055–1095.

Jones-Correa, Michael. 1998. *Between Two Nations: The Political Predicament of Latinos in New York City.* Ithaca, NY: Cornell University Press.

Judis, John B., and Ruy Teixeira. 2002. *The Emerging Democratic Majority.* New York: Scribner.

Keller, Rudi. 2000. "Bush Gets to Point at UNM." *Albuquerque Journal,* 16 September.

Kelley, Matt. 2000. "Most N.M. Democratic Delegates Are Hispanic." *Albuquerque Tribune,* 12 August.

King, Gary. 1997. *A Solution to the Ecological Inference Problem.* Princeton, NJ: Princeton University Press.

Koenig, David. 2000. "Exit Poll Points to Possible Weaknesses in Bush, Gore Candidacies." *Associated Press State and Local Wire,* 14 March.

Koidin, Michelle. 2000. "Bush Putting up a Fight for Hispanic Voters." *Associated Press State and Local Wire,* 6 April.

Labor Leader. 2000. Interview by Lisa J. Montoya. Austin, TX. August.

Laó-Montes, Agustín, and Arlene Dávila, eds. 2001. *Mambo Montage: The Latinization of New York.* New York: Columbia University Press.

Leib, Jeffrey. 2000. "Gore Gets Brief Lift from DUI, Poll Says." *Denver Post,* 5 November.

Leighley, Jan E. 2001. *Strength in Numbers? The Political Mobilization of Racial and Ethnic Minorities.* Princeton, NJ: Princeton University Press.

Li, David K. 2000. "A Game of Poker Could Decide N.M." *New York Post,* 14 November.

Lipsher, Steve. 2000. "More Conservative GOP—But More Dems." *Denver Post,* 8 November.

Lublin, David. 2001. "Explaining Support for Gay and Lesbian Rights in the 106th Congress." Unpublished manuscript. Washington, DC: American University.

Maceri, Domenico. 1999. "Se Habla Politics." *La Prensa San Diego,* 23 July.

MacManus, Susan A., Dario Moreno, Richard Scher, and Henry Thomas. 2001. *Florida Election Poll.* April 3–8, 2001, by Schroth and Associates. Tallahassee: Florida Institute of Government.

Maisel, L. Sandy. 2002. *Parties and Elections in America: The Electoral Process,* 3rd. ed. Lanham, MD: Rowman & Littlefield.

Manfuso, Jamie. 2000. "Reforms by Bush Elusive for Voters." *Austin American-Statesman,* 25 June.

Marcus, George E., W. Russell Neuman, and Michael MacKuen. 2000. *Affective Intelligence and Political Judgment.* Chicago: University of Chicago Press.

Marelius, John. 1998. "The Wilson Years: A Governor's Legacy: First of Three Parts." *San Diego Union-Tribune,* 27 December.

Marinucci, Carla. 2000. "Republicans Go All out to Sway the Latino Vote/GOP, Bush Planning Separate Advertising Campaigns." *San Francisco Chronicle,* 14 January.

Marinucci, Carla, and John Wildermuth. 2001. "State GOP Gropes for Way to Revive Defeated Party." *San Francisco Chronicle,* 25 February, A4.

Martinez, Valerie. 1996. "Unrealized Expectations: Latinos and in the 1992 Elections in Texas." In *Ethnic Ironies: Latino Politics and the 1992 Elections,* ed. Rodolfo O. de la Garza and Louis DeSipio, 113–130. Boulder, CO: Westview.

Mayes, Kris. 1999. "Bush Aims for Latino Vote." *Arizona Republic,* 27 June.

Meckler, Laura. 2000a. "Bush, Gore Ads Courting Hispanics." *Associated Press,* 19 October.

———. 2000b. "GOP Courting Hispanics with New Ad." Associated Press Newswire, 5 April.

Mellen, Karen. 2000. "GOP Works to Boost Its Appeal for Hispanics." *Chicago Tribune,* 12 October.

Mendez, Adolfo. 2000. "Illinois Congressman Leads Amnesty Call for Undocumented Immigrants." *Latino.com,* 11 July.

Mendieta, Ana, Carlos Sadovi, and John Carpenter. 2000. "Hispanic Clout Is Soaring." *Chicago Sun-Times,* 6 March, 6.

Merrill, B. 2000. *KAET Poll: English Immersion Initiative Supported.* Tempe, AZ: KAET.

Metro-Dade Elections Department. 1980. "Official Elections Results." Miami, FL: Miami-Dade County Elections.

———. 1984. "Official Elections Results." Miami, FL: Miami-Dade County Elections.

———. 1988. "Official Elections Results." Miami, FL: Miami-Dade County Elections.

———. 1992. "Official Elections Results." Miami, FL: Miami-Dade County Elections.

———. 1996. "Official Elections Results." Miami, FL: Miami-Dade County Elections.

———. 2000. "Official Elections Results." Miami, FL: Miami-Dade County Elections.

Mexican American Legal Defense and Education Fund. 2000. *Policy Issues for the Presidential Candidates in the 2000 Presidential Campaign.* Washington, DC: Mexican American Legal Defense and Education Fund.

Michelson, Melissa. 2001. "Competing Vote Cues and the Authenticity of Representation: Latino Support for Anglo Democrats and Latino Republicans." Paper presented at the annual meeting of the Midwest Political Science Association, Chicago, April 25–28.

———. 2003a. "Getting out the Latino Vote: How Door-to-Door Canvassing Influences Voter Turnout in Rural Central California." *Political Behavior* 25 (September): 247–263.

———. 2003b. "The Corrosive Effect of Acculturation: How Mexican Americans Lose Political Trust." *Social Science Quarterly* 84 (December): 918–933.

Michelson, Melissa, and Enia Leon. 2001. "Does Ethnicity Trump Party? Latino Voting Behavior in California's 20th District." Paper prepared at the annual meeting of the Western Political Science Association, Las Vegas, March.

Minnite, Lorraine C., Jennifer Holdaway, and Ronald Hayduk. 1999. "The Political Incorporation of Immigrants in New York." Paper presented at the annual meeting of the American Political Science Association, Atlanta, September.

Minnite, Lorraine, Robert Y. Shapiro, and Ester R. Fuchs. 1997. "Political Participation and Political Representation in New York City, with a Special Focus on Latino New Yorkers." New York: Barnard-Columbia Center for Urban Policy.

Mollenkopf, John, and Luis A. Miranda Jr. 2002. *Latino Political Participation in New York City: A Report of the Hispanic Federation.* New York: Hispanic Federation.

Mollenkopf, John, David Olson, and Timothy Ross. 2001. "Immigrant Politics Participation in New York and Los Angeles." In *Governing American Cities: Inter-ethnic Coalitions, Competition, and Conflict,* ed. Michael Jones-Correa, 17–70. New York: Russell Sage Foundation.

Montoya, Lisa. 1999. "Senor Smith Didn't Go to Washington: Latinos and the 1996 Texas Elections." In *Awash in the Mainstream: Latino Politics in the 1996 Election,* ed. Rodolfo O. de la Garza and Louis DeSipio, 131–145. Boulder, CO: Westview.

Moreno, Dario, and Christopher Warren. 1992. "The Conservative Enclave: Cubans in Florida." In *From Rhetoric to Reality: Latino Politics in the 1988 Elections,* ed. Rodolfo O. de la Garza and Louis DeSipio, 127–146. Boulder, CO: Westview.

————. 1996. "The Conservative Enclave Revisited: Cuban Americans in Florida." In *Ethnic Ironies: Latino Politics in the 1992 Elections,* ed. Rodolfo de la Garza and Louis DeSipio, 169–184. Boulder, CO: Westview.

————. 1999. "Pragmatism and Strategic Realignment in the 1996 Election: Florida's Cuban Americans." In *Awash in the Mainstream: Latino Politics in the 1996 Election,* ed. Rodolfo O. de la Garza and Louis DeSipio, 211–238. Boulder, CO: Westview.

National Association of Latino Elected and Appointed Officials Educational Fund. 1990. *National Roster of Hispanic Elected Officials.* Los Angeles: National Association of Latino Elected and Appointed Officials Educational Fund.

————. 2000. "Latinos Grab Seats in State Houses Nationwide: Foundation Set for Redistricting and Future Latino Political Progress." Press release, 9 November.

————. 2001. Personal communication with Harry Pachon.

————. 2002. *Latino Election Handbook.* Los Angeles: National Association of Latino Elected and Appointed Officials Educational Fund.

National Hispanic Leadership Agenda. 2000. *2000 Policy Agenda: An Agenda for the Advancement of Hispanic Americans.* Washington, DC: National Hispanic Leadership Agenda.

Navarro, Mireya. 2000. "Puerto Rican Presence Wanes in New York." *New York Times,* 28 February.

Neal, Steve. 1999a. "Del Valle Throws Support to Bradley." *Chicago Sun-Times,* 29 September, 8.

————. 1999b. "Gutierrez Supports Bradley Campaign." *Chicago Sun-Times,* 28 December, 1.

Nevins, Buddy. 2002. "The Influential, the Reformers and the Philanthropists—Their Faces Change, But Role Stays Constant." *Sun-Sentinel,* 30 June, H1.

Newton, Lina. 2000. "Why Some Latinos Supported Proposition 187: Testing Economic Threat and Cultural Identity Hypotheses." *Social Science Quarterly* 81, no. 1 (March).

Nie, Norman H., Jane Junn, and Kenneth Stehlik-Barry. 1996. *Education and Democratic Citizenship in America.* Chicago: University of Chicago Press.

Noonan, Peggy. 2000. *The Case against Hillary Clinton.* New York: Regan.

Novak, Robert. 2000. "Golden State Attracts Green." *Chicago Sun-Times,* 22 October.

Nye, Joseph, Philip Zelikow, and David King, eds. 1997. *Why People Don't Trust Government.* Cambridge, MA: Harvard University Press.

Olinger, David. 2001. "See How We've Grown: Front Range Drives Statewide Boom." *Denver Post,* 20 March.

Olson, Barbara. 1999. *Hell to Pay: The Unfolding Story of Hillary Rodham Clinton.* Washington, DC: Regnery.

Orlov, Rick. 2000. "Bush Splits with Wilson on Prop. 187." *L.A. Daily News,* 8 April.

Orosco, Cynthia. 2000. "Republicans Pledge Increased Latino Participation, Visibility at Convention." *Hispanic Link Weekly Report* 18, no. 30 (July 31): 1.

Ortiz, P. 2000. "Hard Job: Get New Latino Voters to Polls." *Arizona Republic,* 16 October, B1.

Pachon, Harry. 1998. "Latino Politics in the Golden State: Ready for the 21st Century?" In *Racial and Ethnic Politics in California,* ed. Michael B. Preston, Bruce E. Cain, and Sandra Bass, 411–438. 2nd ed. Berkeley, CA: IGS Press.

Pachon, Harry, and Lourdes Arguelles. 1994. "Grass Roots Politics in an East Los Angeles Barrio." In *Barrio Ballots: Latino Politics in the 1990 Elections,* ed. Rodolfo de la Garza, Martha Menchaca, and Louis DeSipio, 137–160. Boulder, CO: Westview.

Pachon, Harry P., and Rodolfo O. de la Garza. 1998. "Why Pollsters Missed the Latino Vote—Again." *Policy Note.* Claremont, CA: Tomás Rivera Policy Institute (July): 1–2.

Padilla, Felix. 1986. *Latino Ethnic Consciousness: The Case of Mexican Americans and Puerto Ricans in Chicago.* Notre Dame, IN: University of Notre Dame Press.

Pantoja, Adrian D., and Gary M. Segura. 2003. "Fear and Loathing in California: Contextual Threat and Political Sophistication among Latino Voters." *Political Behavior* 25 (September): 265–286.

Pantoja, Adrian, Ricardo Ramírez, and Gary M. Segura. 2001. "Citizens by Choice, Voters by Necessity: Patterns in Political Mobilization by Naturalized Latinos." *Political Research Quarterly* 54, no. 4 (December): 729–750.

Park, David K., and Carlos Vargas-Ramos. 2002. "Paradigms of Minority Political Participation in the United States." In *Research in Micropolitics,* vol. 6, *Political Decision Making, Deliberation and Participation,* ed. Michael X. Delli Carpini, Leonie Huddy, and Robert Y. Shapiro. New York: Elsevier.

Pérez Viera, Edgardo. 2002. *Victoria de un Pueblo: Crónica del Grito de Vieques.* San Juan: Editorial Cultural.

Perez, Miguel. 2000. "Politicians Stake Ground in Battle for Latino Vote." *The Record—Northern New Jersey,* 1 January.

Pitts, David. 2000. "Hispanic Vote in U.S. Growing Larger, But Diverse." *Election 2000 Campaign Spotlight,* 1 March.

Plotz, David. 2000. "Energy Secretary Bill Richardson: He Schmoozes. He Loses." *Slate,* 22 June.

Popkin, Samuel L. 1994. *The Reasoning Voter: Communication and Persuasion in Presidential Campaigns.* Chicago: University of Chicago Press.

Public Broadcasting Service. 2000. "Public Broadcasters to Release Results of National Latino Poll." Press release, 26 July, www.latinopoll2000.com (accessed July 16, 2001).

Puente, Teresa. 2000. "Candidates Take Pass on Latino Conference." *Chicago Tribune,* 30 September.

Purdum, Todd S. 1997. "California G.O.P. Faces a Crisis as Hispanic Voters Turn Away." *New York Times,* 9 December.

Putnam, Robert D. 1995. "Tuning in, Tuning Out: The Strange Disappearance of Social Capital in American." *PS: Political Science and Politics* 28 (December): 664–683.

———. 2000. *Bowling Alone: The Collapse and Renewal of American Community.* New York: Simon and Schuster.

Pycior, Julie Leininger. 1997. *LBJ and Mexican Americans: The Paradox of Power.* Austin: University of Texas Press.

"Race Summary Report." 2000. General Election. Austin: Texas Secretary of State, http://204.65.104.19/elchist.exe (accessed June 11, 2003).

Ramírez, Ricardo. 2002. "Getting out the Vote: The Impact of Non-partisan Voter Mobilization Efforts in Low Turnout Latino Precincts." Paper presented at the annual meeting of the American Political Science Association, Boston, Massachusetts, August 28–September 1.

Rangel, Irma. 2001. Interview by Lisa J. Montoya. Austin, TX. May.

Ratcliffe, R. G. 2000. "Good Economic Times Give Gore an Edge over Bush, Polls Show." *Houston Chronicle,* 26 September.

Reich, Robert. 1997. *Locked in the Cabinet.* New York: Knopf.

Rey, Roberto. 1996. "Leverage without Influence: Illinois Latino Politics in 1992." In *Ethnic Ironies: Latino Politics in the 1992 Elections,* ed. Rodolfo O. de la Garza and Louis DeSipio, 149–168. Boulder, CO: Westview.

Roberts, Chris. 2000. "Gore Tries to Sway Undecided N.M. Voters." *Albuquerque Journal,* 29 April.

Robison, Clay. 2000a. "Bush Can Afford to Shun Texas Shindig." *Houston Chronicle,* 28 May.

———. 2000b. "Bush Leads Gore by Wide Margin among Texas Voters, Poll Shows." *Houston Chronicle,* 25 June.

Rodríguez, Alex. 1999. "Hispanic Voters Absent: Despite Numbers, Group Lacks Clout." *Chicago Sun-Times,* 18 January, 1.

Rosales, Rodolfo O. 2000. *The Illusion of Inclusion: The Untold Political Story of San Antonio.* Austin: University of Texas Press.

Rosenstone, Steven J., and John Mark Hansen. 1993. *Mobilization, Participation, and Democracy in America.* New York: Macmillan.

Schneider, William. 1999. "Prop 187's Backlash: It's Still Ferocious." *National Journal* (August).

Segura, Gary, Dennis Falcón, and Harry Pachon. 1997. "Dynamics of Latino Partisanship in California: Immigration, Issue Salience, and Their Implications." *Harvard Journal of Hispanic Policy* 10:62–80.

Segura, Gary, Chris Garcia, Rodolfo O. de la Garza, and Harry Pachon. 1999. "Social Capital and the Latino Community: Are Latinos Really Bowling Alone?" *Policy Note.* Claremont, CA: Tomás Rivera Policy Institute (February): 1–2.

Shaw, Daron, Rodolfo O. de la Garza, and Jongho Lee. 2000. "Examining Latino Turnout in 1996: A Three-State, Validated Survey Approach." *American Journal of Political Science* 44 (April): 338–346.

Sherwood, R. 2000. "Ruling OKs Internet Voting in State Dem Primary." *Arizona Republic,* 1 March, A1.

Sierra, Christine Marie. 1992. "Hispanos and the 1988 General Election in New Mexico." In *From Rhetoric to Reality: Latino Politics in the 1988 Elections,* ed. Rodolfo O. de la Garza and Louis DeSipio, 43–68. Boulder, CO: Westview.

Sierra, Christine Marie, Sylvia Rodriguez, and Felipe Gonzales. 1999. *This Town Is Not for Sale: The 1994 Santa Fe Mayoral Election.* Albuquerque: KNME-TV5. Videocassette.

Silva, Mark. 2000. "Bush's Approval Rating Still High." *Miami Herald,* 1 March, 1B–2B.

Smith, Dan. 1998. "Wilson's on Latino Hot Seat—Unlike Potential Foe Gov. George Bush." *Sacramento Bee,* 28 June.

Sosa, Lionel. 2002. Interviews by Robert Marbut Jr. San Antonio, TX. 1998–2002.

"The Spanish Test." 1999. *New York Times Magazine,* 8 August.

"Special Report: A Mercury News Poll of Latinos." 2000. *San Jose Mercury News,* www.mercurycenter.com/local/center/polldata.htm.

Stansberry, Jack. 2002. Interview by Rodney Hero and Patricia Jaramillo. Denver, CO. June.

State of New Mexico. 2000. *Official 2000 General Election Results.* Santa Fe: Secretary of State.

Stutz, Terrence. 1994. "Lawmakers, Bush Oppose Denying Aliens Education—No Backing Seen for California-Type Bill." *Dallas Morning News,* 23 November.

Sylvester, Sherry. 2000. "Hispanic Vote Efforts Hard to See." *San Antonio Express-News,* 15 October.

Tapper, Jake. 2000. "California Dreaming." *Salon,* 31 October.

"They'll Be Back." 2001. *Economist,* 24 February.

Tomás Rivera Policy Institute. 2000a. *TRPI Pre-election Survey of Latino Registered Voters, October 2000.* Unpublished data. Claremont, CA: The Tomás Rivera Policy Institute.

———. 2000b. "Most Latinos Favor Gore for President, Favor Democrats for Congress." Press release, 1 November, www.trpi.org/press/110100.html (accessed January 31, 2004).

Torres, Maria de los Angeles. 1991. "The Commission on Latino Affairs: A Case Study of Community Empowerment." In *Harold Washington and the Neighborhoods: Progressive City Government in Chicago, 1983–1987,* ed. Pierre Clavel and Wim Wiewel, 165–186. New Brunswick, NJ: Rutgers University Press.

United Press International. 2000. "Even Bush Can't Lure Hispanics to GOP." *United Press International,* 8 November.

U.S. Bureau of the Census. 1978. "Voting and Registration in the Election of November 1976." Series P-20 #322. Washington, D.C.: U.S. Bureau of the Census.

———. 1982. "Voting and Registration in the Election of November 1980." Series P-20 #370. Washington, D.C.: U.S. Bureau of the Census.

———. 1986. "Voting and Registration in the Election of November 1984." Series P-20 #405. Washington, D.C.: U.S. Bureau of the Census.

———. 1990. "Voting and Registration in the Election of November 1988." Series P-20 #414. Washington, D.C.: U.S. Bureau of the Census.

———. 1994. "Voting and Registration in the Election of November 1992." Series P-20 #466. Washington, D.C.: U.S. Bureau of the Census.

———. 1996. "Voting and Registration in the Election of November 1994." Series PPL-25RV. www.census.gov/population/www/socdemo/voting/vote-wtabcon.html (accessed March 9, 2004).

———. 1998. "Voting and Registration in the Election of November 1996." www.census.gov/prod/3/98pubs/p20–504u.pdf (accessed June 19, 2002).

———. 2000a. "Population Estimates for States by Race Hispanic Origin: July 1, 1999." Population Estimates Program, Population Division, U.S. Bureau of the Census. Release date, 30 August.

———. 2000b. *Census 2000 Redistricting Data (PL94–171).* Summary File Matrices PL1, PL2, PL3, and PL4. Washington, DC: U.S. Bureau of the Census.

———. 2000c. *Voting and Registration in the Election of November 1998.* Detailed tables. Series P-20 #523. Washington, DC: U.S. Bureau of the Census.

———. 2001. "State and County Quickfacts-Colorado." Http://quickfacts.census .gov/qfd/states/08000.html (accessed December 14, 2001).

———. 2002a. "Voting and Registration in the Election of November 2000." www.census.gov/population/www/socdem/voting/p20–542.pdf (accessed June 19, 2002).

————. 2002b. "American Fact Finder." Http://quickfacts.census.gov/qfd/index.html (accessed June 21, 2002).

————. 2002c. *Voting and Registration in the Election of November 2000.* Detailed tables. Series P-20 #542. Washington, DC: U.S. Bureau of the Census, www.census.gov/population/www/socdemo/voting/p20–542.html (accessed February 15, 2003).

————. 2002d. "State and County Quickfacts." Washington, D.C.: U.S. Bureau of the Census. Http://quickfacts.census.gov/qfd/states/06000.html (accessed March 9, 2004).

U.S. Department of Commerce. 1999. *Falling through the Net: Defining the Digital Divide.* Washington, DC: U.S. Department of Commerce.

Vargas-Ramos, Carlos. 2003. "The Political Participation of Puerto Ricans in New York City." *CENTRO: Journal of the Center for Puerto Rican Studies* 15 (Spring): 40–71.

Valadez, John. 1994. "Latino Politics in Chicago: Latino Politics in Pilsen." In *Barrio Ballots: Latino Politics in the 1990 Election,* ed. Rodolfo O. de la Garza, Martha Menchaca, and Louis DeSipio, 115–136. Boulder, CO: Westview.

Verba, Sidney, Kay Lehman Schlozman, and Henry E. Brady. 1995. *Voice and Equality: Civic Voluntarism in American Politics.* Cambridge, MA: Harvard University Press.

Vigil, Maurilio. 1985. *The Hispanics of New Mexico: Essays on History and Culture.* Bristol, IN: Wyndham Hall.

Voter News Service. 2000. *Presidential Exit Polls, 2000.* New York: Voter News Service.

Waldman, Amy. 2000. "New Yorkers Stand out in Protests over Vieques." *New York Times,* 5 May.

Webb, Andrew. 2000. "Bush Pushes Education Plan During U. New Mexico Speech." *New Mexico Daily Lobo,* 18 September.

Werner, Erica. 2000. "Hispanic Voters Rush to Polls." Associated Press, 9 November.

"Who Voted: A Portrait of American Politics, 1976–2000." 2000. *New York Times,* 12 November, 4.

Wilhelm, Anthony G. 2000. *Democracy in the Digital Age: Challenges to Political Life in Cyberspace.* New York: Routledge.

Willie C. Velasquez Institute. 2000a. "Gore Expands Support among Latino Voters." Press release, 6 October.

————. 2000b. "Kay Bailey Hutchison Wins Latino Vote by Small Margin." www.wcvi.org/press_room/press_releases/tx/pr_txexitpoll_112200.html (accessed June 10, 2003).

————. 2000c. "Gore Wins Latino Vote in Texas." www.wcvi.org/press_room/press_releases/tx/pr_txexitpoll_00.html (accessed June 10, 2003).

————. 2000d. "Latino Vote Hit [*sic*] One Million in Texas." www.wcvi.org/press_room/press_releases/tx/pr_txexitpoll_00_2.html (accessed June 10, 2003).

————. 2000e. "Support for Bush Weak among Hispanos in New Mexico." Press release, 5 October.

————. 2000f. "Support for Bush Plummets among Latinos in Illinois." Press release, 3 October.

Wolfinger, Raymond, and Steven Rosenstone. 1980. *Who Votes?* New Haven, CT: Yale University Press.

Zuckman, Jill, and Mark Stricherz. 2000. "Gutierrez Takes Place in Forefront of Leading Latinos. *Chicago Tribune,* 4 September.

Index

~~~~~~

Note: Page numbers in *italic* type refer to figures or tables.

About the Contributors

~~~~~~

Manuel Avalos is vice provost for research and faculty development and associate professor of political science at Arizona State University, West. He has published articles in *Sociological Perspectives, Policy Studies Journal,* and the *Harvard Journal of Hispanic Policy.* His research focuses on questions of social, political, and economic inequality of racial and ethnic groups in the Americas.

Matt A. Barreto is a graduate student in the Ph.D. program at the University of California, Irvine, and a research associate at the Tomás Rivera Policy Institute. He is published in the *American Political Science Review* and the *Harvard Journal of Hispanic Policy.*

Rodolfo O. de la Garza is Eaton Professor of Administrative Law and Municipal Science and professor of political science at Columbia University. He also serves as vice president of the Tomás Rivera Policy Institute. He is the author or editor of sixteen books and more than sixty journal articles and book chapters including, most recently, "Latino Politics," a review of the Latino politics research for the *Annual Review of Political Science.*

Louis DeSipio is associate professor of political science and Chicano/Latino studies at the University of California, Irvine. He is the author of *Counting on the Latino Vote: Latinos as a New Electorate* (1996) and the coauthor (with Rodolfo O. de la Garza) of *Making Americans, Remaking America: Immigration and Immigrant Policy* (1998).

Angelo Falcón is the senior policy executive of the Puerto Rican Legal Defense and Education Fund in New York City. He is also adjunct associate professor at the Columbia University School of International and Public Affairs. He has written extensively on Puerto Rican and Latino politics in the United States. His most recent book is *Boricuas in Gotham: Puerto Ricans in the Making of Modern New York City 1945–2000* (forthcoming), which he coedited.

Luis Ricardo Fraga is associate professor in the Department of Political Science at Stanford University. He is coeditor of *Ethnic and Racial Minorities in Advanced Industrial Democracies* (1992). He is currently completing two other book manuscripts: *The Changing Urban Regime: Toward an Informed Public Interest*, a study of racial and ethnic representation in San Antonio, Texas, and *Missed Opportunities: The Politics of Schools in San Francisco*.

F. Chris Garcia is professor of political science at the University of New Mexico, where he served as president during the 2002–2003 school year. He is the author or editor of ten books and numerous book chapters and scholarly articles. His books include *Pursuing Power: Latinos and the Political System* (1997) and *New Mexico Government* (1994).

Rodney Hero is Packey J. Dee Professor of American Democracy and professor of political science at the University of Notre Dame, and also serves as department chair. He is the author of *Latinos and the U.S. Political System: Two-Tiered Pluralism* (1992) and *Faces of Inequality: Social Diversity in American Politics* (1998), as well as of numerous scholarly articles.

Kevin A. Hill is associate professor of political science at Florida International University. He is the author (with John E. Hughes) of *Cyberpolitics: Citizen Activism in the Age of the Internet* (1998) as well as of scholarly articles in the *Journal of Urban Affairs*, *Politics and Policy*, and *Hispanic Journal of the Behavioral Sciences*.

Patricia Jaramillo is assistant professor in the Department of Political Science and Geography at the University of Texas, San Antonio, where she teaches courses on political behavior, race and ethnicity, and public policy.

Robert G. Marbut Jr. is a graduate student in the Department of Government at the University of Texas, Austin. He is also chair of the National Governing Bodies' Council of the U.S. Olympic Committee.

Frances Marquez is a graduate student at the Claremont Graduate University, where she has received a Haynes Foundation Dissertation Grant and an Abba P. Schwartz Fellowship from the Kennedy Presidential Library. She launched the California Democratic Party's New Citizen Voter Registration Program and was a field representative for retired U.S. representative Esteban E. Torres.

Lisa J. Montoya is director of research and grant development at the Annette Strauss Institute for Civic Participation at the University of Texas at Austin. She studies racial and ethnic politics, gender and politics, and minority participation and representation in the United States. She is published in *PS: Political Science* and *Politics and the Hispanic Journal of Behavioral Science.*

Dario Moreno is associate professor of political science at Florida International University. He is the author of *The Struggle for Peace in Central America* (1994). He has served as an expert witness on three Voting Rights Act cases: *DeGrandy v. Wetherall* (1992), *Diaz v. Miami Beach* (1993), and *Suarez v. Dade School Board* (1998).

Harry P. Pachon is professor in the School of Policy, Planning, and Development at the University of Southern California and president of the Tomás Rivera Policy Institute. He has authored numerous articles in professional journals and coauthored three books on U.S. Latino politics and political behavior. In 1997, he was appointed to serve as a member of the President's Advisory Commission on Educational Excellence for Hispanic Americans.

Ricardo Ramírez is assistant professor in the Departments of Political Science and American Studies and Ethnicity at the University of Southern California. He is currently working on the book *Continuity and Change: Latinos in American Politics since 1990.* He has been working with the National Association of Latino Elected and

Appointed Officials since February 2001 on a project evaluating elite efforts to mobilize Latino voters.

Gary M. Segura is associate professor of American politics at the University of Iowa. He is widely published in several journals, such as the *Journal of Politics, Political Research Quarterly,* and the *American Political Science Review.* His work focuses on issues of political representation, especially congressional elections, public opinion, the capabilities of citizens, and the mobilization of oppressed and/or minority groups within a society.

Robert Y. Shapiro is professor of political science at Columbia University. He is the coauthor (with Benjamin I. Page) of *The Rational Public: Fifty Years of Trends in American's Policy Preferences* (1992) and (with Lawrence R. Jacobs) *Politicians Don't Pander: Political Manipulation and the Loss of Democratic Responsiveness* (2000). His current research examines American national policy making and political leadership and opinion from 1960 to the present.

Christine Marie Sierra is associate professor of political science at the University of New Mexico. Her publications focus on U.S. Latino politics, immigration policy, Hispanic political behavior in New Mexico, and Chicana/Latina politics. She cowrote and coproduced the video documentary *"This Town Is Not For Sale!": The 1994 Santa Fe Mayoral Election* (1999), featuring the election of Debbie Jaramillo as Santa Fe's first woman mayor. She is the principal investigator of a Ford Foundation–funded project entitled Gender and Multicultural Leadership: The Future of Governance.